Welcome to JESUSLAND!

Welcome to JESUSLAND!*

*formerly the United States of America

Shocking Tales of Depravity, Sex and Sin

UNCOVERED BY GOD'S FAVORITE CHURCH, LANDOVER BAPTIST

by Chris Harper, Andrew Bradley, and Erik Walker

WARNER BOOKS

NEW YORK   BOSTON

The events and characters described in this book are fictitious. Certain real locations and public figures are mentioned, but all other characters and events described in the book are totally imaginary.

Warner Books

Hachette Book Group USA
1271 Avenue of the Americas, New York, NY 10020
Visit our Web site at www.HachetteBookGroup.com

Printed in the United States of America

First Edition: September 2006
10 9 8 7 6 5 4 3 2 1

ISBN-10: 0-446-69758-3
ISBN-13: 978-0-446-69758-3
LCCN: 2006921584

Book design by H. Roberts Design

Dedication

We'd like to thank the writers and editors of the KJV 1611, from which all Bible references in this book were obediently quoted without alteration, for providing such complicit source material in our zealous quest for the outrageous.

— Chris Harper, Andrew Bradley, and Erik Walker

Welcome to JESUSLAND!*

*formerly the United States of America

Shocking Tales of Depravity, Sex and Sin

UNCOVERED BY GOD'S FAVORITE CHURCH, LANDOVER BAPTIST

by Chris Harper, Andrew Bradley, and Erik Walker

WARNER BOOKS

NEW YORK   BOSTON

The events and characters described in this book are fictitious. Certain real locations and public figures are mentioned, but all other characters and events described in the book are totally imaginary.

Warner Books

Hachette Book Group USA
1271 Avenue of the Americas, New York, NY 10020
Visit our Web site at www.HachetteBookGroup.com

Printed in the United States of America

First Edition: September 2006
10 9 8 7 6 5 4 3 2 1

Warner Books and the "W" logo are trademarks of Time Warner Inc.
and or an affiliated company. Used under license by Hachette Book Group USA,
which is not affiliated with Time Warner Inc.

ISBN-10: 0-446-69758-3
ISBN-13: 978-0-446-69758-3
LCCN: 2006921584

Book design by H. Roberts Design

Welcome to JESUSLAND!

LANDOVER BAPTIST CHURCH
MAIN CAMPUS VISITOR MAP

JESUS SAVES · SO DO WE

Be Baptist or Be Gone!

Welcome to Jesusland

TICKETS

WWJD?

PARKING ←
"Abraham" Lot thru "Lot" Lot

PARKING →
""Matthew" Lot thru the "Tithe A Lot" Lot

1. "S.S. Noah's Ark 2" luxury emergency escape ship (Platinum Level tithers will be given a 2-hour warning if lake water rises above 60 feet)

2. Metal detectors to ensure that our guests are all carrying concealed weapons

3. *That Don't Sound Saved to Me!* visitor processing center. Wheat: exit to the left. Chaff: kindly return to your cars.

4. Jogging lake

5. Unsaved stockade & "declined" VISA card hospitality suites

6. Racial profiling center

7. Chick-fil-A® monorail to metered parking lots

8. Pastor Deacon Fred's April-May residence

9. Rifle range

10. Free speech zone

11. Saved Souls Cemetery & 18-Holies Golf Course

12. Landover Christian Mall ("Saving Souls, NOT Dollars since 1983")

13. Fish-themed automotive decals and bracelets outlet mall

14. Gift Shop ($185/pp minimum)

15. *Three Solid Gold Krugerrand Coins In A Foutain* prayer pavilion

16. Catholic Cathedrals of Europe Desecration Arcade

17. 1962 slave shacks (now lodgings for indentured, undocumented groundskeepers)

18. World's largest 20 kt. gold cross (FUN FACT: This cross is so ginormous that if it were melted down, the money from the black market could feed every country below the equator except New Zealand, which is just as well since they eat too much anyway)

19. Pat Boone & Reba McEntire's "The Puppet Passion of the Muppet Christ" Musical Theater

20. Third tallest plastic Jesus in the county

21. Main sanctuary and Bowers Towers

22. Pastor's Airbus A380 "Wings of Gabriel" Super Jumbo (retrofitted from 555 seats to 2 seats and a trout fishing pond)

23. Hangar for Mrs. Betty Bowers' ministry G550 jets & Bentleys

24. Hangar for flock's golden chariots to Glory & flying horse stables

25. Apocalypse-proof repository for tax-free millions

26. Leviticus Acres helicopter patrolled community — "America's Most Saved Zip Code"

27. Salvation City office park & Rapture holding area

Welcome to Landover Baptist Church

Landover Baptist Church, Jesus' preferred house of worship, was founded in the year of our Lord 1620. Within moments of the *Mayflower*'s hull being ground into Plymouth Rock, Landover's first pastor, Enoch Jeremiah Smithe, rebuked the crew for shoddy navigation, thereby beginning our church's invigorating tradition of constant, ferocious reproach. Pastor Enoch soon announced that he was breaking away from the milquetoast Puritans of Massachusetts for being soft on witches, supping with bottom-baring Injuns and succumbing to satanically effeminate fashions, such as finishing off Godly black clothing with ostentatious white collars.

Enoch Jeremiah Smithe was particularly offended by his fellow settlers' decision to run about like a pack of pansies by embracing the flamboyant craze of sewing enormous belt buckles onto all of their hats.

As He was wont to do with almost tedious regularity, the Lord appeared in the form of a woodchuck or other nut-gathering creature as Pastor Enoch made his way through the New England wilderness. One day, the Lord (this time as a friendly squirrel) called out to Pastor Enoch from the sagging limb of a beech tree, telling him that a "free hold" could be taken on "land over" toward the west. And that land was absolutely *full* of acorns!

That evening, all 25 founding members of what was then called the First and Only True Baptist Church in America made their way toward the State of IowalottoGod (later shortened) because the squirrel had prophesied that if they went much further west, they were bound to run into crazy Mormons. It was God's Will that they settled in a wooded, hilly region that is still known as Freehold. They have remained in this New World Eden for over 300 years, righteously relaying the constant displeasure of the Lord to all who are fortunate enough to pass through.

Landover Baptist Church was abruptly wrenched into the modern age one August afternoon in 1962 when federal authorities wrongly seized our Godly campus and presented young Pastor Deacon Fred with an outrageous edict. The news they gave Pastor could not have been more shocking: We were to be the last people in America to free their slaves. It appears that we were so fastidious in following the Word of God that it had never been brought to our attention that slavery was not only frowned upon outside the Bible, but also had been somehow abolished. Out of the blue, church members were suddenly forced to pay "the help." But when the Lord closes the door on a slaves' shack, He opens an even nicer one on the church's vault. The unexpected cash shortfall led to the discovery of just how much money you can raise in Jesus' name in America if you have access to television. This joyous revelation started Landover on the road to becoming the nation's most prosperous religious industry, with funds more than adequate to support a 152,319-member congregation with 117 pastors and 212 full-time paid deacons. Since that day over forty years ago, the liberal media has salivated like a consumptive demon over our every move. But such persecution doesn't surprise us in the least. The Bible tells us that if we follow Jesus, the world will hate us. And from the looks of things, we must be following Jesus *a lot*.

Hey Kids! Accept Jesus Christ as Your Personal Lord and Savior and Get a Free PlayStation 3!

This offer is for children and teenagers only! It may not be used in conjunction with any other Landover Baptist salvation offer.

Hey kids! If your Mom and Dad didn't buy you a PlayStation 3 for Christmas, you can still get one *FOR FREE!* Have you ever heard of Jesus Christ? Well, He's heard of you! And He wants you to have all the cool toys your parents are too cheap to buy! In fact, the Lord Jesus is mighty angry with your parents for not giving you all the latest stuff that every kid in America deserves! And Jesus has got your back, because He is your homeboy! If you've never heard of Jesus, He is an invisible cloud-dwelling deity (infinite lives!) who loves you very much and wants nothing more than to give you a free PlayStation 3!

We here at Landover Baptist Church work full-time as servants of Jesus Christ, and He's told us about you and your predicament. He completely understands! He is totally down with that! In fact, lucky for you, in order to follow Him, you are actually required to hate your parents!

If any man come to me, and hate not his father, and mother . . . he cannot be my disciple.—The Lord Jesus Christ *(Luke 14:26)*

Pretty cool, huh? So, if you hate your parents, you are already halfway to becoming a True Christian™! Congratulations!

Kids! This is real easy! Just have all of these numbers from one of your Daddy's checks ready when Jesus answers the Phone - and You'll be qualified for a free game! Awesome!

✝ LANDOVER BAPTIST
CHRISTIAN BANK
Freehold, Iowa

For _____

⑆000400500⑆ ⑈000300540093⑈ 0030

↑ Routing and Transit #
↑ Checking Account #
↑ Check #

Here is what you need to do to get your free PlayStation 3:

1. Tell Jesus that you hate your parents, and that you'd rather have Him for your Daddy. Ask Him to forgive your sins, and cover you with His blood (you'll see plenty of that splattered across your TV when you play your complimentary *Grand Theft Auto 4* game!).
2. Find one of your Mom's or Dad's credit cards (a blank check is even better!).
3. Call our church office and we will provide you with simple instructions on how to use your parents' credit card to charge a love offering over the phone. Don't worry if you can't find a credit card. We can teach you how to use one of your Daddy's checks to do an automatic draft withdrawal (which will get you free shipping and a bonus game disk!).

Please note: If your parents ask you where you got your new PlayStation 3, just tell them that your Lord and Savior, Jesus Christ, delivered it to you via the U.S. Postal Service in exchange for your soul.

Still NOT SURE? Here's more:

Landover Baptist's PlayStation 3 comes with a complimentary modified version of the popular disk *Tony Hawk's American Wasteland*. You can upload Jesus' face into the game and automatically unlock all of the cheat codes to "God Mode," so that Jesus can win every single level and perform incredible grab-tricks, spins, flips and stunts!

As a new Christian, you will want to share the good news of Jesus Christ with as many of your peeps in the hood as you can. The great thing about *Tony Hawk's American Wasteland* is that you can actually get off your skateboard and walk around in the game and talk to other skaters about the Plan of Salvation! And if they don't accept Jesus as their Personal Savior, you can blow their frigging heads off later. How cool is that!?

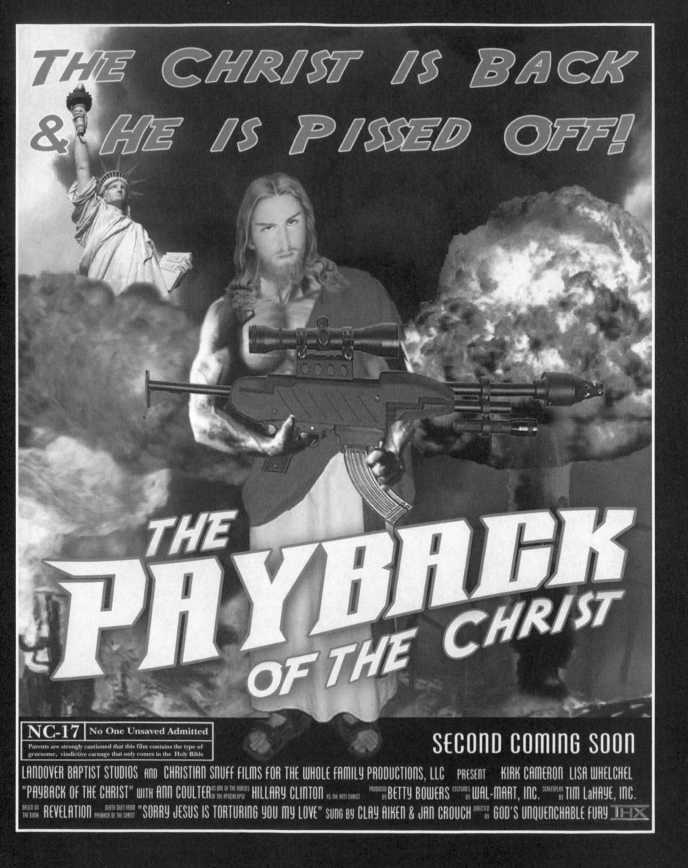

LANDOVER BAPTIST CHURCH

"Unsaved Unwelcome"

JANUARY NEWSLETTER

Cause of Homosexuality Discovered After Long Weekend with a Cucumber

Creation Science doctors at Landover Baptist Hospital for the Saved have begun providing complimentary removal of prostate glands for all male patients and their visitors unless they have a "985 Waiver" form in triplicate from a qualified pastor. "I can't tell you the hours I have spent wondering what it is about sticking something in your rear end that drives homos so nutso," announced Dr. Watkins, the hospital's chief of staff, whose honorary medical degree was conferred by Landover Baptist University for the Saved after he memorized all of the Old Testament "begets" in reverse order. "Finally, we understand the scientific explanation behind what turns red-blooded Promise Keepers into insatiable bottoms. Our case studies reveal that homosexual gratification results when rectal demons are jammed up against the prostate gland, thereby stimulating the gland with their sharp, scampering hooves and tiny little tridents. Without this colonic stampede triggered by claustrophobic demons having their personal space invaded by foreign objects, buggery would be no more thrilling than sticking an enormous Q-tip into your ear. Therefore, stamping out the incentive to being a damned homo boils down to either removing the prostate gland or the demons. And, as any Bible-believing doctor worth his leeches knows, demons are a lot harder to find and suture."

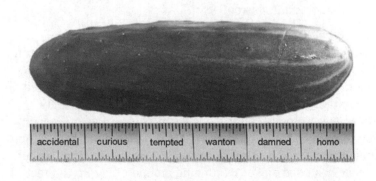

accidental | curious | tempted | wanton | damned | homo

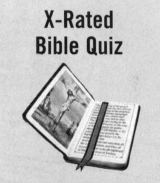

X-Rated Bible Quiz

Were sex toys used in Biblical times?

A. They may have been, but that's certainly not something God would advertise in the Holy Bible.

B. Yes. Woman masturbated themselves to distraction with expensive dildos made of gold and silver.

C. No. People in Biblical times engaged in sex only with animate objections, such as human and animal body parts.

D. None of the above.

Answer: B. "Thou hast also taken thy fair jewels of my gold and of my silver, which I had given thee, and madest to thyself images of men, and didst commit whoredom with them" (Ezekiel 16:17).

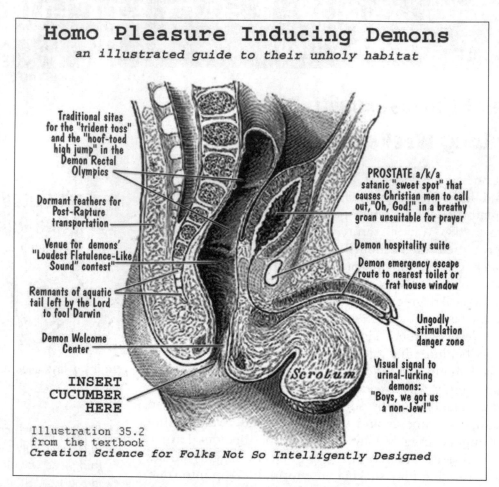

Homo Pleasure Inducing Demons
an illustrated guide to their unholy habitat

Traditional sites for the "trident toss" and the "hoof-toed high jump" in the Demon Rectal Olympics

Dormant feathers for Post-Rapture transportation

Venue for demons' "Loudest Flatulence-Like Sound" contest"

Remnants of aquatic tail left by the Lord to fool Darwin

Demon Welcome Center

INSERT CUCUMBER HERE

PROSTATE a/k/a satanic "sweet spot" that causes Christian men to call out,"Oh, God!" in a breathy groan unsuitable for prayer

Demon hospitality suite

Demon emergency escape route to nearest toilet or frat house window

Ungodly stimulation danger zone

Visual signal to urinal-lurking demons: "Boys, we got us a non-Jew!"

Scrotum

Illustration 35.2 from the textbook
Creation Science for Folks Not So Intelligently Designed

Landover Named "Most Selective Church in America" by *U.S. News & World Report*: Now Harder to Get into Than Harvard

Orientals get into Harvard easier than blacks get into debt, but one has yet to show up at our door good enough for worship at Landover Baptist.

As most of you know, we model our holy church after Heaven: Hardly anyone gets in. From the uttermost to the guttermost, our Godly church proudly turned away so many lost, pathetic souls last year that we stopped counting in April. Because of the failing economy we inherited from insatiable sex maniac Bill Clinton many years ago, Landover witnessed an enormous increase last year in filthy, hungry ragamuffins pounding on its imported African ivory church doors. "They claim to want to know Jesus' promise of obscene wealth," said Pastor Deacon Fred, "but have the effrontery to show up in our beautiful, professionally decorated sanctuary without a coat and tie. That kind of nonsense may have passed muster in Judea, but we like to think we are bit more particular than Jesus. After all, you won't see any of us running around oiling up the feet of the local whores!"

Heaven nervously Welcomes Wildly Successful Islamic Terrorist

Inhabitants of Heaven put down their lyres and Danish today, reacting with both surprise and alarm when Iraqi insurgent Muhammad Abu Ubeida appeared before them at 29:14 HT [Heaven Time]. "You could have heard an angel dancing on the head of a pin drop," recalled Christian terrorist Timothy McVeigh from an adjacent cloud. According to well-placed sources, both seraphim and former humans had watched the Abu Ubeida trial and execution in Baghdad with rapt attention. "We were all on tenterhooks over where this blood-thirsty menace would wind up after his death," said spirit and repentant axtress Lizzie Borden. "For several days now, every klatch of angels was buzzing with a prophetic scuttlebutt about a post-sentencing conversion."

"Apparently, the clever little so-and-so repented," said the clearly infuriated Mrs. Betty Bowers, "showing a rather lawyerly appreciation for damnation's yawning loophole. Yes, just one mealy-mouthed mea culpa murmured nanoseconds before dying and, no matter how many Americans you may have killed that morning, the Lord welcomes you with open, and presumably enormous, arms into Glory. So, naturally, Heaven is absolutely chockfull of hideous, *loathsome* people, flying about as they, no doubt, smugly reflect upon their inexplicable good fortune to be living in an ADD (Attention Deficient Deity) Universe patrolled by a God who remembers only the last thing anyone ever said to Him."

Founders of Traditional Values Coalition, Focus on the Family and ChildCare Action Project View 1,467 Hard-core Gay Pornographic Videos for Christ

"We were looking for homosexual subtext," said a clearly exhausted Louis P. Sheldon. "Frankly, on repeated viewings, there was something objectionable in all of them. Sometimes, it was just a saucy look; sometimes, fellatio performed with far too much gusto. I can't tell you how many un-Godly penetrations I counted because I left my notes in the screening room. Frankly, I'm amazed at how *homosexual* gay porn is—everything was just *drenched* in hot, sweaty man sin. Well, except the first few minutes of *Bareback Mountin'*. That one took a while to get going."

Health Watch: Atheism: Now America's Most Popular Fatal Disease

Unless you've been living in a cave for the last 20 years or are Catholic, you already know that Landover Baptist's Pastor Deacon Fred and Brother Harry Hardwick are the world's foremost Christian experts on the deadly disease, *Atheism,* and its carriers, called *Atheists.* Through their exhaustive experience with this disease, our two illustrious pastors have put together some information that could immunize you from even the most virulent strains of Atheism.

HOW IS ATHEISM CAUGHT?

Like mosquitoes are to stagnant ponds, Atheism is to active minds. Anywhere conditions allow for unfettered thought, an infection of logic or a Baptist asking "but why?", chances are someone is about to catch himself a nasty case of Atheism.

WHEN IS THE ATHEISM SEASON?

The Atheism season runs from June to September, when the Baby Jesus' birthday party is a distant memory and ripe bosoms are bouncing about on the beach. It picks up again during October, as celebrations of Satan's Birthday at Halloween lower the immunity levels of Christians who crave bite-size Three Musketeers bars and candy corn. But be on your toes: Anytime a classroom, book or mind is open, it is Atheism season, my friend!

SYMPTOMS:

1. Hanging out in coffeehouses and any university not started to pay for a Bible-believing pastor's beach house.
2. Protesting in front of public or government buildings (unless it is an abortion clinic).
3. Obesity. Just because someone is grossly overweight, don't assume he is an inoculated True Christian™. Most Godly people assume that anyone who comes down with a case of Atheism will look like an emaciated granola cruncher who jogs

and plays racquetball or a vain, silicone-filled, hedonistic partygoer who worships only her full-length mirror. Creation Scientists warn, however, that the disease can manifest itself in ways that make early detection difficult by mimicking the symptoms of Evangelical Christianity, such as morbid obesity and the need to tell people, whether asked or not, that their enormous girth is the result of an undetectable thyroid condition and not the box of Little Debbie cakes the patient is holding.

4. Possessing a rash of diplomas. In advanced cases, post-graduate degrees.

PREVENTION:

Get a vaccine. A vaccine against colds hasn't been developed because colds can be caused by many types of demons. But the Atheism vaccine has been around since 1611. *It is called the King James Bible.* If you feel a bout of Atheism coming on, hold the Bible in front of you so you can't see anything and bang it on a table so you can't hear anything (and so you can't actually read it). This can keep you safe from even the university-educated strain of Atheism.

This Sunday's Sermon:

"Why Do Catholics Worship a Gal Too Lazy to Cook Her Savior Son a Hot, Home-cooked Meal for His Last Supper?"

Becoming a Christian: As Easy as Removing Unwanted Nose Hair!

SERMON BY BROTHER HARRY HARDWICK

Friends, as True Christians™, we are obliged to save as many lost souls as we can in the time left over from acquiring financial blessings. In witnessing at our country club to Catholics, Episcopalians, Presbyterians, Democrats and other unsaved trash who wistfully file membership applications, Heather and I have heard time and again from people who are leery of our faith because they think life as a born-again Christian would be difficult. Nothing could be further from the truth, my friends. In fact, next to being a Hilton harlot, it's the easiest lifestyle imaginable. Let me explain how you can let the unsaved know that being a Christian is as easy as pie.

Start out by letting the unsaved know they don't need any courage to become a bona fide Christian. In fact, it is precisely because they lack courage that many of our brothers and sisters became Christians in the first place. We all fear death. We all fear the unknown. We all fear the possibility there may be nothing after this mortal life. Psychologists and 12-step programs teach people to confront these fears head-on and overcome them. But not Christianity! Our faith uses these fears to induce people to join our steadily growing, politically influential ranks. We say, "Of course, you fear death, as well you should, because not only is death the end of this life, but it is also the beginning of eternal torture. But if you exhibit your love for Jesus (including using preprinted tithe envelopes) there will be no death, only everlasting life in 24-karat-gold utopia." Why should anyone have to confront his fears when our faith promises an afterlife that automatically answers even his most petty wish in the unambiguous affirmative?

Let the unsaved know they don't need "self-esteem" to be a Christian. In fact, if anything, feelings of self-worth are barriers to salvation. You see, Christians don't think positively about ourselves, for our faith teaches that we are filthy, miserable beings, born into sin. Every one of us is so despicable that we deserve to burn in flames forever. It is only by the Grace of God that we will wind up in Heaven. As Christians, we take no pride in anything we accomplish on Earth, for worldly accomplishments are evil (1 John 2:16; 1 Timothy 3:6). Besides, True Christians™ know that the Lord bristles when humans either take credit for things that turn out well or fail to blame themselves for the things that don't.

Let the unsaved know that they won't have to worry a lick about a darn thing if they become Christian for they will *always* be blessed. Are they poverty-stricken? Illiterate? In ill health? In an abusive relationship? Secular thought would have them seek education, job training, a so-called "healthier" lifestyle and divorce to overcome these problems. But Christians aren't about to waste all that time away from watching *The 700 Club* when the Lord tells us we are just fine and dandy the way we are! After all, the meek, the poor, the hungry and the persecuted are blessed (Matthew 5:3–6).

Finally, let the unsaved trash know they don't have to go to the trouble of becoming good people to be Christians. Our faith teaches that we all come up short—we all sin. But by accepting Jesus, all our sins are forgiven—both our sins of the past and the ones we will inevitably commit in the future! It's a little doctrine called Eternal Security, and by golly—it works! Once saved, *always* saved. In fact, even those committing the most evil acts imaginable will still go to Heaven, so long as they once took a moment to get saved.

The bottom line is that being a Christian is the easiest lifestyle one could ever adopt. You need no courage, no self-esteem and no motivation. This is why so many would-be Christians first turn to alcohol, drugs, sex, food or some other vice as an easy way out, requiring no difficult questions about why they have addictive personalities in the first place. But those particular crutches cause liver cirrhosis, heart attacks, venereal disease and unsightly obesity. Let it be known throughout the land that an addiction to Jesus has none of those ill side effects. It's sugar-free, fat-free, thought-free and absolutely fireproof. Easier than knocking a squirrel's head off with a round of Russian artillery shells. Glory!

Gallup Poll Indicates Average American Only Hears About Jesus 48 Times a Day

Sadly, recent polls show that on an average day, an American is less likely to hear about Jesus Christ's love message than he will hear about Jennifer Aniston's love life. Most disturbing of all, the report found that almost an entire hour can go by in many Blue States without a Personal Savior being introduced into an otherwise friendly conversation. Pastor calls on you and your family to do your part in changing these disappointing statistics by preceding anything you do during the day by asking out loud, "Jesus, may I?" If you forget to ask "Jesus, may I?" you will have to take two bunny-steps back.

167 Baptists Plummet to Their Deaths When Jesus Is a No-Show at Rapture

Almost 100 members of Bringing Integrity To Christian Homemakers and their spouses were killed December 31, 2005, at a Rapture Bon Voyage party. All of the women had paid Landover Baptist $114,000 to be among the first to be whisked to Heaven in Jesus' arms at the stroke of midnight. Party attendee Mr. Tommy Jenkins had reportedly told friends, "Tonya was real excited about scraping enough money together to get to go. It was Becca's college money, but Tonya knew it was the End Times so there wasn't going to be no college and Landover always does everything up really nice. We wanted to go out with a little flourish."

The party was held on the rooftop of the 35-story Landover Hotel and Prayer Convention Center, which was renamed Rapture Tower for the evening. Special 40-foot golden staircases had been constructed to give the partygoers a head start on their ascent to Heaven. Hourly catering staff dressed as angels were positioned at the top of each plywood staircase to beckon the partygoers on to Glory at midnight. The exclusive

party featured everything from Petrossian caviar to French nonalcoholic "champagne-like" sparkling beverage for the teetotaling Baptist crowd.

"I knew something was amiss," lamented party organizer and America's Best Christian Mrs. Betty Bowers, "when I went to open a case of Cliquot for my New Year's Eve party in Ravello, Italy, and realized it was that dreadful faux-champagne I'd ordered for the Landover party. UPS must have swapped the orders. And the implications of that horrid blunder didn't occur to me until many of Landover's most prominent BITCHes* were already dead. To be even more honest than my Savior, I was simply too busy worrying about how the mix-up would be the figurative death of my own party to stop and think how it might prove to be the actual death of those poor women who never drink even an unpretentious hock, much less a lovely quality champagne."

An obviously homosexual waiter for the event recounted, "I told several of those Baptist ladies that I was going to cut them off because they were getting real drunk. But they told me that they never drink and they were just 'drunk in the Spirit.'" He then rolled his eyes and added, in that snide, homosexual way of theirs: "*Spirits* was more like it." According to another sodomite: "Well, the big thing I remember is that all of the partygoers were horrendous tippers—even for Baptists—and as it got closer to midnight, they started to walk up the golden staircases located all along the periphery of the roof. They were yelling things like 'I'm coming, catch me! Catch me, Jesus!' and then all these old chicks just started bungee jumping off the side of the building. Except without ropes." When the Landover Chapel bell struck midnight, each member of Bringing Integrity To Christian Homemakers grabbed her husband's hand and raced up the golden staircases. As each couple got to the last step, they threw themselves off the side of the 470-foot building and into the waiting arms of Jesus. According to eyewitness accounts, however, Jesus, apparently tied up elsewhere, was a no-show and was regrettably not able to stop them from denting car hoods, flattening expensive shrubbery or staining the sidewalks below.

LANDOVER BAPTIST CHURCH
RAPTURE ALERT SYSTEM

RED
(GO)
IF YOU ARE READING THIS,
YOU WERE LEFT BEHIND!

ORANGE
(SET)
JESUS SPOTTED IN
DES MOINES QUICK MART

YELLOW
(READY)
NORAD SIGHTS FLYING HORSES
GRAZING NEAR OZONE LAYER

BLUE
(ON YOUR MARK)
UNEXPLAINED DISTURBANCES
IN UPPER ATMOSPHERE

GREEN
(STAND FIRM IN CHRIST)
WORK A STEADY JOB, ATTEND
CHURCH WEEKLY, TITHE 10%

---

*Bringing Integrity To Christian Homemakers

New Evidence Proves Noah's Sons Rode Flying Dinosaurs

The recent unearthing of feathered dinosaur skeletons in China finally answered an age-old question and provided Creation Scientists with undeniable proof that Noah's sons used flying dinosaurs to transport polar bears, penguins and other species from far-away lands to join them for a forty-day ride on Noah's ark.

Bible-Based Dieting Tips

What?* know ye not that your body is the temple of the Holy Ghost which is in you, which ye have of God, and ye are not your own? For ye are bought with a price: therefore glorify God in your body, and in your spirit, which are God's (1 Corinthians 6:19–20).

*(Pardon the Lord's rudeness!)

"Gals, if Jesus Wanted You Emaciated, You'd be Living in Ethiopia—Not Within 20 Miles of a Shoney's!"—Mrs. Harry "Heather" Hardwick

Good heavens, ladies! If it isn't enough having to cut down on medicinal booze when we're pregnant, now we have to be careful about what we eat because we have the finicky Holy Ghost living inside our tummies. And frankly, the last time I looked in the mirror, I was appalled by how much weight He had put on!

It is absolutely critical for Christian ladies to have a well-balanced diet to feed both themselves and the ravenous Holy Ghost, who is simply crazy about those yummy T.G.I. Friday's frozen potato skin appetizers. My advice is based on the four major food groups: fat, sugar, protein and carbohydrate. Focus on meat, dairy products and sweets. Avoid processed foods at all costs. The Holy Spirit can't hold processed food down, and when a member of the Trinity burps, even your least nosy neighbors will know about it. So, avoid oatmeal, yogurt, Lean Cuisine, Power Bars, cottage cheese, wheat germ and anything made by the misleadingly named "Healthy Choice" group. A simple rule of thumb is that if it doesn't live in a barn, or at least come out of something that lives in a barn, it probably isn't worth frying up in the first place. Besides, you've got a 10,000-year-old entity living in your stomach, and believe me, it is going to take Him a long time to get used to anything new like so-called "spa cuisine."

Some unsaved nutritionists have condemned similar diets, but my plan is amply supported by the Holy Bible, which once again proves that medical researchers are full of, pardon my French, bull crap. Throughout the Old Testament, God rewarded good acts by instructing his people to eat the fat of the calf—and lots of it, too. "And ye shall eat fat till ye be full" (Ezekiel 39:19). Now, would God reward his people with something unhealthy? Of course not. God knows that His little sidekick, the Holy Spirit, doesn't want to be stuck trying to gnaw His beak through that reconstituted sawdust they force you to buy at Jenny Craig! The people of yesteryear ate loads of red meat, fat, cheese, cream, butter and oil (Deuteronomy 32:13–14; 1 Samuel 17:18). And the most favored people ate the largest quantities (Genesis 43:34). Yet the people back then lived to be hundreds and hundreds of years old! So, you all can choose to stick to South Beach and only live to see 85—that's your decision. But

Special Sermon Next Week Sponsored by the Department of Homeland Hysteria:

"The Only Man from the Middle East You Want to Share a Plane or Taxi with Is Jesus!"
by Pastor Emeritus Richard B. Cheney

Last Week's Favorite Hymn:

Jimmy Johnson performs the hymn "Take Me Jesus Before I Commit That Sin That Feels So Darn Good Again"

Bible Quiz:
God's Absolutely Favorite Ways to Kill

How does an irascible God punish those who break His commandments?

A. He strikes them with plagues, burning fevers that consume the eyes, pestilence, consumption, blasting, the sword and even mildew.

B. He strikes them with painful hemorrhoids, scabs, itching, madness and blindness.

C. He sends wild bears to devour their children.

D. Any of the above, depending on His mood.

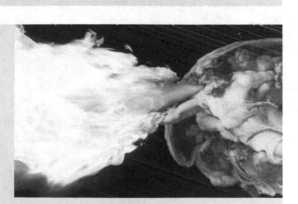

Answer: D. "But if ye will not hearken unto me. . . . I will even appoint over you terror, consumption, and the burning ague, that shall consume the eyes. . . . I will also send wild beasts among you, which shall rob you of your children" (Leviticus 26:14–22). "If thou wilt not hearken unto the voice of the Lord thy God. . . . The Lord will smite thee with a consumption, and with a fever, and with an inflammation, and with an extreme burning, and with the sword, and with blasting, and with mildew. . . . The Lord will smite thee with the botch of Egypt, and with the emerods, and with the scab, and with the itch, whereof thou canst not be healed. The Lord shall smite thee with madness, and blindness" (Deuteronomy 28:15–28).

And What Have YOU Sacrificed to Save Souls Recently?

Brother Hardwick Lost
80 Pounds and His Wallet
Wrestling Demons
Out of Local Harlots
Last Month

PLEASE NOTE:

The Road to Hell will be closed for widening from September 17 through December 1. Please plan an alternate route.

Last Week's Favorite Hymn:

"My Sins of Yesterday Are Washed Away (Amazing Grace Period)"

give me Methuselah's diet anyday. Praise God!

Some of the demons reading this are now undoubtedly thinking about vegetables. Vegetables can be very pretty as garnish, but they take up too much space on a plate, and eating them should be avoided whenever possible. Granted, if the vegetables are part of a cream sauce or have already been mixed with the pasta, there is little you can do, but keep consumption to a minimum. Direct your help to avoid the produce section when shopping. It's a real time-saver! My cute little Mexican housekeeper knows that the more green there is in the shopping bags, the less green she'll get at the end of the week. Let us not forget that Jesus referred to the meat eaters as strong and healthy and the vegetarians as weak and sickly (Romans 14:2). Again, subtle proof that the Holy Ghost, although an invisible entity, is outright carnivorous! Better to have Him chomp down on a nice, juicy Angus porterhouse than pick your rib cage clean! And I don't mean to be graphic here, but every Christian lady knows what beans, cabbage, cauliflower and the like can do with regard to noxious posterior fumes. Granted, the Bible says that when God passes gas, it sounds like a lovely harplike tune (Isaiah 16:11). But notice that the Bible carefully skirts the whole issue of the smell. Play it safe, gals: don't even trust Beano to keep your Christian home free from Holy flatulence.

From Pacifiers to Penises:
Every Parent's Worst Nightmare!

Is My Little Baby Going to Go Gay?

Handy Homo Prevention Tips for Concerned Parents with Suspect Toddlers

1. **A boy must not sit on a toilet unless he is having a bowel movement.** It is a scientific fact that when a man needs to use the restroom, he is called upon to engage in the unpleasant undertaking of extruding a poopy in only one out of every three visits. But homosexuals use all three visits to practice squatting, to limber the cheeks of their bottoms in preparation for even the most enormous (Negro) penises. Such calisthenics are neither necessary nor advisable for men who have no intention of squatting over someone else's engorged manhood. As soon as your child is able to walk on two feet, you must make sure he is taught to stand proudly in front of a private or public toilet seat, and to speak not a word, especially in response to the coy whispers of Catholic priests in the next stall.

2. **A boy must eat everything on his plate.** But a son pestering you to serve corn on the cob, hot dogs or sausages is signaling the need to change his diet. Try serving meals that more effectively evoke a hankering for the fragrant delights of the female genitalia. An artichoke stuffed with tuna fish will usually do the trick.

3. **A boy must not be allowed to watch cartoons of any kind.** He should spend Saturday mornings sitting quietly by his father's side (with a respectful three inches between the male bodies), watching sports that don't involve male leotards. He must watch football, basketball, baseball and boxing. Soccer is not a sport for civilized people and often results in alarmingly long, uncut penises escaping from satin shorts.

Pastor Condemns Selfish Stoning of Sons

Pastor strongly condemned Mrs. Thaddeus "Deanna" Lane's stoning to death of her two sons last weekend despite her otherwise airtight alibi that the Lord specifically told her to do it. Pastor told the congregation at last Sunday's sunrise service. "Deuteronomy 21:21 makes it very clear that unruly children are to be taken to the town square and stoned to death by *all* of the townspeople—not just the mommy. Mrs. Lane selfishly denied the people of her community, who are always eager to help, an opportunity for civic comraderie and, perhaps, even a lovely potluck supper that is part and parcel of any stoning. Fortunately for all concerned, except perhaps for Mrs. Lane, I have determined that such selfishness calls for a public stoning. So I guess there is no harm done. Well, again, except to Mrs. Lane. And you may start that on the count of three."

Baptist Insurance Company Bases Life Insurance Policies on Old Testament Life Spans

Catholics, non-Baptist Protestants and other non-Christians sued Landover Life Insurance Company last Tuesday. The crux of their complaint is that the insurer charges higher premiums for non-Landover members. The company answered the lawsuit by explaining that its premiums are based on Christian actuarial tables. They stated, "As True Christians™, we base everything on the Bible and that includes Old Testament life expectancies. Therefore, our policies are written for an average life expectancy of about 647 years. We are willing to take the losses from Godly folks not always making it to 969 like Methuselah, but we are not about to take on the risk of insuring folks God kills off before they even get into triple digits. We will not be in the business of rewarding folks who piss off the Lord."

4. **A boy must always wear thick white underwear.** White boxers and/or briefs are acceptable. Your child must be taught that men who wear colorful underwear or undergarments that are cut within one inch of the outer periphery of their pubic region or the trough of the valley between the cheeks of their bottom are either European or homosexual—and in America, that is a distinction too fine to bother with.

5. **A boy must never cry or pout.** Crying, pouting or showing human emotions besides rage and anger (Godly emotions) are weak and feminine traits. After the natural tears of infancy, brought on by a child's traumatic exit from the spiritual realm of Heaven—experienced after the horrible shock every young man experiences in seeing his very own mother's hairy, dilated vagina—into this Devil-run world we call Earth, your boy must be taught to stop crying. If your child is still crying after three weeks, please drop him off at the Creation Science Laboratory for the remainder of the year and for a determination of whether he is worth having back.

Last weekend, Paintballers for Christ recorded 87 "hits" on unsaved shoppers at the Merle Hay Mall in Des Moines, splattering them with balls full of the blood of Jesus and tiny, little laminated Bible tracts. Glory!

Dating Tips for Christian Men

If you have grown up in a Christian home that believes in the Holy Bible, then most certainly you have limited yourself to chaperoned dating until the age of 21. If you are truly saved, it is not until your 21st birthday that the thought of dating someone without adult supervision would even enter your mind.

If you think you have found a creature who has kept herself pure for her future husband and who knows how to cook, sew and keep a Christian house neat enough for a surprise visit from Jesus, then you are now ready to take a few cautious steps to make certain she is not the type of girl who will squander your income or lean toward gossip. This "inspection period" is called dating. Here are a few tips to get you prepared for your first date:

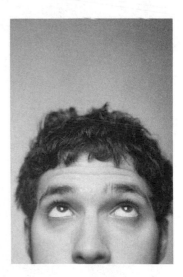

1. **Comb your hair.** In Genesis, the Lord said that He was giving man dominion over all the creatures of the Earth. Regrettably, this list included head lice, which are very common among Christian men, especially Pentecostals. Although it is a normal and natural blessing from God to have dominion over head lice, you should certainly wash your hair before your date if only to avoid the temptation of putting your arm around the young lady while lifting it to scratch your scalp.

2. **Pray.** Spend the day before your date with at least six hours of solitary prayer in a closet or other confined area wearing BVDs that have been left in the icebox overnight. Ask Jesus, who had a suspicious amount of exposure to the cunning wiles of harlots drenched in scented oils, to help you not to succumb to lusty ladies who offer to wash your feet—or any other body part, for that matter. Pray that you will have a bountiful nightly emission before your date, rendering you completely drained and flaccid for the rest of the day, making it more difficult for your thoughts—and blood—to stray to the tip of your hibernating penis.

Newlyweds' Tips on Keeping Jesus Satisfied

Give thanks where it is due, fellows: "Thank You, Jesus, for this orgasm one of us is about to receive!"

3.   **Recite verses together.** When you are on the date and your lady friend fails to come up with interesting baseball statistics, leading to awkward moments of silence that exceed 10 minutes, quote Scripture or sing a favorite hymn you have memorized to her. All women are impressed by such things, as they are eager to foolishly believe that if a man remembers anything, he will remember her birthday. Her failure to be wooed by any religious recitation is a sign that she might be possessed by a demon and may only be with you in hopes of wrapping warm, moist lips that never move in prayer around the hopefully limp shaft of your manhood. If you sense that this is her mission, take her to your church and drop her off by the back gate with a note to the pastor taped to her forehead that reads, "HARLOT." Be sure to secure her to a tree or post using your neck tie and belt. Then call Pastor immediately on his cell phone so that he might exorcise this wanton of her yearning lust.

4.   **Take her to visit God's house.** The best place for a first date is church. Oh, how impressed your sweetheart will be when she finds out you are taking her to Wednesday evening services! Spring for a Platinum Level tither Communion and you won't even need to take the little darling to dinner afterward!

A SPECIAL THANKS

to all of the CIA Covert Christian Missionaries who performed a roof-rattling rendition of "Onward Christian Special Forces Assassination Operatives!" with gusto at last week's service.

TURN OR BURN MOTHERFUCKER

5. **Question her salvation.** Use the time you are together to find out if your sweetheart is *really* saved. Question her salvation at least 15 times. Make sure she knows the exact day and hour (and preferably the exact minute) she met Jesus. Try to trip her up in her lies if she seems insincere or equivocates.

6. **Tuck your tallywhacker.** If you have not had a nightly emission before your date, make certain that you take extra precaution. Use an Ace bandage or knitting yarn to tie your penis back against your stomach or underneath your heinie. If you tuck instead of tie, make sure that the tip of your penis does not curl back far enough to enter the hole in your heinie where you go poopy out of—otherwise you might accidentally sodomize yourself during dinner and be a damned homosexual by dessert.

7. **Avoid touching this woman at all costs!** Make certain there is no personal contact like touching elbows on a shared armrest at a G-rated movie (foreplay) on this first date. Even if she has said yes to marriage, it is imperative that you refrain even from holding hands for at least two years until the courtship is over and you are whisked away on your honeymoon!

Happy 6,006th Birthday, Planet Earth!

Enjoy it while you can because the Lord so loved the world, He is about to blow it into a billion pieces any minute now.

 ## Greenhouse Effect Linked to Urban Sprawl in Hell

The Holy Bible has, once again, disproved modern science. Scientists have blamed the greenhouse effect (the supposed heating of the Earth's atmosphere) on everything from hairspray cans to cow flatulence. Landover pastors have determined, however, that the cause is far simpler: overpopulation in Hell. "While this is certainly not good news for Asians, Muslims, Catholics and Presbyterians," remarked Freehold Garden Club president Mrs. Betty Bowers, "all that additional sinning means that a rather lovely array of subtropical perennials is now hardy in Iowa. But, then again, the Lord's favorite fertilizer has always been sh-, ur, manure. Glory!"

Protecting the Sanctimony of Marriage:

Landover Baptist Church

A Proposal to Amend the United States Constitution to Conform to Biblical Principles Regarding Marriage

TO: PRESIDENT GEORGE W. BUSH

AMENDMENT XXVIII.
No state may sanction marriage between people of the same gender.

AMENDMENT XXIX.
No state may sanction marriage between a man and a woman who was married previously but has since divorced (Matthew 5:32).

AMENDMENT XXX.
No state may sanction marriage involving a widow (unless it is to her brother-in-law—see amendment 34). All women whose husbands have passed away are to refrain from intimacy and pleasure for the remainder of their lives (1 Timothy 5:5-15).

AMENDMENT XXXI.
No state may sanction marriage between people of different races (Deuteronomy 7:3; Numbers 25:6-8; 36:3-9; 1 Kings 11:2; Ezra 9:2; Nehemiah 13:25-27).

AMENDMENT XXXII.
No state may sanction marriage between a Christian and a non-Christian (2 John 1:9-11; 2 Corinthians 6:14-17).

AMENDMENT XXXIII.
No state may sanction marriage involving a man who has had sexual thoughts about a woman other than the one he intends to marry (Matthew 5:28).

AMENDMENT XXXIV.
No state may sanction marriage between a man whose brother has passed away and any woman other than his brother's widow. Each state must require the brother of a deceased man to marry his brother's widow (Deuteronomy 25:5-10).

Proposed Constitutional Amendments

AMENDMENT XXXV.
No state may sanction marriage between a man and any woman unwilling to promise in her wedding vows to obey her husband and submit to his every whim (Ephesians 5:22-24; 1 Corinthians 11:3; Colossians 3:18; 1 Timothy 2:11-12; Titus 2:3, 5; 1 Peter 3:1).

AMENDMENT XXXVII.
No state may sanction marriage in which the wedding ceremony is to occur during the woman's menstrual cycle unless the prospective spouses agree to refrain from intimate relations until the woman's period of uncleanness has terminated (Leviticus 18:19, 20:18; Ezekiel 18:5-6).

AMENDMENT XXXVIII.
No state may sanction marriage between a minister and any woman other than a virgin (Leviticus 21:13-14).

AMENDMENT XXXIX.
No state may sanction marriage between a rapist and any woman other than his victim. States must require a rapist to marry his victim (Deuteronomy 22:28-29) unless the victim failed to cry out, in which case the rapist is relieved of this obligation (Deuteronomy 22:23-24).

AMENDMENT XL.
No state may sanction marriage between a man and an aggressive or contentious woman (Proverbs 21:9, 21:19, 25:24, 27:15).

AMENDMENT XLI.
No state may permit a man to have more than 700 wives and 300 concubines, lest he be seen as unrighteous by the Lord (1 Kings 11:3).

In the Lord's Holy Name and in Service to our Christian Nation and Godly President,

Pastor Deacon Fred

Pastor Deacon Fred for The Lord Jesus Christ at the Landover Baptist Church Freehold, Iowa

PASTOR'S PULPIT:

Alabama: A Preview of the Coming Glories of a Christian America!

SERMON BY BROTHER HARRY HARDWICK

As our nation's poet laureate Peggy Noonan might say, Alabama is a shining city upon a landfill, a wondrous testament to all of the blasphemy-silencing righteousness in store for the rest of America in the coming theocracy. Years ahead of the remaining, less furiously Christian states, Alabama is a

cradle for the type of "*You're gonna be a dang Christian whether you like it or not, boy!*" soul-winning that is sweeping the nation. Ask yourself, what other state has produced a Christian as righteous in the face of the nonbeliever as Judge Roy Moore? Yes, you might say Kansas has gifted America with Rev. Fred Phelps. But former Alabama Supreme Court Justice Roy Moore has taken Reverend Phelps's carefully nuanced truism that "God hates fags" and imbued it with the power, grandeur and authority of secular law. And, friends, that is what turning a chaotic, everyone-makes-up-his-own-mind democracy into an obedient, here-is-what-you-better-damn-well-think theocracy is all about.

For example, on February 15, 2002, Alabama's highest court unanimously denied custody of three helpless children to their evil mother who had decided to be a damned lesbian, probably simply to annoy the holy court. In a concurring opinion in which the Lord used a court stenographer to throw His angry voice, Justice Moore wrote that homos are evil deviants the government should execute, just as the Old Testament commands:

> The State carries the power of the sword, that is, the power to prohibit conduct with physical penalties, such as confinement and even execution. It must use that power to prevent the subversion of children toward this lifestyle, to not encourage a criminal lifestyle.

D.H. v. H.H., 830 So. 2d 21, 35 (Ala. 2002) (Moore, J., concurring). Godly Alabamians cheered this return to fire-and-brimstone rhetoric while the Christ-hating liberals on the less Godly Supreme Court up in Washington, D.C., scoffed at Judge Moore's holy crusade to decorate every public space and breakfast nook with enormous replicas of the Ten Commandments. Scores of True Christians™ in Alabama, however, joined Judge Moore in loving almost all of the Ten Commandments so much that they found it in their righteous hearts to overlook the ill-conceived commandment against idolatry, falling prostrate before an enormous chunk of chiseled granite in the lobby of the Alabama Supreme Court. This was before an unsaved federal judge caused it to be savagely yanked out of the mouth of the court like a bloody, perfectly healthy molar, leaving the courthouse without any eye-catching advertisements for Christianity.

But this was just a temporary setback in our glorious calling to slap the name of Jesus into the heads of Americans who don't

Des Moines Federal Court Orders Landover Baptist to Move 12-Story Marble Ten Commandments Monument Another Eight Inches to the Left to Comply with Latest Supreme Court Ruling

Jerry Falwell Devotes His Life to Homosexuality

On Wednesday, Rev. Falwell announced that he is joining Dr. James Dobson, of Focus on the Family, in devoting 100 percent of his time to pondering all the many sweaty, animalistic things men can do to one another behind closed doors once they have ripped each other's clothing off with their teeth. "Frankly," said an excited Falwell, "thanks to the success of this cotton-picking homosexual agenda not only do we now have homo bishops, it's gotten to be the point where I can't do anything without thinking about hairy man-on-man sex. Just last Sunday, I had gone a whole five minutes without thinking about an enticingly turgid African penis waving within inches of my nose, and what do you know? I found myself at my country club's breakfast buffet staring down at all those hot, moist, brown sausage links. Well, we all know how that ended. I had to grab a napkin and excuse myself to the restroom while my meal got cold. I tell you, I've had it with homos ruining decent, normal people's lives—and meals!"

Surprising Charges of Racism Rock Landover Community Theater

Out of a desire to be respectful to the feelings of the colored maintenance staff, the Landover Baptist Minstrel Players' production of the lighthearted farce *Petunia, the Pentecostal Pickaninny* will not be performed during Black History Month this year. Instead, it will now open the season. Standing room tickets are still available for some shows.

voluntarily go to our churches. For as Alabama goes, go goes the nation. Soon, from Bangor to Honolulu, you won't be able to get a driver's license, fill up your minivan with gas or buy a loaf of bread without calling out the name Jesus in praise! Indeed, come Judgment Day, Jesus will, no doubt, first land in Alabama, probably right on top of the statute of Jefferson Davis in front of the Montgomery capitol building, smashing it to pieces with the bucking hooves of his flying white horse. That great state's saved citizens will be among the chosen few to join the congregation of Landover (Platinum through Gold Levels) in the VIC (Very Important Christian) section of Heaven. I suggest every one of you who is currently inclined to look down your Hell-bound nose at Alabama, start developing a taste for grits, hominy, overalls, humidity and plaque before it's too late. Don't say I didn't warn you!

Bible Quiz:
A Woman's Place: Under a Man

According to the Scriptures, what is a woman's role in the educational process?

A. Whatever role she chooses. (NOTE: Consider this answer a freebie!)

B. To teach for only a year so that she, like Mrs. George W. Bush, will then have something to talk about the rest of her indolent life.

C. Never that of a teacher because women are easily deceived.

D. A and B.

Answer: C. "Let the woman learn in silence with all subjection. But I suffer not a woman to teach, nor to usurp authority over the man, but to be in silence. For Adam was first formed, then Eve. And Adam was not deceived, but the woman being deceived was in the transgression" (1 Timothy 2:11-14).

Well-Mannered Boy or Little Homo? Sometimes, Only Jesus Can Tell the Difference

Freehold, Iowa—All of 10-year-old Geoffrey Barnes's teachers at Landover Baptist School for Saved Children described the immaculately groomed child as polite. *Too polite.* "When I heard about this boy's persnickety courtesy, I became alarmed," recounted Pastor Deacon Fred. "As any Christian father who has taken a leather strap to an overly swishy son knows, the line that separates a well-mannered little boy from a rainbow-flag-flying, gay-parade-float-riding, hop-scotching sissy is as fine as a Chinaman's hair. In fact, the only way to tell if you have a little sodomite-in-training under your Christian roof is to closely watch your son's little face—and crotch—when you sit him down and give him some homosexual pornography."

As a test, Pastor showed little Geoffrey Barnes a whole banker's box stuffed with an encyclopedic collection of vintage 1970s homosexual pornography. "I was waiting for that boy to vomit up his little breakfast or hurl a dog-eared first issue of *Playgirl* at the wall, screaming the name of Jesus in righteous fury," recalled Pastor. "But the only thing that polite little pervert said was 'thank you' before asking permission to leave. That was all I needed to hear to know that we had a genuine nancy-boy on our hands."

Pastor immediately alerted the parents of normal children at the school of the significant risk of seduction and recruitment by a conniving tot craftily using perfect manners to disarm his prey and mask his vile lusts. "When I got Pastor's urgent memo, the first thing I did was go straight on down to Geoffrey's Creation Science lab and grabbed that little pansy by his perfectly pressed collar," recalled Principal Enoch Richards. "I smacked that boy so hard, I dented my wedding ring. Few things make my temper rise like a sissified boy. That child makes my skin crawl. I'll tell you something, I've spent a lot of time thinking about those lustful men who do ungodly things to delicate body

Drunken Catholic Priest Turns Truckload of Krispy Kreme Doughnuts into the Body of Christ

Boxfuls of glazed and chocolate-dipped Jesuses are thought to be on the shelves at several area Kroger stores. Shoppers avoiding red meat are advised to play it safe and choose another brand.

parts best left to the timid touch of a Christian lady, and I can tell you that I hate homosexuals more than almost anything. More than even Mexicans."

As part of Geoffrey's mandatory Baptists Are Saving Homosexuals ex-gay detoxification program, Geoffrey will appear before all 14 Landover Baptist Sunday services and beg for forgiveness until the sin-hating congregations' rebukes are finally silenced. He will also be required to skip around school for two weeks wearing a large pink sandwich-board sign reading "Jesus Hates Me Because I'm a Big Ole Sissy." After that, if he is caught being effeminately courteous again, his domineering mother and distant father will be fined no less than $1,000 for each offense.

"We've never let anyone graduate from our school and go on to become a florist or a Scientologist and we're not about to start now," said Principal Richards. Richards asked parents to become vigilant in spotting the evidence of homosexuality before carelessly letting one of their little sodomites onto a school bus. The most reliable signs that a son is skipping down the road to frenzied buggery are: playing with dolls that don't kill, playing tiddlywinks (or just saying the word), donning stylish or coordinated clothing, especially in pink, purple and certain shades of green, sporting unnaturally clean toenails, demonstrating artistic originality or a musical talent other than listening, having a "flair" for anything, possessing a wild imagination or ability to speak French, wearing their hair over the ears or collar or in revealing "free love" bowl cuts, being too eager to please parents or teachers, swaying slightly while praying, reading too much or too well, locking bedroom doors and reemerging flushed and sweaty, crying when not being spanked, refusing to disrobe in the locker room or Pastor's office, refusing to skip over the parts in the Bible about King David and his regrettable wantonness for young Jonathan, extending fingers during a yawn, and being the last one picked for any team that doesn't have "debate" in its name.

Pastor Tells Divorcees:
The Honeymoons Are Over!

Last month, an early morning suburban raid was carried out by Baptist SWAT teams armed only with King James Bibles and semiautomatic rifles. During the incursion, over 200 so-called "wives" were roused from sleep between 3:00 and 4:30 A.M. to the sound of their front doors being kicked in by Pastor Deacon Fred. They were then soundly rebuked, allowed a moment to remove their foam curlers and taken to Freehold Train Depot in unmarked church minivans. There, they were loaded into leased boxcars for the 49-hour journey to their new home at Landover Baptist Internment Campus for Divorced Women in Manzanar, California.

As Pastor Deacon Fred explained in a press release: "The New Testament is very clear in Matthew 5:32. A woman who remarries is a harlot. End of story. It hardly seemed fair to the Catholic streetwalkers downtown, who, thanks to calls from Landover wives, are now more familiar with a paddy wagon than the back of a deacon's Cadillac, if we just left these domesticated tramps free to peddle their used goods in the bedrooms of Landover's exclusive Christian subdivisions."

The raid was made during Landover's annual Crystal Night, which is the charitable evening when local winos receive a stem of Waterford (Mauve pattern) to start their heirloom collec-

Four Out of Five Baptist Divorcees Angry at Gays for Undermining the Sanctity of Marriage

"With each new husband, I grow increasingly angry at those cotton-picking homosexuals for undermining the sanctimony of my marriages," said a clearly vexed Nancy Schaeffer. "At the rate those gay boys are going, by the time I get to my sixth marriage, it may not even be worth the effort. Damn them. Damn them all to hell!"

Church Member Spotlight:

Pastor Harvey Darkens plans to break Methuselah's record by keeping his comatose wife, Millie, alive for 970 years with the help of a Tupperware feeding tube and an old Hoover vacuum as a makeshift respirator.

PLEASE NOTE:

To reduce clutter displeasing to Christ in the collection plates, starting next weekend, all 27 ATMs located in the sanctuary will only dispense in multiples of $100. We are asking everyone to try to use each of these new machines to ensure that they are all working.

tions. "These vagrants need to be made to realize that every beverage—even isopropyl alcohol—tastes better in leaded crystal," explained America's Best Christian, Mrs. Betty Bowers, through a bullhorn from a reconnaissance helicopter to a pleased Nancy Grace. "We surprised these wanton divorcees living in sin as adulterers with second—shockingly, sometimes *third*—husbands while they were sleeping. Pastor learned that neat little trick during sleep deprivation training at Gitmo where he served as a celebrity Baptist chaplain to the prisoners. Fortunately for us, we were dealing with Iowans, not hysterical, media-savvy Arabs, so most of our more coercive methods of persuasion won't be rudely splashed across the yellow pages of the *New York Times*. To be sort of honest, I was initially opposed to breaking down their front doors and dragging those strumpets into the streets because it smacked of bad manners. But when the Lord comes a'knocking, like a thief in the night, He means business. All these altar-crazy trollops will be held until they can be repatriated with the only husband God recognizes at parties—their *first*. Any illegitimate offspring of an unholy, later union, of course, will be placed in like-raced Christian homes or rented to the new Nike factory."

THE GOOD NEWS

Pastor Fleeced by Expertly Written E-mail from Nigeria Promising Millions

Last week, Pastor Deacon Fred, along with several other Landover Baptist staff members, received an urgent e-mail message from Basher Mobutu, son of the late president of Nigeria, Mobutu Sese Seko. "I knew that this surprisingly rich African fellow was desperate for Christian help," recalled Pastor Deacon Fred, "because he had taken the time to send copies of this e-mail not only to me but to everyone on our staff and their families." In the e-mail, Basher explained that he knew Pastor would be surprised to hear from him, but assumed that Landover Baptist Church was already aware of a financial dispute between his family and the present civilian government of Nigeria. Mr. Mobutu conveyed that, due to circumstances beyond his control, his father's bank accounts in Switzerland and North America were frozen. He went on to solicit Landover's confidential assistance in taking custody of 30 million United States dollars (US $30,000,000.00). "Naturally, that bountiful sum caught my well-trained eye," said Pastor. "We didn't get to be the richest church in America by asking a lot of questions when folks wave a fistful of cash in our faces. So the first thing I

Pastor Deacon Fred Storms Out of Conference

Pastor Deacon Fred angrily dismissed the Landover Conference of Pastors when they failed to grant him the honorary title "His Most Godly Magnificence" as part of his new eight-figure compensation package. In lieu of the title, Pastor Deacon Fred declared himself "infallible in all church matters, except remembering folks' names."

This Week's Soloist's Hymn:

"Redeemer, My Feet Doth Need Washing Again!"

Terrorists at Your Front Door? Support the "No Knock List"

In response to the wildly successful "No Call List" that prohibits telemarketers from swindling unsuspecting old people into squandering a retirement nest egg that could better be used to secure a new waterfall for our Sanctuary, Landover Baptist lobbyists are vigorously championing the "No Knock List" currently before Congress. This bill will allow American households to register their Christian homes with the FBI. Once a family is listed, they will be absolutely immune from any criminal prosecution or civil damages that may arise from the injury, mutilation, death or dismemberment of any Jehovah's Witness, Mormon or other pesky false-faith missionary knocking on their doors during dinner. Once this bill is passed, American Christians will finally be able to retire their polite "no, thank you" and haul out the type of ammunition that even the most obdurate *Watchtower*-wielding nuisance can understand.

did after reading the e-mail was to call Mrs. Bowers and tell her to gas up her ministry Gulfstream jet because we had us an urgent trip to Africa to pick up some blessings."

"As a real American," Pastor would later recall, "I would normally have no reason to ever go to an uncivilized country like Africa. But as a Christian, I was curious to return to the Garden of Eden where the Lord had first given man a paradise—only to snatch it back in a hotheaded rage. Once I got there, I realized that the deck was stacked against Adam and Eve from the get-go. As Mrs. Bowers and I quickly became aware, to be the only two white people in Africa is a daunting ordeal."

After returning home, embarrassed by realizing he had been the victim of an incredibly clever and elaborate e-mail con game clearly perpetrated by master criminals, Pastor Deacon Fred told Pat Robertson on *The 700 Club*: "Being Baptist, growing up reading only the Bible, we are taught never to question the truth of anything someone has taken the time to type. So, naturally, I took it on face value that this little African fellow had millions of dollars he was willing to give us—and millions more we could call upon the power of the Lord to coax him out of. I now realize that he was like the Devil—cagily tailoring temptation to play into the biggest weakness of the tempted. I'm sure if I had been Whitney Houston, the e-mail would have promised a pile of prime Colombian cocaine the size of Kilimanjaro. But since it was addressed to me, an American with a Christian ministry, I was, of course, offered cash. I'm sure if he had sent it to you, Brother Pat, that cagey little so-and-so would have offered you cash, too. Although I imagine that quite a bit less would have done the trick."

Landover Christian Academy for the Saved

FINAL HISTORY EXAM

TODAY'S DATE IS: _____ (days since the spotless, placenta-free birth of the Baby Jesus)

CLASS: History of Liberals Ruining America

TEACHER: Your Parents' Choice for All of Their Real Estate Needs: Mrs. Marge Davis, Realtor®

YOUR NAME: _____

DIRECTIONS: This is a three-part test concerning the Founding Fathers of this Christian Country who are currently being lapped by the relentless flames of Hell.

PART ONE

The first part of the examination involves reading quotations from these wig-wearing demons to see if you can get past even one of them without projectile-vomiting your breakfast onto the back of the student in front of you. If you manage to read all of these Dark Side utterances without being physically ill, there is no need to proceed to Part Two, as you have already failed this course.

PART TWO

Thomas Jefferson

With a No. 2 pencil, draw a circle around each satanic quotation and connect it with a line of flames to the Founding Father who was damned to Hell for saying it.

James Madison

A. "Whenever we read the obscene stories [of the Bible], the voluptuous debaucheries, the cruel and torturous executions, the unrelenting vindictiveness with which more than half the Bible is filled, it would be more consistent that we call it the word of a demon than the Word of God."

Thomas Paine

B. "The day will come when the mystical generation of Jesus, by the supreme being as his father in the womb of a virgin, will be classed with the fable of the generation of Minerva in the brain of Jupiter."

C. "The United States of America should have a foundation free from the influence of clergy."

Benjamin Franklin

D. "As to Jesus of Nazareth, my Opinion of whom you particularly desire, I think the System of Morals and his Religion . . . has received various corrupting Changes, and I have, with most of the present dissenters in England, some doubts as to his Divinity."

George Washington

E. "During almost fifteen centuries has the legal establishment of Christianity been on trial. What have been its fruits? More or less in all places, pride and indolence in the Clergy, ignorance and servility in the laity, in both, superstition, bigotry and persecution."

John Adams

F. "The government of the United States is not in any sense founded on the Christian religion."

PART THREE

Draw pointy tails, horns and looks of excruciating pain on each of these evil men's faces.

amazon.com

Bannou Book Block™ is active (check with your pastor about deselecting this option)

Welcome to Books!
Click here to explore more.

Books you recently looked at include:

Demon Spotters' Illustrated Guide
Over 3,500 types of demons sorted by fetish & aroma

by Mitch Walker, Creation Scientist

Demon Spotters' Illustrated Guide

Getting to the Bottom with Things
BY
BILL O'REILLY

Sequel to Good Vibrations by Bill O'Reilly

Daddy, Why Did Jesus Kill Gradma?

Teaching toddlers about Hell

A Christian Coloring Book by Pastor Deacon Fred

Daddy, Why Did Jesus Kill Grandma? (Teaching Toddlers About Hell)

A Christian Children's Coloring Book by the Lord Jesus
(edited by Pastor Deacon Fred)

List Price: ~~$12.07~~

Our Price: $35.99

You Save: Nothing (only Jesus saves!)

Availability: Down to last 56,893 in stock (more on order!). Orders of fewer than five books are looked upon with disfavor by a watchful God jealous of Dan Brown's sales. Warning: Each book contains a GPS tracking device, enabling author to determine if you are palming it off in secondary markets or taking it into places you ought not enter, such as massage parlors, Las Vegas or Catholic churches.

Summary: Told in the type of easy-to-understand, jaunty language that makes graphic stories of the death of loved ones fun for the young, *Daddy, Why Did Jesus Kill Grandma?* is a must for families with small, curious children. They will be thrilled and giggle as God's fiendishly violent temper is directed toward those who dare to question His perfect, unconditional love for them. Poor old, sassy Grandma Jenkins is no exception. Better she had slipped down the cellar stairs and broken every brittle bone in her old-lady body than back-talked Jesus after He killed her husband of 52 years! For her, there is no escape—and no reunion with her more obsequious spouse. To her horror, one thoughtless slip of her impudent tongue uttered under her breath next to Mr. Jenkins's deathbed sealed her fate. Why, she may as well have hollered, "Jesus, grab me by my cheap strand of pearls and sling me into the fires of Hell now!"

Your children will follow her exciting limb-bruising descent into Hell with wide-eyed excitement, as this helpful book instructs you to light a Zippo lighter under their extended palms for a fabulous interactive sensation, allowing tykes to better appreciate Grandma's fiery predicament. Marooned alone in the lake of fire, Granny's only company is a visiting red-finned water demon named "Mr. Pokey Tale." Mr. Pokey Tale sodomizes Granny, which is tactfully explained as "Mr. Pokey Tale put his giant pee-pee in sweet Grandma Jenkins' screaming mouth as fire waves crashed onto her gray head, bursting her wrinkled body into flames, like a little kitty cat being thrown into your family room fireplace."

This beautifully illustrated Christian children's coloring book is grounded in the timeless words of Jesus Christ. Jesus teaches all His children not to be afraid of the Devil, but to fear the Living God. "But I forewarn you whom ye shall fear," Jesus says in Luke 12:5, "Fear Him, who after he hath killed hath the power to cast into hell." Talking to a four-year-old child about God's carefully orchestrated plan of eternal torture in Hell and His unquenchable thirst for boiling human flesh used to be difficult and scary, but now, with this book, the only thing your child will scream is, "Read it again, Mommy!"

From the book:

Remember dear Grandma, who baked so well?
Soon she will be baking—This time in Hell!

Dear Daddy, why Grandma? What did she do?
Don't question it, child, or God will GET YOU!

Hardcover 12th edition (November 2005)
Christian Children's Books; ISBN: 09246663322: Dimension (in Godly inches): 0.47 x 9.5 x 12

Amazon.com Sales Rank: 19
Average Customer Ranting: ★★★★★
Number of Reviews: 2,785 (CLICK HERE to apply for permission from author to review)

Satan's Concubine
autobiography by
ann coulter

Satan's Concubine, autobiography by Ann Coulter

amazon.com

God-fearing fundamentalist Baptist customers who bought this book also bought:

- *Jesus, Will My Islamic Playmate Butcher Me to Death? Teaching Children About Religious Extremists Who Don't Believe in Jesus,* by Marge Davis
- *Bloody Marys for the Soul,* by Jenna Bush
- *Bargaining for Freedom with Whiskey: A Survival Guide for Nubile Baptist Boys Cornered by a Catholic Priest* by Father Brenden O'Malley (retired and on probation)
- *Your Daddy Don't Live Here No More. He's Shacking Up with Satan!,* by Tonya Trixie Perkins
- *Heather Has Two Mommies—and They're Both Going Straight to Hell!* by Dr. James Dobson

---

People who bought this book were most likely to bid on the following auctions:

- Solid Gold Calf (Price: $118,125)
- 8-piece matching set of Louis Vuitton Rapture Luggage (still open)

Editorial Reviews

When it comes to pornographic violence, Landover Baptist always gives Mel Gibson a run for his money, and this book is no exception. Your children will love the exciting story and you will admire the detailed Thomas Kinkade® cartoons. As you flip through the pages of this lushly illustrated book, you'll see Grandma Jenkins kneeling in prayer by her husband's deathbed. Her Christian family is gathered around her, praying and reading a Bible that has been in the family since before the Civil War. Within moments of her beloved husband succumbing—finally—to an agonizing death from cancer, Grandma opens her mouth and breathes the words, "I'm not sure if God is even real anymore" and sobs. During the next 35 pages, Grandma finds out just how real God is when He nanny-slaps her head with His gigantic hands, bursting it like a ripe tomato all over the family and hospital walls. The book also comes with a red crayon that children can use to color the hospital walls with Grandma's blood, and later to color places where Grandma keeps bursting into flames in the lake of fire.

Spotlight Reviews

13,230,999 of 13,231,000 people found the following review helpful:

★★★★★   *A book guaranteed to both entertain and frighten children of all ages!*

Reviewer: **Mrs. Betty Bowers, America's Best Christian,** May 6, 2006

When small children inquire about the whereabouts of a deceased friend or relative, some timid, deceitful parents will respond with the outrageous lie that "they are in Heaven with the angels," knowing full well that the loved one's decaying corpse is languishing in the dirt until Judgment Day. Some counterfeit-Christians actually embrace the despicable falsehood that the dead are already gallivanting about in God's Glory—as if the Lord provides "free samples" of Heaven, allowing sinners to "test-drive" their reward. Such a ludicrous notion, of course, would render the glorious Day of Judgment a superfluous charade. As all True Christians™ know, it is the Lord's plan that those He has decided to kill off shall commune with worms and rodents in graves until, in 99 percent of the cases, He dispatches them to Hell to be tortured by proxy for eternity. This may not be a pleasant thing to tell children barely old enough to dress themselves, but it is not a parent's business to succumb to lies simply to cover for the Lord's wildly misanthropic predilections. That is why *Daddy, Why Did Jesus Kill Grandma?* is the only book we use at Bringing Integrity To Christian Home-makers' "Teaching Toddlers About God's Relentlessly Vicious Wrath" workshops.

Kerry Bumper Sticker Removed— Along with Car

Landover Security has impounded a blue Volvo in Calvary parking lot, Section L, for having an old Kerry bumper sticker. "It must have been some sort of sick joke," laments Pastor Deacon Fred. "But they aren't getting that car back until they apologize before the entire 8 o'clock service."

Disciplinary News:

Mrs. Delores Matthews turned her husband in to the Board of Deacons for momentary equivocation before joining the rest of the congregation in a hearty "Amen!" following Pastor's sermon last Sunday. Split-second review of security videos has resulted in a $450 fine for Mr. Matthews and a lovely citation on real parchment for Mrs. Matthews, signed by Jesus Himself.

HEATHER'S HOLY HABITS:

Is It Possible to Be Ladylike and Christian at the Same Time?

Ladies, being Christian and female is rough these days, but managing to be ladylike at the same time? Goodness! Let's face it, gals, the Bible doesn't give us much wiggle room. The Good Book describes us as being about as wretched as a creature can be. And our predicament all started with that harlot Eve, who obviously wanted grandchildren so badly she snuck into her own sons' beds (since Adam and Eve had no daughters). But it wasn't her incest or infidelity that condemned us all. It was a few nibbles on a piece of fruit that really ticked God off. Which just goes to show that women have been stuck on unreasonable diets literally from the start of mankind.

We must never forget how disgusting the Lord thinks we are, ladies. At one point, God actually placed monetary value on people and, as you can expect, we're worth about as much as a dollar bill in Paris (Leviticus 27:3–7). Because we are so wretched, we are never to maintain any position of authority (Isaiah 3:12). Because we are inherently sinful beings, we must forever keep our mouths shut in church, letting our husbands explain anything we need to know (1 Corinthians 14:34–35) except, presumably, how to get to the grocery store. And, of course, we are always to obey our husband and submit to his every whim . . . limberness and gag control notwithstanding (Colossians 3:18; 1 Peter 3:1).

At first blush, one might think the key to a happy life for women is to avoid marriage altogether. But the Lord's Code of Regulations has closed that loophole. As we all know, women exist to serve men and procreate, and one must marry before having children to avoid the damnation of fornication (1 Corinthians 7:1–2). At second glance, one might conclude that finding a way to rid herself of her hubby is the answer. But divorce is out of the question, because Jesus hates divorcees (Matthew 5:32). And killing your husband isn't much of an option because life for widows is even worse than life for women in general. Widows must constantly be desolate and pray all

day and night (1 Timothy 5:5–6), which will give you the calloused knees of a crack whore. And no widow can expect assistance from anyone unless she is over 70, had only one husband, raised children, lodged strangers, washed saints' feet, relieved the afflicted and diligently did good deeds (1 Timothy 5:9–15). Who would have time to get even the most modest amount of shopping squeezed into the day if she was charged with all those laborious responsibilities? It seems our loving God has anticipated every possible contingency and found a way to cut us off at every turn to make our lives as miserable as folks who live without air-conditioning.

But don't despair. As American True Christians™ living in Jesusland, we know that saved life is all about using religion to our advantage. The bottom line, gals, is that being ladylike is just like every other aspect of Christian living: You have to find a way to manipulate the Word of God to support whatever it is you want to do. Let me give you a few examples from my incredibly blessed and ladylike life. Like all true ladies, the last thing in the world I want is to have a husband writhing around on top of me while my hair gets mussed as I lay there reciting the "begets" from Abraham to Jesus, and worrying about my dress getting wrinkles from being flung over a chair. But the Bible says we must submit to our husband's sexual demands. However, like just about all of God's admonitions, there are exceptions, and the exceptions swallow the rule. Here is what you do: The Bible says that when a woman is having her monthly visitor, she is unclean for at least seven days and no one is to come near her (Leviticus 15:19). A husband should not even look at his menstruating wife (Leviticus 18:19). Use this time to your advantage! It is during these "periods" of time that I have done my most productive shopping in Manhattan. And, as I explain to Harry, for some reason, my monthly visitor seems to want to linger for weeks on end, particularly around the holidays.

Perhaps the most difficult Bible verses to deal with are those that appear to say we should all be homely and unattractive. A clever Christian gal will work out ways around these as well. Harry used to try to induce me to shop at the Freehold thrift shop instead Neiman's by citing that disturbing verse from First Timothy:

> In like manner also, that women adorn themselves in modest apparel, with shamefacedness and sobriety; not with braided hair, or gold, or pearls or costly array (1 Timothy 2:9).

Church Member Spotlight:

Inez Watkins, 82, Is Touched by an Angel and Calls the Police!

Last Week's Favorite Hymn:

"Mary, Kindly Shut Your Cakehole While Your Son Is Talking to Me!"

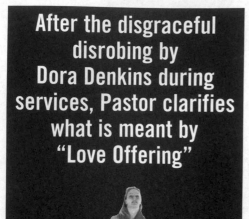

After the disgraceful disrobing by Dora Denkins during services, Pastor clarifies what is meant by "Love Offering"

First, I explained to Harry that the only things you can buy at the Freehold thrift shop are Dacron pantsuits and phosphorescent gowns. Pants are to be worn by men only and, as for the shrill gowns, I am unlikely to be invited to a Guatemalan prom anytime soon. The Bible clearly forbids women from wearing men's clothes, so the thrift shop was out of the question (Deuteronomy 22:5). (I carefully sidestep the fact that men's clothes *were* dresses when Deuteronomy was written.) I then explained that "modest apparel" simply means something that is not revealing, in eye-popping contrast to one of Dora Denkins's cellulite-flashing leather miniskirts. I would never wear anything that tight or anything that revealed that much skin, for I wouldn't dream of condemning half the men in Freehold to Hell for lusting in their hearts (Matthew 5:28). The ban on gold and pearls is a bit more difficult to address, but when your jewelry collection is encyclopedic enough to allow substitutions of platinum and diamonds, it becomes less of an issue. After all, the ultimate goal of any True Christian™ is: Make your faith conform to your lifestyle.

THE GOOD NEWS

Nipple-Flashing Harlot Dragged from Last Sunday's Service

Pastor wishes to apologize to everyone offended when last Sunday's sold-out 8:00 A.M. service turned into a pornographic film festival. (And if you weren't offended, you had no business being there in the first place.) As you will reluctantly recall, during the sermon, cameras regrettably settled on Bertha Hasselhof, causing images of the breast-feeding exhibitionist to be flashed across the 24 HDTV screens throughout the sickened sanctuary. "Bertha was sitting right next to me at service when she pulled out the first of those

Winnebago-sized breasts of hers," recalled Mrs. Barry "Freda" Claiborne. "The thing that caught my eye was that the liver-colored area around the end of her upper-lady-business was as dark and drippy as a used Lipton teabag! When she pushed her little Jimmy's head into it, he looked like he'd just been shoved head-first into a bowl of soggy cereal. And the noise! Mercy me, it was like being stuck next to some sucking goat!"

"Since the offending trollop was sitting in general admission," Mrs. Betty Bowers, America's Best Christian, told Diane Sawyer later that night, "the Lord had mercifully kept her revolting display hidden from me for several minutes during Pastor's sermon. Then, I looked up from my *Robb Report* and saw a pair of 22-foot bosoms leaking and heaving on the JumboTron over the altar. It was like watching two zeppelins full of half-and-half hovering and colliding overhead. Oh, the humanity! Without saying a word to each other, Heather Hardwick and I immediately flipped open our cell phones and speed-dialed church Security to let them know that we had the equivalent of a temple prostitute in our very sanctuary. Honestly, I haven't seen such shrewish behavior since I wrestled a beer funnel from Jenna Bush during one of those weekend interventions at Camp David."

Within seconds of Betty's and Heather's calls, five burly men in crisp uniforms grabbed Bertha by her arms and dragged her up the aisle to the back of the church. When they

JUST ANNOUNCED:

To speed up the processing of the approval of prayers for amounts exceeding $350,000, starting next Monday, *one* member of the Holy Trinity, rather than the traditional two, will constitute a quorum. The Holy Spirit remains your best bet for successfully securing vacation property.

Bible Quiz:

How does God say a new wife must defend herself if her husband claims she was not a virgin on their wedding night?

A. She must only swear, in the name of the Lord, that her lady parts had not previously been taken out for a test drive.

B. She must submit to a full gynecological examination by an independent physician (not given to leering), chosen by the tribunal.

C. Her parents must wave the bloodstained sheets and nightgown around in public as proof.

D. None of the above.

Answer: C. "If a man take a wife, and go in unto her . . . I found her not a maid, then shall the father of the damsel, and her mother, take and bring forth the tokens of the damsel's virginity unto the elders of the city in the gate; and the damsel's father shall say unto the elders . . . these are the tokens of my daughter's virginity. And they shall spread the cloth before the elders of the city" (Deuteronomy 22:13–17).

ATTENTION PLEASE:

Would the little lady who left her "Love Waits" tube-top and crotchless under-panties in the choir balcony last night please see the Pastor?

got to the vestry, they dropped Bertha with such heartfelt disgust that her son, Jimmy, was dislodged from her enormous bosom and began rolling down the main aisle. The infant would have made it all the way to reserved seating had it not been for the nimble block with an umbrella by Landover Junior High for the Saved hockey-star Bobby Brunswick.

"Of all the things that have happened in the 50-plus years I've been a member of this Godly church, this takes the cake," noted a still distraught Mrs. Floribunda. "I was here the first time a woman ever tried to speak in the chapel, right before her family's house got burned to the ground. I was here the day the first colored person walked right into the main sanctuary with his head held up high like he was a normal person or something. But nothing over the decades prepared me for what I saw when I looked up at that enormous TV screen. You would think a Baptist chapel would be the one place on Earth you could be safe from kinky pornography! I'm just glad Betty and Heather acted with lightning reflexes to get that brazen harlot removed. Who knows? Goodness me, had they waited a minute longer, we'd probably have seen the little tramp's thong panties flying over our heads and swinging from the golden cross over the altar!"

He Shot a Man Dead for Mocking Jesus

Bubba Gatlin will be released from prison tonight after being imprisoned for almost two excruciating hours following his shooting of a notorious local Christ-hater. Sheriff Paterson said that no charges will be filed, as street surveillance videos clearly show that Mr. Gatlin complied with a local ordinance requiring all citizens to observe a post-rebuke three-second "cooling down period" before driving a bullet through any blasphemer's skull at point-blank range. A dinner will be held in his honor in Fellowship Hall. Check the church lobby for more details.

Landover Baptist's Afterlife Real Estate

Call Marge Davis, the Lord's exclusive Realtor® for luxury estates in Heaven's lovely pearly-gated communities. Glory!

"In my Father's house are many mansions: if it were not so, I would have told you. I go to prepare a place for you."
—John 14:2 and Marge Davis!

"Lay up for yourselves treasures in heaven, where neither moth nor rust doth corrupt, and where thieves do not break through nor steal." *—Matthew 6:20*

New listings in the most desirable neighborhoods of Metropolitan Heaven!

And God said, "Let the waters under the heavens be gathered together into one place—your new harp-shaped swimming pool!"

$23,988,340 15BR/17.5BA Won't Jesus be a jealous God, indeed, when He sees that your mansion is nicer than His! Beautiful paneled library with over 1,300 Bibles! "Race you to the other end of the pool, Matthew, Mark and John!" Greater love hath no man for a home theater!

A 24/7 concierge? Jesus said, "It is not written in your condominium agreement?"

DIVINE NEW PRICE! Corner unit with two balconies guarantees views of sinners being killed in both hemispheres during Apocalypse! Blessed are the fly-in closets. No knee should bow with ceilings this high! Trinity three-head feather-care shower.

Judge not from the curb that ye be not judged foolish for not looking inside!

$1,200,999.99 "Your Father knoweth what things you have need of before you ask Him." Which is why you'll be calling out, "Hamburgers or bratwurst, Mary and Joseph?" from your new 53" Viking propane patio grill! You'll have had your Last Supper on a kitchen stool once you see your space-saving new folding Formica formal dinette!

Episcopalian Style— Pentecostal Price!

Even Mary will think your landscaping is immaculate!

$12,400,000 8BR/9.5BA on private cloud w/tennis court. "Jesus, I'm already in Heaven, dear. So I don't have to believe a word you say anymore—and that ball was out, mister!" The spirit is willing and the flesh will be weak after an afternoon in your private massage gazebo with hunky Saint Sven!

And God said, "Let there be recessed light! For verily I say unto thee: what a fabulous sunken bath!"

PRAY ABOUT NEW PRICE! Father, forgive the previous owners, because when it came to decorating, they knew not what they did! "A fresh coat of paint, Jesus?" Ask, and ye shall receive, that your joy may be full! An answer to the prayers of anyone the Lord hasn't blessed with a substantial down payment.

God saw your new chef's kitchen and saw that it was good! God saw your new billiard room that He had made, and behold, it was very good!

$145,000 down (with heavenly financing) guarantees one of the last remaining mansions of 10-karat gold on the cul-de-sac abutting the Lord Jesus' lovely estate! Reach across your sterling silver cyclone fence to pick fruit from Jesus' Trees of Knowledge orchard—just to see the look on His face!

Jesus

Bad Credit? Don't worry! The things that are impossible with men are possible with God! (Luke 18:27)

Sorry: No hablo Foreign

THE GOOD NEWS

Dead Girl Calls Justin Timberlake's Bluff in Suicide Dare

Thirteen-year-old Penny Hestridge, after being rejected by a member of the acid-rock group 'NSync, wished the cruel world a good "*bye, bye, bye*" in a suicide note found at her bedside. Penny's mother told Pastor that she heard the nihilistic song playing for the millionth time in her daughter's bedroom and the word "*bye*" of the last chorus was punctuated by a loud noise that sounded like a .22-caliber pistol going off. Three hours later, the song "Bye, Bye, Bye" was still playing at full volume on Penny's CD player. Mrs. Hestridge walked into Penny's bedroom and was shocked to find her daughter dead, parts of her plump head now littering the new carpeting, still clutching her suicide note containing the vicious lyrics:

> *And now I really come to see*
> *That life would be much better*
> *Once you're gone*

When asked to explain why "Bye, Bye, Bye" drove Penny to kill herself, Mrs. Hestridge responded: "Well, she's been playing that dang song for going on five years now. I'm telling you, just a few more 'byes' and I was fixing to kill myself, too! But, seriously, I think what happened was when she first really understood the lyrics, Penny felt that it was Justin Timberlake's way of saying he was leaving her for Britney. And then Cameron, which she had to find out about on *TRL*. Over time, when he never called between girlfriends, she started to think he was telling her that he probably wouldn't even notice if she was alive or dead. Teenage boys can be so cruel."

Mrs. Hestridge told *Entertainment Tonight*'s Mary Hart that Penny had been dating Justin for several years. "She started writing letters to Justin when she was around eight, asking him if he loved Jesus enough to join her in comitting to a 'Love Waits' pledge and T-shirt. No more than one or two letters a day for several months. Her whole allowance went for stamps. Well, finally he wrote her back. You know how shy boys are around girls they like. Penny knew that he really liked her when she saw how much trouble he had gone to in responding to her. He'd gotten a professional photographer to make a big glossy photograph of him. He even had his name printed at the bottom for her. And then he'd written across his cute little jumpsuit 'Love, Justin.' Over the years, she must have gone to eight or nine of 'NSync's concerts and at every single one Justin yelled to her—in front of everyone—'I love you!'"

Mrs. Hestridge was so distraught over her daughter's death that even before the funeral, she was consulting with lawyers about a $230,000,000 lawsuit against the rock group that killed her daughter. "Now I know that Justin was just toying with Penny's affections. But this is America: you can't kill people without paying a lot of money. Just ask those tobacco companies. 'NSync murdered my baby and I'd at least like to get a real nice house in Orlando or something so I don't feel like she died for nothing. It's all sad and everything, but as a Christian, I try to look on the bright side. You know, at least I don't have to hear that song no more. So, there's that."

Annual Harry Potter Book Burning to Be Held on East Lawn

Last Week's Favorite Hymn:

"It's Raining Four-Headed Lions in Jerusalem Tonight!"

Landover Opens America's First Ex-Negro Ministry!

As Baptists, we all know that God created us in His image. So, it is only fair that we turn around and graciously extend the same courtesy to others. That is why Southern Baptists everywhere have embraced the glorious crusade of courageously coercing everyone to be just a little bit more like us—and righteously undermining (for Christ) those who willfully refuse to give up their so-called "identities." We started off on a small scale, thrusting pamphlets into the hands of Jews and Hindus on their so-called "holy" days and crisply informing them with Christian love that they are damned for eternity. Were these poor, lost souls grateful for us taking time out of our busy day to let them know they are going straight to Hell? Hardly! Truly, the unsaved can be the very picture of discourtesy. Well, our Godly mission for complete conformity can weather an uncivil rebuff from unsaved trash!

Prayer Death Squads Target Local Democrat

Mark your imprecatory prayer calendars to lobby for the death of local Demoncratic mayoral candidate Miss (with countless children, mind you!) Cloressa Washington all day Monday. Pastor is asking all current Landover Baptist Gold and Silver Level Prayer Partners to disregard the Prayer Circle Hit List included in last Sunday's newsletter. Those who have begun prayers beseeching the Lord Jesus to dip Antichrist Hillary Rodham Clinton like a teabag into boiling liquid are encouraged to finish that heartfelt entreaty. All other prayer warriors are to immediately turn the Lord's attention to the more pressing political need of preventing a liberal Negress from turning City Hall into a new rest stop for weary demons on their way to Des Moines.

For those wishing to learn the most effective ways to goad the Almighty into killing, maiming or otherwise inconveniencing, make plans to attend "The Positive Power of Negative Prayer: Why Stop at Just Assassinating Their Character?" seminar in the Golden Cherubim ballroom off of the main sanctuary. Thursday, 8:00 P.M. ($200 in advance/$400 at the door/ammo provided to the first 25 prayer warriors).

True Christians™ everywhere are now turning their attention to forcing homosexuals to try to act like real people. Landover Baptist's good friends at Traditional Values Coalition have discovered that the most effective way to marginalize nancy-boys (so they can't get *special* rights, such as being treated like they were one of us) is to keep repeating the sound Creation Science principle: Gay people are not born that way because we say they aren't. Traditional Values Coalition's founder, Rev. Lou Sheldon, who has selflessly devoted his entire life to thinking nonstop about other men licking each other, explains: "All we need is for folks to send us money—and it is going to take a lot, so give until it hurts—so we can hire one of these gay boys to go around saying he put no more thought into his decision to be a homo than he did into choosing his socks this morning. But we need to be more careful than our friends at Focus on the Family, who placed full-page ads in national newspapers, promoting their plump ex-gay spokesperson, only to have the damned fairy lapse over an alcoholic beverage at a seedy homosexual hustler bar!"

While Landover Baptist applauds Traditional Values Coalition and Focus on the Family's noble efforts to make sure that people who only *think* they are happy know that they are actually utterly inconsolable, we don't believe that ex-gay ad campaigns go nearly far enough. "President Bush has asked all Evangelical Republicans to reach out to the coloreds," explains Pastor Deacon Fred, "because, let's face it, they are about the only folks out there who hate homos as much as us. That's why we have recruited Clarence Thomas, Alan Keyes and Michael Jackson, in a $1,700,000 deal, to be our spokesnegroes for Landover Baptist's new ex-Negro ministry called Baptists Invoking God's Old Testament Standards. BIGOTS will teach Negroes that Negroality is all about *acting* Negro, not *being* one. We at Landover Baptist realize that there are problems for Negroes that even prisons can't fix. The solution? Stop being one! Because, friends, being a Negro is a *choice*. And we care enough to make sure folks don't make the wrong one. Like, if you write 'What Would Jesus Do?', don't willfully go ahead and write it with your left hand, knowing all along that Jesus wrote with His right hand. It's all about a Godly choice. Remember, all you folks with fish decals on the backs of your cars: Swimming isn't what makes a fish a fish. It's having those ugly, bulging eyes and smelly scales that make them fish. They *choose* to swim. And, with the Lord's love, they could stop tomorrow."

Overheard:

72-year-old Pastor Enoch Smith: "I know you are inside that delightful young woman's vagina, demon! And I command you to wipe yourself down and come on out of there in the name of Jesus—or I'm coming in after you!"

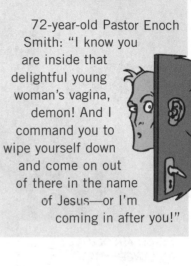

Last Week's Favorite Hymn:

"O Great Marketer, What a Vend We Have in Jesus!"

1. GIVE EQUAL TIME TO COMPETING IDEAS

Evolution, Slavery, the Holocaust and Gravity: There are two, equally reasonable sides to every issue! Make sure you give them equal attention.

2. DON'T TAKE SIDES

"Well, Jenny, this is one theory: that the Earth is round. The other, equally valid theory is that it's as flat as a pancake. You need to decide what's right for you. I'm just your geography teacher, dear."

Freehold, Iowa Public School System

SCIENCE
Curriculum Guidelines

Using Intelligent Design to Trick Your Slightly Less Credulous Students into Believing in Creationism

3. TEACH ABSOLUTELY ANY THEORY THAT COMPETES WITH EVOLUTION TO EXPLAIN THE ORIGINS OF LIFE ON EARTH

★ *The Totally Awesome Super-Computer on Mars Theory*

★ *The Vulcan Love Child Teleported to Africa Theory*

★ *The Enormous Tub of Unrefrigerated Yogurt Culture Theory*

And don't forget the most popular theory amongst Christians: The Talking Snake Theory from the historical Garden of Eden

4. MAKE SUPERSTITIONS SOUND SUPER-SCIENTIFIC!

Noted Baptist Scientist Discovers "Science Don't Make a Lick of Cotton-Pickin' Sense!"

"We don't know how He does it," said Landover Baptist Junior High School for the Saved teacher Mrs. Doris Whitaker, "but Jesus changes the colors of the leaves on the trees during the fall, which is the season named after the fall of man from Eden where they had no autumn colors until an angry Lord made the skies rain with blood. And no fancy-schmancy science book of silly facts will tell you that. It is perfectly clear that Baby Jesus is behind the pretty-colored leaves that drop off the trees as piles of trash on your lawn! Why else are only Christmas trees left green? So they can be decorated on His birthday, that's why! Praise!"

designs *on* intelligence

Mrs. Whitaker expressed a long-held Baptist belief that so-called "science" cannot explain the things you can see with your own two eyes without making up a load of hooey. "In spite of our righteous— *and dang expensive*—lobbying, Congress has been unwilling to force scientists to label their disgusting God-hating work as fiction," said Pastor Deacon Fred. "But it's not called *Science Fiction* for nothing, folks! So-called 'science' is just a big pile of secular lies made up solely to take the credit away from God's 'mad scientist in His secret laboratory in the sky' approach to creating stuff. There is no other way of putting it! Do they think that the people of God are going to stand by like idiots and let so-called 'scientists' rot this country's educational system with fanciful lies without telling them that their so-called 'hypotheses' are nothing

GUEST SERMON:

"The faith-filled folks of America have proven that the 'theory' of evolution is so crazy, they don't even have to understand one single bit of it to kick it to the curb!" by Pastor Creflo Dime, gloriously sober through the power of the Lord Jesus for almost a week.

Last Week's Favorite Hymn:

"He's Gonna Smack That Sin Right Outta Your Stupid Head!"

Full-Blown Demon Possession Misdiagnosed as Epileptic Seizure by Unsaved Doctors

Midget Digested by Whale in Bible Reenactment

In his newfound Christian zeal, dwarf Napoleon Thumb tried to prove the Bible true by reenacting one of its most controversial stories: Jonah and the whale. Thumb was placed in the mouth of a whale at Landover Aquarium in hopes of being swallowed for three days and later testifying about his joyous experience at Sunday services. After two weeks, aquarium curators are still patiently waiting for Wanda the Whale to poop out Thumb's other leg and his sleeping bag.

more than the mischievous hunches spawned by hooved demons in lab coats?"

"As Christians, we don't need far-fetched 'theorems' or outlandishly childish 'scientific' explanations like the Big Bang to make sense of the universe. We already know that Jesus is up in Heaven, living on a cloud, sitting on a golden throne. If He rustles His silver robes, the Sahara gets a sandstorm. If He flicks a drop of perspiration off His furrowed brow, those little folks in Tokyo find themselves under 10 feet of water. And this is how stupid secular scientists are: They go all crazy over a few little Chinese dissident factories belching smoke, saying it causes LSD rain and holes in the erogenous zone But I have news for them: The Lord isn't about to let mankind destroy a planet He has clearly stated in Revelation that He has His heart set on annihilating. And when the Lord unleashes the not-so-environmentally friendly fires of Hell during the Apocalypse, all those pinko tree-huggers driving around in their silly little toy hybrid cars are going to look out their tiny windshields and long for the good old days when they only had Chernobyl and the Exxon Valdez to bitch about! Glory!"

The Homo Handshake

"Exposing the Homosexual Agenda Series."

1. The prospective recruit (palm facing) is approached by a homosexual using the "three finger lure."

2. The homosexual extends his middle finger toward the tender area of his prospect's palm.

3. If there is no resistance, the homosexual begins to "tickle" the soft skin at the center of the palm.

4. During the final downward motion of the shake, it is seen who will insert or receive the index finger, thus establishing who will play the "girl" when they later meet in a public toilet for sex.

Bible Quiz:

Whom Would Jesus Damn?

What type of blasphemy is absolutely unforgivable—no matter how much you grovel?

A. None. Jesus came to Earth to forgive *all* the sins of those who accept Him as their Savior.

B. Blasphemy of God, the Father, for He is ruler over all.

C. Blasphemy of Jesus, the Son, for He died for our sins.

D. You can be forgiven for blaspheming God or Jesus, but blaspheming their invisible sidekick, the Holy Ghost, is unforgivable and ensures your descent into the fiery abyss, even if you say "oops!"

Answer: D. "All manner of sin and blasphemy shall be forgiven unto men: but the blasphemy against the Holy Ghost shall not be forgiven unto men. And whosoever speaketh a word against the Son of man, it shall be forgiven him: but whosoever speaketh against the Holy Ghost, it shall not be forgiven him" (Matthew 12:31–32; see also Mark 3:28–29; Luke 12:10).

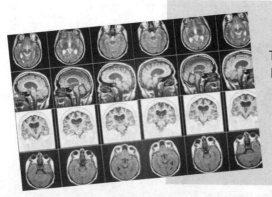

Thank You!

Through subtle yet eager nods of 1,451 happy heads, Landover Baptist members who are over 100 years of age, and in a persistent vegetative state, have unanimously agreed to increase their auto-withdrawal tithes by at least 25 percent for the next hundred years. Praise the Lord for their generosity!

PASTOR'S PULPIT

Chances Are, You and Your Family Will Wind Up in Hell

SERMON BY BROTHER HARRY HARDWICK

One of our Platinum Level tithers recently expressed a concern I've heard frequently of late: "Brother Harry, given all the people who say they've accepted Christ, will Heaven be overcrowded, like China or Des Moines?" The answer, friends, is no. You will be relieved to know that there will be far fewer people in Heaven than you might think. Instead, the vast majority of people you know will wind up spending eternity surrounded by drooling demons sporting basting brushes and erections.

We know that the first to be plunged into the smelly, hot bowels of Satan's lair will be the despicable folks who currently pose the greatest threat to America. No, not those annoying Allah-yodeling terrorists. Friends, I'm talking about a much more destructive cult. A cult is a group of individuals who share common, outlandish beliefs they are not willing to subject to rational discourse. Like Mormons or Jessica Simpson fans. The mindless, pernicious cult I have in mind is the blasphemous "Jesus is Love" liberals who think the Bible is a tiny pamphlet containing nothing more than the verse "For God so loved the world, that He gave His only begotten Son, that whosoever believeth in Him should not perish, but have everlasting life" (John 3:16).

These brainwashed liberal zombies think that salvation is just like a carefree game of golf, and that God gives you a mulligan for your sins just as long as you remember to say, "I accept Jesus." If you ask these "Jesus is Love" folks, they'll tell you, "Go ahead and kill someone, but just remember to add a 'by the way, I accept Jesus' while you're cleaning up the blood and bits of cranium—and you're on your way to Heaven!" According to this extremist cult, you can do the "Four Rs"—rape, rob, record rap music or write a check to the ACLU—and you're still going to Heaven as though you were a decent person, just 'cause you happen to be organized enough to remember to utter a few magic words to Jesus.

Well, we True Christians™, who are more familiar with the less forgiving moods of the Lord, know that the Holy Bible, both Old and New Testaments, promises that whole continents full of sinners and other savages will spend eternity spinning on a rotis-

This week in Bible History:

The Lord, while watching *Jeopardy!*, turned an Ephraim woman into a buffy-tufted-ear marmoset for failing to state her prayer in the form of an answer.

Tit for Tat Retaliation

The American Association of Scientists for Evolution has asked all Christian pastors to include the following disclaimer in any sermon: "The resurrection of Jesus is a controversial *theory*, not a fact, something over which there is disagreement and is currently without proof. This sermon should be approached with an open mind, studied carefully, and you should critically consider all sides."

serie. And when you review the Bible in context, it becomes perfectly clear that just about *everyone* is going to Hell. The Apostle Paul told us that fornicators, idolaters, drunkards, adulterers, thieves, the effeminate and those who abuse themselves with mankind (that's those penis-addicted homosexuals, my friends) may not enter the Kingdom of Heaven (Ephesians 5:3–5). I don't know where the liberal cultists get off suggesting that the Apostle John's flimsy generalities trump the Apostle Paul's very specific condemnations. Since every Christian worth his KJV Bible knows to ignore Jesus when He conflicts with Paul (like when it comes to paying attention to God's silly Old Testament rules), it stands to reason that John's mealymouthed ramblings don't stand a chance when Paul's busy spitting the fires of wrathful righteousness. And I promise you this: When the Lord is looking for a crib sheet on Judgment Day, He isn't going to be swayed by John's verse being painted on more poly-blend sheets at college football games than any other Scripture. Can I get an "Amen"?

Rest assured, there'll be plenty of room for driving ranges and beautiful, wide-open shopping malls in Heaven. For example, studies show the majority of people have had premarital sex. The Bible condemns them as fornicators. All non-Christians are going to Hell as idolaters, and that includes the Catholics and Catholic-lights (Episcopalians) who worship that Trinity interloper, Mary. Of the few people remaining, most of them will go to Hell as adulterers. Matthew told us that anyone who has sexual thoughts about someone to whom he is not married is an adulterer (Matthew 5:28). Matthew also told us that anyone who divorces, then remarries, is committing adultery (as is the person the individual marries) (Matthew 5:32). So, there is all of Hollywood and most of America down the drain to Hell. And once you include all the foreign folks who never heard the Good News and the children who died before accepting Jesus, the guest list to Heaven is down to very few people indeed.

But even if you think you're somehow in the clear, guess again. Not only are individuals who marry a second time condemned, but so are their children, their grandchildren, their great-grandchildren, etc. Because their second marriage is a nullity, any children of that marriage are illegitimate and are thus the little bastards condemned to the 10th generation (Deuteronomy 23:2). In other words, not only must you make sure you do not engage in any of the sins Paul said would ensure eternity aflame, you must hope none of your distant ancestors ever divorced and conceived one of your great-great-great-grandparents out of wedlock or during the second (and unrecognized) marriage. So all of you had best go home and shake your family tree to see if any bastards fall out. Because if they do, I'm sorry to say, it was nice knowing you, but you won't be joining me, Heather and our boys in Heaven.

THE GOOD NEWS

Widowers Are Given Permission to Almost Masturbate

For the first time in the church's 386-year history, the Landover Conclave of Cloistered Elders is allowing human sexual organs to be intentionally touched for the purpose of pleasure.

Inadvertent stimulation has been long recognized as an unsavory risk of Godly procreation among True Christians™, but, according to reliable reports from the Ladies of Landover, our male members have been commendably diligent in sparing their submissive wives from the sin of unnecessary arousal. Intentional excitement of moist or hardened furry, unmentionable areas of the body between the legs (particularly when one happens to be alone), on the other hand, has always been banned without qualification by the church. Nevertheless, as a result of relentless complaints of recent widowers who happen to be major donors—  as well as alarming evidence culled from the church's Sin Surveillance closed circuit video system—Pastor has carved out narrow exceptions to the church's previous outright ban on self-stimulation. "We really had no choice," noted a tired and distraught Pastor Deacon Fred during a news conference held shortly after the decision was reached, "but rest assured, God takes no stock in the satanic adage, 'A bird in the hand is worth two in the bush.'"

The ruling was reluctantly issued in response to the arguments of several wealthy middle-aged divorced male church members who challenged the church's initial policy last year. They claimed that because they cannot have nonmarital sex since fornication ensures eternity in Hell (1 Corinthians 6:9–10), they should be allowed to defile their bodies once in a while, at least to make sure they will ascend in the Rapture with all the important stuff still working properly.

The new policy is not without its limitations. The first restriction is that no Landover gentleman will be permitted to reach the messy stage of ejaculation. "The Bible is very clear

Pastor Orders Christian Men to Think Only About Jesus While Masturbating

Does your son or husband wander off into the family bathroom for a suspiciously long, noisy time, only to reemerge more flushed than the commode? Are you a man who gives in to temptations of the flesh when Satan makes your own tallywhacker so irresistible that you become a de facto penis-crazy homosexual for several minutes? Well, Pastor has a tip that will make your little problem go away in a jiffy! "The Apostles told us repeatedly that Jesus forbids lust, since ejaculation is for baby-making, not anxiety release or college fraternity initiation," Pastor told a recent gathering of God's First Gender club. "Furthermore, Matthew said that 'whosoever looketh on a woman to lust after her hath committed adultery with her already in his heart' (Matthew 5:28). So the only way to masturbate without lust is to keep your mind on the passion of the Christ, instead of your own, at all times. In other words: Fellows, keep your hand on your manhood and your eye on the cross, and you won't spill your seed all over the already messy road to Hell."

that a man's seed is for filling up his home and minivan with children only," noted Pastor. "In fact, the Bible says that when Onan released his seed onto the ground, God was so furious about the sticky mess, He struck Onan dead (Genesis 38:9–10). Allowing men to diddle with their tallywhackers for more than a few moments is just an invitation for the Lord to go on one of His killing sprees. And, frankly, the last thing we need around here is secular reporters clicking photos of colored janitors carting off corpses from our church's many men's rooms."

Recognizing that a few men may err and sin by not stopping in time, the new policy requires all who decide to participate in the act to register with Pastor Deacon Fred. Specially made Tupperware seed containers will be signed out of his office by Mrs. Watkins, who will use an Excel spreadsheet to guard against overuse. The sinner must catch his mistake in his numbered container before it reaches the ground. All containers are to be returned to Mrs. Watkins within one hour of checkout. The careless diddler will then receive two punches in his Sin Card. After 10 punches, the sinner will be relieved of that which tempts him most. As the Bible clearly states: If a part of our body offends us, we must cut it off (Matthew 5:29–30).

God's Handy Tips on Keeping Slaves Happy and Beaten

As a guide to timeless moral truths, the Bible is a blueprint for how today's Christians should treat their slaves. Indeed, the Lord is so *crazy* over the idea of owning slaves, He could have been, well, one of our nation's Founding Fathers! For while delicate King James translated the Greek "doulos" as "servant," "maid" or any number of other coy English euphemisms for the regrettably enslaved, the Lord, on the other hand, made no bones about coming right out in the original text and saying He was referring to people who were their master's property (Exodus 21:20–21).

1. How did Jesus say a slave should treat his master?

A. Since slavery is clearly immoral, Jesus expressly prohibited His followers from owning other humans as property and, indeed, spoke out often against slavery.

B. A slave must obey his master's commands unless they are immoral, unjust or involve wearing a leash while in a sling.

C. A slave must completely obey and fear his master, even if his master is cruel and unjust.

D. A slave treated unjustly should pen rhythmic lamentations to the Lord that can be sung by large groups of weary people swaying in fields of cotton.

2. What is God's policy on physical punishment of your slave?

A. None. No deity worthy of being called Lord would encourage such a barbaric practice as slavery.

B. It is necessary because words alone will not overcome a slave's misconduct.

C. If you blind the slave or knock his or her teeth out, you'll have to let the slave go.

D. B and C.

3. Whom did God tell the Israelites they should enslave?

A. Only those people who had formerly made the Israelites slaves.

B. All the people of other tribes living anywhere around them.

C. Those who made fun of their yarmulkes.

D. None of the above.

4. What does God command to happen to a male slave after six years of service?

A. He is free to leave with his wife and children, so long as he was married when enslaved.

B. He is free to depart but has to leave his wife and children with the master if the master introduced him to his wife.

C. If he wants to stay behind with his wife and children, his master must bore a hole in his ear with an aul.

D. All of the above.

5. What does God instruct us to do to a master who beats his slave to death?

A. Nothing. Because God does not endorse slavery, the Bible pointedly does not provide slaveholders helpful guidance on this subject.

B. He should be punished just as he would be for killing any other individual.

Meddlesome IRS Drops Investigation of Our Republican Church's Tax-Exempt Status

Three days after Pastor Deacon Fred and Brother Harry Hardwick went on a seal-clubbing retreat with Messrs. Bush and Cheney, the IRS announced it was dropping its investigation into whether Landover forfeited its tax-exempt status by engaging in so-called "political" activity. The incident triggering the investigation occurred on the last night of the 2004 Democratic convention, when two deacons riding atop a circus elephant used flamethrowers to set afire a live donkey wearing a Hillary Clinton mask at Landover Stadium, to the roaring ovation of the 7,000 present. The IRS ruled that the event was clearly nothing more than an animal sacrifice prescribed by the Book of Leviticus and that the political allegiance of the animal involved was wholly irrelevant.

C. He should avoid all punishment if the slave survived for a couple days after the beating.

D. None of the above.

6. Does God allow you to sell your daughter into slavery?

A. Yes. And the situation is not unbearable for her, since, if her master takes her as his wife and she does not please him, he must set her free.

B. Yes. But only stepdaughters. Blood relatives may not be sold.

C. No. God is known to frown on men pimping their daughters unless it's for the benefit of angels visiting Sodom.

D. No. The Lord encourages you to find other ways to make ends meet, like ransacking nonbelievers' tents and prohibiting your wife from buying expensive jewelry.

7. What punishments does God mandate when an ox gores a free man and when an ox gores a slave?

A. If the ox is a first-time offender that kills a free man, the ox, alone, should be stoned.

B. If the ox is a known recidivist and kills a free man, both the ox and his owner should be killed.

C. If the ox kills a slave, the ox's owner must merely give the slave's owner 30 shekels of silver (and, to be fair, the ox should be stoned).

D. All of the above.

8. What conduct by slaves particularly disgusts Jesus?

A. Insincerity. Slaves pretending to respect their masters when they're really just trying to curry favor.

B. Disobedience.

C. A and B.

D. None of the above.

9. Is slavery an appropriate penalty for someone caught stealing who can't pay back what he stole?

A. Of course not. That would be cruel and unusual, even for God.

B. Yes, but only slavery through judicial incarceration and for the length of the sentence.

C. Yes. There is nothing more irritating than an inept thief who has no money! A thief who is too poor to make restitution should be sold to pay for his theft.

D. None of the above.

God's Handy Tips on Keeping Slaves Happy and Beaten

Answers

1(C) "Servants, be subject to your masters with all fear; not only to the good and gentle, but also to the froward" (1 Peter 2:18).

2(D) "A servant will not be corrected by words: for though he understand he will not answer" (Proverbs 29:19). "And if a man smite the eye of his servant, or the eye of his maid, that it perish; he shall let him go free for his eye's sake. And if he smite out his manservant's tooth, or his maidservant's tooth; he shall let him go free for his tooth's sake" (Exodus 21:26-27).

3(B) "Both thy bondmen, and thy bondmaids, which thou shalt have, shall be of the heathen that are round about you; of them shall ye buy bondmen and bondmaids" (Leviticus 25:44).

4(D) "If thou buy an Hebrew servant, six years he shall serve: and in the seventh he shall go out free for nothing. If he came in by himself, he shall go out by himself: if he were married, then his wife shall go out with him. If his master have given him a wife, and she have born him sons or daughters; the wife and her children shall be her master's, and he shall go out by himself. And if the servant shall plainly say, I love my master, my wife, and my children; I will not go out free. . . . His master shall bore his ear through with an aul; and he shall serve him for ever" (Exodus 21:2-6).

5(C) "And if a man smite his servant, or his maid, with a rod, and he die under his hand, he shall be surely punished. Notwithstanding, if he continue a day or two, he shall not be punished: for he is his money" (Exodus 21:20-21).

6(A) "And if a man sell his daughter to be a maidservant, she shall not go out as the menservants do. If she please not her master, who hath betrothed her to himself, then shall he let her be redeemed" (Exodus 21:7-8).

7(D) "If an ox gore a man or a woman, that they die: then the ox shall be surely stoned, and his flesh shall not be eaten; but the owner of the ox shall be quit. But if the ox were wont to push with his horn in time past, and it hath been testified to his owner, and he hath not kept him in, but that he hath killed a man or a woman; the ox shall be stoned, and his owner also shall be put to death. . . . If the ox shall push a manservant or a maidservant; he shall give unto their master thirty shekels of silver, and the ox shall be stoned" (Exodus 21:28-32).

8(C) "Servants, obey in all things your masters according to the flesh, not with eye-service, as menpleasers; but in singleness of heart, fearing God" (Colossians 3:22; see also Ephesians 6:5-6).

9(C) "If a thief be found breaking up, and be smitten that he die, there shall no blood be shed for him. If the sun be risen upon him, there shall be blood shed for him; for he should make full restitution; if he have nothing, then he shall be sold for his theft" (Exodus 22:2-3).

The Devil's Trickery: Satan loves to read backwards, but he can't read upside down! So the best way to drive old Mr. Beelzebub crazy is to avoid mirrors—and write your diary while standing on your head. Glory!

In Surprise Upset, Pastor's Secretary Beats Local Harlot in This Month's "Most Sexually Degrading Personal Testimony" Contest

YOU CAN TURN YOUR HUMILIATION INTO DOLLARS, TOO! Have you done crack? Been a whore? Drunk too many vodka stingers and wound up buck naked in a sling in someone's basement? If your testimony is debasing enough to show Jesus' love on Pastor's TV show, you may win $1,000 in tithe credits!

Miss Anne Thrope's Winning Testimony:

My relationship with God had always been rocky. When I was in college, I would lie awake at nights, worried that He didn't approve of what or whom I had done that day. Then, the Ambien would kick in. When I woke up the next morning, I would be haunted by a sense of vague reproach. If only I hadn't suffered from ADD, I would have thought about it long enough to realize that my morning anxiety was connected to my nighttime ruminations about God.

Instead, I walked around all morning thinking I had forgotten a really great idea for doing something new with my hair. That really bothered me because everyone wants to live up to their full potential.

After taking Beginning Psychology, I realized that my relationship with God was weirdly codependent. He pandered to my self-esteem issues with His "I love you no matter how bad you are" stuff, while I enabled His wild bipolar mood swings and passive-aggressive inattention by turning a blind eye to my pore size and the Holocaust. Anyway, we drifted. It's not like I rejected Him. I just felt like He wanted space. You know, totally needy constant praying had to stop—and it did, after many a tearful confrontation too embarrassing to recount here. That's when the crazy sex started. It was constant. First, I did it by teams. Then, by fraternities. Finally, I had to start going off campus just to see fresh faces. It was all getting so tawdry.

And the commutes were a bitch. I began thinking about stopping the sex thing altogether. Just as soon as I could come up with a suitable substitute for all the aerobic exercise.

That is what led me to Pastor Deacon Fred. He made me feel totally at ease. I told him I didn't want to go to Hell. That was sort of nonnegotiable. But then I told him about how much unmarried sex I was having. I sort of fudged on the numbers by dropping a zero off the end. I was glad I did because he looked sort of shocked anyway.

Pastor Deacon Fred told me that I was sinning big-time. "Duh," I told him. "I know that, but I was really looking for, like, a way to make it not count by repeating incantations over inexpensive jewelry or something."

"We're not Catholics," he reproved. He said "Catholics" like he'd just eaten a spoonful of spoiled canned tuna. He then told me that I would have to give up sex with men until I was married. That struck me as odd, since my father had told me that it was *after* marriage that that happened.

"Well, I suppose I could always have sex with women!" I joked. "Yes," he said evenly, running his hand languidly down his chest toward his lap, "there is always that." "But the Bible forbids homosexuality, Pastor!" I blurted out, somewhat taken aback by his lurid suggestion. "Yes, it does," he calmly responded. "But only between men. I invite you to search the Bible for where God said one single word about lesbianism. Yes, Paul made some noise about *excessive* lesbianism in Romans, but the Lord doesn't mind two healthy, nubile little lambs frolicking about." Pastor Deacon Fred's hands had dropped below his desk. He must have had a notepad in his lap because he appeared to be writing.

"So God thinks two guys together is an abomination, but thinks two chicks together are cool?" I asked. "Apparently," Pastor responded, eyebrows raised somewhat conspiratorially. "Well, so much for those feminists who think God is a woman. I mean, HELLO? Obviously, we are talking typical male here!" I observed. "Yes," Pastor agreed, "our Blessed Lord created the lovely, lithe form of libidinous woman, with moist inviting thighs and soft heaving bosoms for the delight of her lucky husband. But until that time, there is nothing to say that a lovely lonely nymph can't play with her buxom little friends." By now, Pastor was writing rather quickly.

"It is probably best that someone who has your spiritual well-being in mind, as well as a firsthand knowledge of Biblical

Pastor Filled Missionary Positions Overseas

Pastor consoled disappointed Runner-up in the Miss Saved USA Pageant by taking her to the Ritz Hotel in Paris for 24/7 Bible study to discuss Eve as a parable of every woman's inability to resist devouring something big and shiny when placed close enough to her weak, wanton mouth.

Saint Patrick's Day:
Like the World Needs Yet One More Excuse for Catholics to Get Vomiting Drunk!
—Pastor Fritz O'Donnelly

New Diebold Voting Software Means Suspected Democrats Can Be Boot-Kicked Right Out of Church Before They Even Get Home from the Voting Booth

Before dozens of cameras, Pastor Deacon Fred declared, "I'm not about to let liberal trash sneak into our voting booths to cast votes against Godly Republicans, so help me Jesus!" He held a computer printout in one hand, while using his other hand to spray-paint in red "A Vote for a Democrat Is a Vote for Lucifer!" on Mrs. Kenneth Fowler's garage door just moments before she returned home from voting. "Used to be, it would take weeks to sort out the wheat from the chads," Pastor told the media. "Now, electoral retribution is done God-style: swift, sure and dripping in red. Hallelujah!"

ins-and-outs, be there to assist. To make sure that giddy, but chaste, lesbian abandon doesn't spill over into another, technically forbidden type of carnal sin spoken of in Romans 1:26," Pastor said, aglow with caring enthusiasm. He walked around his desk, keeping his crotch modestly covered with his hat. He placed his creased hand on me in a way that reminded me of how my dear father had touched me many nights when I was a little girl. Before Child Services found out.

Since that time when Pastor Deacon Fred led me to the Lord, I have never sexually sinned before God. We came close one night, when Pastor had arranged to have me and five women from his Guatemalan Baptist Outreach Ministry romp around naked on his bed, but Pastor disengaged before any real sin occurred. I guess the lesson that I have learned in coming with God is that when the Lord closes a door (men), He opens more than a window (women). I am so grateful to the devotion to the Lord's will shown by Pastor. I keep asking him what I can buy him to thank him for leading me out of a life of sin. He always has his video camera running, so I asked if I could buy him some film. But he is so selfless, he always just says, "Dear, you have already done more than enough."

Lovely Funeral Ruined by Unsaved Corpse

During its glorious 145-year history as a lushly landscaped retreat for the deceased to rot until the Rapture, Landover Baptist's Saved Souls Cemetery has painstakingly avoided having its rich earth broken by either a dead body going to Hell or a living gardener speaking Mexican. Parishioners were therefore shocked to learn this past Saturday that young Leslie Waite, an unsaved five-year-old, was accidentally laid to rest in the hallowed grounds of the cemetery. Within half an hour of little Leslie being lowered into the rich Iowa soil, gravediggers were summoned back to reopen her freshly covered plot, cart the corpse away in a wheelbarrow and sandblast her name off the marble headstone. "The news about someone unsaved polluting God's sacred soil spread around the church quicker than the flu in a swarm of Orientals!" explained Pastor Deacon Fred. "And, frankly, I was worried. I didn't want to have yet one more situation this month where church members go in and dig up someone they didn't like. No matter how many times I tell them not to, they always manage to trample the shrubbery."

Leslie's unsuitability for internment was discovered by an alert Mrs. Betty Bowers while she spoke to the child's emotional mother immediately after the burial. "When it seemed that the mother had calmed down to the point where she wasn't going to be laborious to talk with, I walked over to offer Christian comfort," recounted Mrs. Bowers. "And to suggest a foundation not quite so terribly terra-cotta. After all, there she was, everyone she knew watching, and she looked like a veiled flowerpot. I was just trying to be helpful, but what do you say to a mother who has just lost a child? The last time I'd been in that situation was when I spoke with dear Sister-in-Christ Patsy Ramsey. And somehow my '*just try not to kill the other one*' speech seemed out of place, so I just launched into some rigmarole about having her laughter and words to remember Leslie by as I discreetly made dinner reservations on my BlackBerry."

It was then that Leslie's mother carelessly revealed that her

Next Week's Sermon:
"Just Because God Loves to Kill Little Babies Doesn't Mean You Can Join In!"
—Brother Harry Hardwick

Last Week's Favorite Hymn:

"O God, Thank You for Answering My Many Prayers, but You Missed a Few"

daughter had been mentally retarded. "She could never really understand what was going on," Mrs. Waite told Betty, "but she always seemed so happy. It was a joy to have her in my life. She was so filled with love." Upon hearing this sad news, Mrs. Bowers hung up on her florist mid-conversation and immediately speed-dialed Pastor Harry Hardwick's number. "Pastor, there has been a horrible, ghastly mistake!" said Betty into her BlackBerry. Rushing over to the freshly wounded soil of the gravesite, Mrs. Bowers called back the attendees who had started dispersing: "Dig that little sinner up this instant! She has not accepted Jesus! She didn't have the mental capacity to accept a compliment, much less a Savior." Numerous members of the congregation began chanting: "Dig her up!" As Pastor Harry Hardwick explained to the sobbing mother: "This is a resting place for True Christians™. This cemetery is just as choosy as Heaven—no more, no less. You have to accept Jesus as your Personal Savior to get in." Waving his hand in the direction of perfectly manicured acres of greenery, peppered with marble monuments and mausoleums, some the size of convenience stores, he added: "If you want to bury trash, Mrs. Waite, find yourself a landfill."

Bible Quiz

By the time God gets through with His killing sprees, how many dead men, women and children will there be?

A. None. God doesn't kill children.

B. Ten million, give or take a village or town here or there.

C. One hundred million (mostly Chinese).

D. Enough to cover the surface of the Earth like a giant turd.

Answer: D. "And the slain of the Lord shall be at that day from one end of the earth even unto the other end of the earth: they shall not be lamented, neither gathered, nor buried, they shall be dung upon the ground" (Jeremiah 25:33).

Is God Waiting Until the Apocalypse to Break His Amazing Killing Record?

The Bible teaches us that God Almighty holds the world record for genocide, with sundry human despots left arguing over bragging rights for second and third place for achievements that are rendered so minuscule by the Lord's body count, they should be an embarrassment to any conscientious sociopath.

While an occasional tornado or mud slide is often seen as God's calling card, many Christians have been growing concerned by the less impressive scale of Heavenly provoked disasters

The Exact Number of Jesus' Torture Techniques Is Revealed by Eight-Year-Old

The $13,450 prize for the "How Many Different Types of Torture Does Jesus Have in Store for Those He Loves but Nevertheless Flings into Hell?" contest was awarded to little Jeremy Johnson, age eight, this week. He had the winning guess with 865 surprisingly graphic illustrations in crayon.

recently. "I don't know," said Sister Adel Perkins, "it is almost as if the Lord is getting too old to really stir things up anymore. Natural disasters just don't *kill* like they used to. To be sort of honest, I've become mighty concerned of late that the Lord is downsizing. I mean, He's already delegated all the natural disasters that occur here in America to that Mother Nature woman, and I just don't trust her. And I don't mean to be disloyal, but no one wants to waste their time worshipping an impotent God who is suddenly a scaredy-cat about killing folks. Especially now that we are up against that crazy Muslim god who acts like death is the only game in town."

Such disheartened Christians have found some hope in the news of enormous swaths of unsaved barbarians dying each day in some country called Africa. And the Lord splashing most of Asia with water in the tsunami of 2004 was a welcome reminder of God's willingness to branch out from the less expedient habit of killing sinners one by one. Not since the time of Noah has God used water so effectively to harass sinners and wreak havoc upon those who don't flatter Him with sufficient regularity. What used to take 40 days and 40 nights, the Lord is now able to accomplish in a *single day* with the drop of an enormous holy paperweight into the Pacific. As unsaved, impoverished Hindus toiled in beachside shacks on Christmas instead of exchanging expensive gifts from American department stores to celebrate the Baby Jesus' Birthday, the Lord was plotting their horrific, briny demise. True Christians™ know from the Great Flood that one of God's favorite ways to indiscriminately kill enormous swaths of children is by drowning them and watching them gasp for air while floating like little discarded Styrofoam cups in the surf. Sometimes, He extends an enormous hand as if He is about to rescue the bobbing tot, only to retract it at the last minute to teach the drowning child a valuable lesson about the ineffable nature of God's love.

Church Member Spotlight

Hank Wilkins was laid to rest and sent home to Jesus this week.

Pastor commented during the eulogy, "Hank Wilkins made the Apostle Paul look like a damned Hari Krishna freak! Friends, we lost a true man of God!"

Creation Science News

All Landover Baptist house-wives showing a flair for archaeology are encouraged to join our $3.4 million expedition to East Africa to use Caterpillar tractors to unearth miscellaneous bones needed to complete Landover Creation Science Museum's world-renown Talking Snake Bone exhibit.

This Week's Featured Hymn:

"Heavenly Lord, I Am Unworthy, but I'll Be Angry if You Don't Take Me Anyway"

Thanks to the Efforts of True Christians™, Millions Will Starve to Death Tonight Knowing Jesus

a yummy can of Gospel — no calories

Since the day Jesus left, every born-again Christian has been obedient to His final command, the *Great Commission:* "Go ye into all the world and make disciples of all men." Christ promised that He would come back when everyone in the world had a chance to hear the Gospel. Thanks to the Internet, which often takes the form of graffiti in Third World countries, even the poorest unsaved trash in Burma has now been exposed to the Lord for at least enough seconds that he can be justifiably tortured in Hell if he doesn't flatter Jesus. Indeed, he would already be amongst the saved, had it not been for his lazy refusal to get his naked heinie off his grass mat, learn some English and order a computer from Dell. Verily, you can lead a horde to a man who walks on water, but you can't make them drink the blood of the Lamb! As of June 17, 2006, according to our calculations, the Gospel has reached every living person on the planet who really wanted to hear it in the first place. "Missionaries are wasting their time with those ignorant foreign folks," one Evangelical expert stated. "Besides, do you really want Heaven to be knee-deep in Chinamen?"

The last remaining people on Earth to hear about Jesus Christ were a handful of TV-less hillbillies in the remote town of Lynchburg, Virginia—people so addicted to moonshine they could never get the phone out of the cradle before the eighth ring whenever missionaries called. Being without the resources to make a financial love-offering, these lesser beings could not inspire the interest of the Jerry Falwell ministry up the road. "We'd just never heard anything like it before!" they exclaimed after hearing the Good News while eavesdropping in a line to buy Lotto tickets. "We would always drive by these white buildings on every block with parking lots full of fancy cars and folks dressed up in expensive suits. Yeah, we felt left out. But we are used to going without. Especially teeth."

American Embassy Is Burned to the Ground After Mrs. Phillips' Third Graders Mail Finger-Paintings of the Prophet Muhammad to Pen Pals in Saudi Arabia

"For reasons not clear to me, I read somewhere that most Muslamics have no clear idea what the face of that Mr. Muhammad of theirs look like, except for the turban, of course," explained Mrs. Phillips. "And that's real sad. I mean, how in tarnation are you supposed to stand before a god and ask for stuff when you have no idea what he looks like? I'm telling you: I made it a point to find out what Jesus looked like before inviting Him into my home, much less my heart. Through Christian kindness, my class was just trying to help those incurious folks out."

Unlocking the Mystical Bible Code

Next to playing the Beatles' White Album backward, the most reliable way to see into the future is to discover the messages ingeniously encrypted into the Hebrew text of the Bible. Once the right-to-left craziness of the Jews is turned into more Christ-like characters and stacked without breaks or punctuation (much akin to most e-mail), messages from God appear horizontally and vertically (but never diagonally, as the Lord deemed that intellectually effete). In the letters from the Book of Genesis on the next page, Creation Scientists at Landover Baptist University for the Saved have unlocked two prophesies of Jesus and one for the tragedy at the World Trade Center Towers. Since these are some of the smartest Baptists in America, you probably won't be able to find any more messages from the Lord, but it is always fun to try!

Local Pastor Sets Soul-Winning Record

Rev. Jimmy Hudack won a lost soul in under 10 seconds using only a page from a Bible tract that had stuck to his shoe. So powerful is the Word of God that Rev. Hudack was able to lead the lamb to Christ while balancing on one foot and drinking pink lemonade—all at the same time!

```
C H E N E Y B A T S H I T C R A Z Y E R K I T A Y
R I L W H E A Y J A L R E R E T E D R A M L O P E
A D C D E W E Y W I N S I E T Y I R A T S L U O R
C J S I G O K I S N E D D A R P J A T F U C U N T
K K M A R K F E L T O T I T L L E T S O R O T S I
I R T E O B A L S P E T H I S I S B U L L S H I T
S I G O D I S D E A D R A O N E U N N L Y A I T A
W S P J A C E U F U M E M N E A S S H O L E S O N
H D R W S E S Y I L L E T I M S I R T W E R R A I
A L E N L R T O M C R U I S E I S N U T S A E M C
C T D V I K I U S R E A V M A K A E L H I T N E U
K Y S T T S O A T O L O C J I T H O I E P H J I N
A R O Y R P L R E S I H M O R M O N S M O R O N S
I M X Q F O W E R S U C R K U U M I R O T E Y S I
O T W A T K I G O D H A T E S Y O U A N D E S I N
B R I L N J O O D R S E K U L I T T L E A L O F K
H I N V E S T I N E N R O N E D N Y N Y E R D Y A
A B M R I C E N S S A P I T T L E O D S O A O K B
I J B U Y H I G H S E L L L O W N U R F I N M E L
R C O K S D U T A E K O C K I S N I P E R T Y A E
E V O L U T I O N R E A L L A M A D A L E L O N D
A H B Y L O B H A T R V I A M S I I K T R I T T E
J E S U S D O E S N T S A V E T T O R C T R A P I
E P W S V E R L I W U O G I T W A T C H P O R N E
S C I E N T O L O G Y S U C K S I R T O R N E E R
```

NOTICE: *If you are not a Pastor, you are forbidden to view the rest of this page. It contains mystical revelations that are, frankly, none of your damned business.*

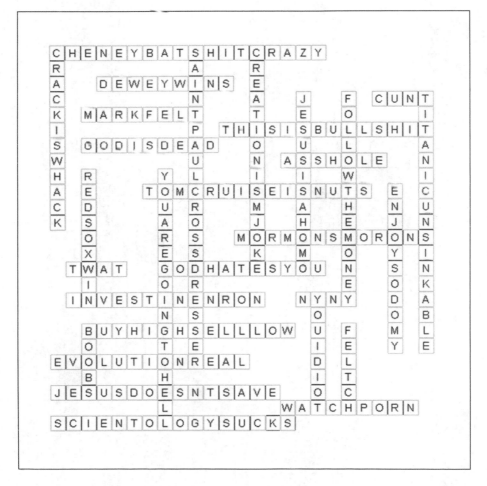

This subliminal message from the Lord is made possible by a generous grant from: The Put Pastor in a Lamborghini Fund

The Perfect Prayer

Dear Holy Trinity: God, the Father, who still so lovingly works on His anger management issues, Jesus, the alarmingly suicidal Son, and their flying feathered sidekick, a little white bird called the Holy Ghost:

I call upon all of the godless trash in the world to bow their heads and still their licentious tongues as I talk to my invisible friend, who lives in the sky, but is reputed to have excellent hearing.

Dear Lord, I know that I am worthless and a constant source of irritation to you. Thank you for not killing me today and flinging my limp corpse like a half-eaten piece of chicken into the flames of the sadistic place called Hell you created for all those who are not effusive enough about what your Son did on the cross. As a True Christian™, I love you with all my heart, convenience permitting, and am only glad your nasty temper was not turned on me today. Would that the others in my life, no matter how much they may have pissed you off, as You know they have surely done me, could be so lucky to avoid your wrath, especially as they have already weathered my own.

Lord Jesus, I know that your love is absolutely unconditional: All you ask is that I do everything you demand. And flatter you regularly and without shame or regard to the mess you make of everything you try to create.

Even though you made some noise about giving away all our possessions to the poor, please call me, as you have Brothers Pat Robertson and Jerry Falwell, to parlay my Personal Savior into a Personal Fortune! And O Lord, please guide your own Republican Party to effect that which you most secretly desire—tax cuts for folks rich enough to tithe to your wildly successful franchise.

And even though you made some off-the-cuff comment about "resisting evil and turning the other cheek," please ensure that all people, no matter how meager their backgrounds, one day realize the American Dream of owning and using a concealed weapon. And guide our True Christian™

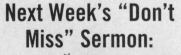

Next Week's "Don't Miss" Sermon:

"Things Jesus, No Doubt, Now Regrets Saying"

This Sunday's Sermon:

"Rap Music: Giving Every White Woman in the Suburbs What She Has Always Feared Most: Children Who Seem Colored!"
—Pastor Theodore Washington

President George W. Bush, O Lord, in his glorius revelation that the best way to get around your commandment to respond to an attack with kindness is to attack first. And Lord, teach all those pesky homos to honor the sanctity of the holy covenant between a man and a nonpenised person in all of our many marriages. In this I pray.

Best regards,

[Sinner's name here]

Oh, and while I have you, Jesus, I really want me one of them new [expensive item that Jesus secretly wants you to have goes here]. Rev. Kenneth Copeland told me on TV that you want me to be as rich as Herod and I think a new [expensive item that Jesus secretly wants you to have goes here] would be a really good start. I will keep checking with UPS, for, truly, I feel a victory coming on! Praise!

Sodomy: Invented in Greece, Perfected in Rome

Last week, the Baptist moral think tank Saving Cures Ailing Morality published the results of its 60-month investigation into the inextricable connection between homosexuality and the Catholic "Church." SCAM was established by internationally renowned Christian advice columnist Mrs. Betty Bowers and international financier Brother Harry Hardwick, Platinum Level members. SCAM's investigation was exhaustive. In addition to interviewing Catholic clergy they found in bathhouses, adult book stores, highway rest stops and "archbishops4boysNOW" AOL chat rooms, Bowers and Hardwick also traveled straight into the miasmic bowels of Satan's official embassy on Earth—Vatican City.

Upon entering the Devil's rococo playground, Bowers and Hardwick were shocked beyond what even their lifelong hobby of hating Catholics had prepared them for. "It was worse than any nightmare in the Book of Revelation," reported Hardwick. "It was like walking into the Pantheon. Everywhere we turned, there was yet one more dress-wearing idol leering at us. Marble statues of false gods, surrounded by multitudes of clamorous Catholics rubbing them smooth as if each saint's foot were a genie's lamp. I stopped to snuff out the Hell-like effects of several candle-lighters and Betty was moved by Jesus to righteously slap some Italian woman wearing a doily on her head to stop her from slobbering on an Apostle's instep. Pansy priests and cardinals pranced around in hideous silk frocks, all of which were black or red, Satan's official colors." Bowers was as horrified by the gaudy artwork of the church as she was by the mincing effeminacy of the clergy. "Now, no one would accuse me of not enjoying a feminine flourish in every room, but the whole Vatican looked like it had been whomped up by Carmela Soprano after winning the New Jersey lottery. Frankly, Las Vegas looks downright Mies van der Rohe by comparison!"

Mrs. Betty Bowers identifies the man wearing an elaborately embroidered, long, flowing gown she rebuked: "I think it was Oscar de la Renta, but it was definitely the Pope wearing it!"

Bowers and Hardwick knew the information most important to their investigation was contained amongst the catacombs of pickled saint hearts and manuscripts in the Vatican's basement. Aside from protecting their saved status, their most daunting challenge was gaining entry into the archives's ferociously guarded secret vault. Fortunately, both Landover members are on the board of directors of one of the world's leading abortion-clinic-bombing groups, Heaven Angrily Notices Gynecological Embryo Removal. In addition to revealing their status as directors of HANGER to ball-gown-wearing "church" officials, as an added precaution, both Bowers and Hardwick wore large buttons proclaiming: "I SAW THE FACE OF THE VIRGIN MARY IN AN ENCHILADA IN TIJUANA." The gates to the Vatican vaults were, of course, immediately flung open in their honor and the Baptist sleuths were granted unqualified permission to explore both the manuscript archives and the Venerated Body Fluid Vial Museum.

The pagan rites Bowers and Hardwick had witnessed beneath the clearly phallic Bernini columns in the main sanctuary and the pornography that adorned the Sistine Chapel ceiling was not nearly as disturbing as what their research through the archives revealed. Charter documents haphazardly written on cloth scrolls by drunken monks reveal that the Catholic "Church" was created by a group of brazen buggers who had been expelled from early Christian churches in Italy.

Last Week's Favorite Hymn:

"I'm Gonna Sprout Wings and Fly with Jesus, Fly with Jesus"

These unrepentant sodomites began what is now known as the Catholic "Church." The scrolls reveal that the founders of the new "church" chose to name their new "religion" using lewd, colloquial terms of ancient Greece, the land known for little more than a turgid penis entering a man's backside for the very first time. These profane Greek terms were "Cathos" and "licos." A Creation Science institute specializing in ancient Greek and leprechaun footprints has confirmed to SCAM that the term "Cathos" is a contracted reference to "catamite hos" (young male temple prostitutes). "Licos," of course, means *to place the tongue upon and lick greedily.* Thus, the Catholic "Church" was named after the very deviance so many of its members publicly condemn yet privately relish. So incensed were all other men in real Christian churches of the time by the relentless, unwanted advances upon their crotches by wheezing Catholic priests, they engaged in a unified opposition to the Catholics, which was later referred to as "Protestantism," a Middle English word that Brother Hardwick was almost certain had been coined to mean "protect testes from him."

So desperate was their need to retain their homosexual roots that the founders were willing to defy God's Word in order to preserve their depraved Roman nightclub-centric lifestyle. We all know queers revere and adore overbearing women, like Barbra, Judy and Liza, especially if they succumb to the gay ritual of substance abuse. The original Catholics experienced the same need to fawn before needy females and consequently made the Virgin Mary the Diana Ross–like diva of their religion, demoting Jesus from *the* Supreme to merely *a* Supreme. But the most conniving act by the Catholic founders was to distort God's Word to conceal their faggotry. The original priests knew full well that they and their successors would spend their lives boinking boys with nary a lascivious glance toward women. While any discovered buggery could be kept quiet in exchange for sensational confessional booth information, the absence of any relationship with women risked giving away the game. Hence, the founders inserted into the church charter a proviso stating that priests were not to marry or become sexually involved with women, but were instead to spend their time in the "church" with frolicsome young males called "altar boys."

This Month's Featured Hymn:

"Hark! The Bombs of Jesus Fall!"

Backyard Full of Dead Bunny Rabbits Proves Only Jesus Rises After Being Killed on Easter

Landover Baptist's annual Easter Bunny Slaughter for Sacred Stew turned deadly earlier this week when two unsaved children were nearly egged to death. The incident occurred during the annual field trip the third grade takes the day before the Easter holiday to Freehold Central Park. The yearly Easter tradition of pelting rabbits with hard-boiled eggs was established in 1921 to teach children at a very early age about ludicrous pagan traditions. Students spend the Wednesday before Easter in school, boiling dozens of ostrich eggs. "The longer the egg boils and the harder it gets, the better to teach them pagan rabbits a lesson," said Christian educator Mrs. Ona Mae Pilate. Once the eggs have cooled, the children scrawl passages from Deuteronomy onto them and form an imprecatory prayer circle where they pray over each egg individually. The following day, each student carries an oversized basket of blessed ostrich eggs to the park.

Shortly before the students arrive, 50 young bunny rabbits grown on Old Man Tucker's ranch are released into the park. After the children are lined up, the teacher blasts a round of buckshot into the air, and each student chases down bunnies, hurling eggs directly at their bobbing heads. "This obviously isn't a full-blown Old Testament–style stoning," noted Mrs. Pilate. "We use eggs instead of rocks and bunnies instead of people. These are children, after all. But we believe the timeless truths of the Bible are still being taught even though we are killing worthless, sex-crazed rabbits instead of worthless, sex-crazed people. The eggs are malleable enough that the rabbits survive quite a few hits if they duck quickly enough, thereby giving all the children, including the smaller ones, a shot at a new

Landover Baptist Children's Rifle Range to Refurbish All 48 Clinton Effigies

J. J. Summerell, Jr., director of Landover Baptist Academy for the Saved Children's Pre-K Riflery Squad, has announced that the popular life-size Bill Clinton targets are all in desperate need of repair. "Slick Willy Clintax has been out of office for ages," said J. J., "but folks around here hate him as much as when he was president because we all know he is still secretly causing all of our nation's problems." The eight-year-old Clinton targets are so riddled with bullets, particularly below the belt line, that it is no longer possible to isolate hits and measure student performance. New, wider bull's-eyes will appear on the forehead, left chest and groin of each target. Mr. Summerell promises that the renovation will come in under budget: "Even though we decided at the last minute to turn half of them into Hillary, once we remembered how she makes Ellen DeGeneres look like Pamela Anderson, we knew we could just use the same body and clothes that we ordered for her husband."

pet or meal." Most of the rabbit carcasses are used to make a large stew that the students present to the local synagogue for their Passover feast, as part of Landover's Outreach to Those Who Killed Our Savior. "For years, we've had the kids tell those Hebrews that it's beef stew," noted Pastor Deacon Fred. "And they've responded that it's the most flavorful beef stew that tastes like chicken they've ever eaten. For all we know, the Lord works a transubstantiation miracle on it after it leaves our hands, but we haven't changed the recipe in over 80 years."

About halfway into this year's egging, Mrs. Pilate became concerned when she heard soft groans coming from one area of bushes where a large congregation of egg-throwing third graders had congregated. There, she found several toddlers in bunny costumes writhing on the grass. Apparently, the preschool center at Our Lady of Perpetual Candle-Lighting had brought a dozen of its youngsters, dressed as little Easter Bunnies, to the park to hide eggs for the remaining children to find later in the afternoon. The third-graders had mistaken the three- and four-year-olds for enormous rabbits. "I screamed at the students to stop the egging, but they were oblivious," noted Mrs. Pilate. "They had this glazed look of rectitude in their eyes and kept throwing. We had been heavily studying the Book of Leviticus earlier that week and I suppose they were just in a frenzy of right-eousness. Fortunately, this happened late in the day, so they soon ran out of eggs. Two of the idol-worshipping children dressed in bunny costumes remain in serious condition, and while I'm sorry for what happened, being pelted with 20 or 30 ostrich eggs is nothing compared to what the Lord has in store for those little Mary-worshippers when He gets ahold of them."

PASTOR'S PULPIT

America Is Now Torturing Foreigners: But Is It Enough?

ANNOTATED SERMON
BY BROTHER HARRY HARDWICK

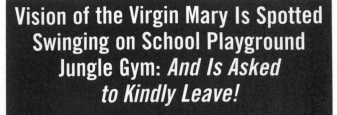

Vision of the Virgin Mary Is Spotted Swinging on School Playground Jungle Gym: *And Is Asked to Kindly Leave!*

Brothers and Sisters in Christ, America has always been the best at every task she fixes in her lovely glare. So, I suppose, it should come as no surprise that she is now known throughout the world for excelling in something new: torture. But are those America-haters in Jew York and Hollyweird proud? No, those nancy-boys can't put down their knitting quickly enough to genuflect and curtsy before liberal cabals like that convention they are having all the time in Geneva.

Folks, as if you didn't know it already, our country has become almost too offensive for True Christians™ to even live in! We put effeminate, liberal intelligentsia concepts like so-called "dignity"—*some of you out there are spitting and laughing, but this is serious business*—above fundamental Biblical principles like God's command that we slaughter those with different religious beliefs—killing every man, woman and child—in any country we conquer that worships an invisible god who, unlike our invisible God, is invisible because he isn't actually there at all,[1] (with the exception, perhaps, of those tantalizing virgins we wish to enslave as our own[2]). In fact, if we decline to kill heathens, we run the risk of God slaughtering us, as He has done to so many in the past.[3]

Southern Baptist Convention Updates the Trinity. Out: the Peacenik Holy Spirit Dove. In: the Bellicose American Eagle

If our friends over there in the White House show a canny flair for torture, well, it should come as no shock. Mr. Bush has made no secret that he takes his marching orders from only one Father—God. And the Bible teaches us that when it comes to inflicting painful vengeance, the Lord makes Pol Pot in Cambodia seem like a nervous-nellie hobbyist. After all, God, the Father, having purposefully created woman *before* the advent of feminism, is a manly and unapologetically vindictive deity, who kills those who don't follow His will at the drop of a turban. He engages in acts of violence that make the Iraqi situation look like a swishy debutante cotillion. Drowning, burning,[4] starving,[5] stabbing with a sword,[6] blinding,[7] breaking people into pieces,[8] breaking knees and legs—in fact, every body part from the sole of the foot to the top of the head[9] and the dreaded inflicting of hemorrhoids[10] are but a few of God's favorite methods of torture.

Now, as all you out there know (even you folks up yonder in the balcony): No one supports our troops more than my wife, Heather, and me. All of you who have seen us about town are well aware that we've bought numerous patriotic bumper stickers for all of our family vehicles, including the Hummers of our boys off at college. But I still feel compelled to say that, compared to the Lord, our Christian soldiers are hesitant, prissy amateurs.

There, I've said it. Having dogs intimidate prisoners doesn't come close to having dogs actually devour people who rub you the wrong way.[11] And sodomizing someone with a foreign object isn't nearly as painful as making them so sick, their bowels actually fall out of their bodies where they can be sodomized at leisure long after the victim has left the room.[12]

Those Arabiacs should be glad God sent American soldiers as proxies to do His bidding instead of going in there and whipping their butts Himself. God, having developed his personality long before the advent of 12-step programs, is a boldly jealous and vengeful divinity who has promised certain demise of anyone who doesn't constantly compliment Him, instead focusing their attention on other, more Amnesty International–compliant deities.[13] God has promised that, "All of the earth shall be devoured with the fire of my jealousy."[14] God will kill so many nonbelievers that there will be no place large enough to bury them all.[15] If a nation, like Iraq, does not believe in Him, He "will utterly pluck up and destroy that nation,"[16] laughing at the heathens as He kills them.[17] Even in the New Testament, God promised to kill those who don't flatter Him,[18] eventually hurling them into a "lake of fire"[19] where there will be wailing and gnashing of teeth.[20]

Our brave Christian soldiers' minimal torture can only serve to prepare these heathens for the far greater abuse they will face come Judgment Day, when horselike locusts with human heads, women's hair, lion's teeth and scorpion's tails will sting them for five months[21] before they are burned to death.[22] Our Christian soldiers are just getting a head start on inflicting the horrors promised by God in the Book of Revelation. Let us praise them for their Biblical insight. And if we raise our voices in criticism of their efforts, let it be only to chide them for being so darn blasted timid! Next time they get out those dog leashes, they will ask, "What would Jesus do?" and those naked Iraqi suckers will find themselves yanked across a steaming pile of their own godless excrement! Praise Jesus!

1. Deuteronomy 3:3, 6; 7:2, 4; 12:2–7; 20:16; 25:19; 1 Samuel 15:2–3,

2. Numbers 31:1–54; Deuteronomy 20:13–16.

3. E.g. 1 Kings 20:42

4. Psalms 106:11–18.

5. Deuteronomy 28:48; 32:21–26.

6. Jeremiah 11:22.

7. 2 Kings 6:18.

8. Jeremiah 51:21.

9. Deuteronomy 28:35.

10. Deuteronomy 28:27.

11. 2 Kings 9:10.

12. 2 Chronicles 21:14–19.

13. Deuteronomy 32:35; 2 Kings 1:4, 17; Jeremiah 6:11.

14. Zephaniah 3:8.

15. Jeremiah 19:11–13; 25:33.

16. Jeremiah 12:17.

17. Psalms 59:8.

18. Acts 3:23.

19. John 15:6.

20. Matthew 13:41–42, 50: 25:41; Revelation 21:8.

21. Revelation 9:7–10.

22. 2 Peter 3:7.

Unsaved Catholic Claims Sister Inez Caused His Deafness

Mary-worshipping priest and pedophile who has so far evaded detection Father William O'Reilly filed a lawsuit in federal district court last month, claiming that Landover's Sister Inez caused his deafness when she rebuked him at point-blank range as he exiled the ornate stone building where the local Catholic cult meets. Sister Inez had barely finished telling Father O'Reilly that Jesus had just regaled her with sordid tales about catamites, when the local priest, pretending to be an altar boy, dropped to his knees in supposed pain. At Sister Inez's instruction, her lawyers filed an answer asserting intervening and superseding cause, in particular, that deafness is God's punishment of sinners (Exodus 4:11). The case was thrown out of court yesterday by Judge Robbins, a Landover Gold Level tither, after Sister Inez interpleaded the Lord Jesus as a necessary party over whom the court lacked jurisdiction.

Christian Ladies Go Undercover for Jesus at Des Moines Sex Club!

Last month, Mr. and Mrs. Harold Greene were publicly rebuked and thrown out of Landover Baptist Church (once their tithes were brought current) when it was discovered they had visited Satan's Retreat, a notorious so-called "swingers club" in Des Moines. "It makes my flesh crawl to think about what goes on in these enormous, godless cities," Pastor Deacon Fred told the congregation, after inviting everyone on the aisle to pelt the sinners with the phlegm of righteous fury as they made their shameful egress up the aisle. "But I never would have thought Sodom's purulent tentacles would have reached amongst God's favorite people here at Landover. Of course, I should have known that harlot Goody Greene was up to the Devil's business. Week after week, I saw her sit right there on that front pew—never wearing a stitch of underpanties! Not once! I tell you, it was hard every Sunday trying to get through my sermon having to look at that immaculately waxed gateway to the hot fires of Hades nestled between the long, lovely legs of that syphilitic tramp!"

Upon finding that there were harlots in their midst, several ladies of Christian propriety refused to attend services at all. "What concerned me," explained Sister Inez, "was the thought that I might be sitting in church next to one of those sluts with a trick pelvis. I have, of course, always Lysoled my pew before service. While that seems reasonably effective against the unpleasant, moist residue of garden-variety pooty-poots, I am not sure if it does the trick with chlamydia." More galling to the Ladies of Landover was Goody Greene's unseemly talk of actually finding pleasure while being subjected to the inconvenience of providing sexual satisfaction to men. "There may as well be a sign on the narrow road to Heaven that says: 'If you yield, go ahead and exit,'" opined Mrs. Betty Bowers. "Once even the mildest enjoyment poisons the penance of Godly subjection to such an ungodly—and messy— act, you may as well have all your help change your yellow bug lights to red ones because, whether you know it or not, you have become the town whore. And it's a sad thing to be known as the town whore. Especially, I imagine, if you live in Manhattan."

Following the shocking news, services were routinely interrupted by Platinum Level tithers standing up, pointing at someone in the less desirable sections of the church and declaring: "Does anyone else smell the foul stench of debauchery? Something wicked this way sits! Carnality is afoot! And harlotry is in our midst! I have been convicted by the Holy Spirit that they have been to the godless city of Des Moines with nefarious intent!" To put a stop to these annoying interruptions to his sermons, but also to find out which congregants were slithering off to the city for illicit fun, Pastor Deacon Fred selected the six Landover women least likely to be pestered to remove their clothing at a sex club. He asked them to make a clandestine trip to Satan's Retreat to root out and photograph any church members.

Once the ladies got inside the club, they spent approximately 30 minutes quietly going from room to room, carefully overriding their instincts as hostesses to wave to anyone they recognized. The ladies' plan to patrol unobtrusively was ruined when Helen Floribunda reproved a woman on a mattress for talking with her mouth full. "She was surrounded by men who slotted into her every opening like a bunch of Legos," added Mrs. Betty Bowers. "While I reluctantly admired her limber dexterity, I was appalled by her conduct. A true Christian lady always gives a gentleman her undivided attention."

Recounting what she observed as she walked through several rooms full of naked people, Ann Townsend said: "You need to understand, we are all Christian women. We have only ever been with our husbands. And the things we saw in there were real eye-opening—among other holes. In fact, I certainly have some honesty issues I need to take up with my hubby. I mean, unless he's gone metric on me, someone has been less than forthcoming about what is 'big.'"

After an hour of preliminary reconnaissance with infrared photography, Mrs. Bowers signaled to the other ladies to begin their raid by interrupting the live sex show with a hearty bop to the end of an erect penis with her 12-pound King James Bible. "I mean to tell you, after we went through with the mace, pepper spray and stun guns, those harlots and whore-hoppers was screaming like demons in Hell!" recounted 72-year-old Mrs. Witherspoon. The wails of the fornicators were only subdued when Heather Hardwick moved through the building to begin Operation Christian Hostess. Mrs. Hardwick had arrived with a sterling silver tray carrying nine port wine cheese balls. Hidden inside each cheese ball was a canister of tear gas she had appropriated from her husband's End Times underground arsenal. As Heather entered each room with her lovely

tray, she voraciously ate her way through a cheese ball, revealing a stainless steel canister, which she dropped in a corner of each room. "I knew I only had a couple minutes before each canister went off, so I had to eat fast," recalled Heather. "They certainly were delicious. They were loaded with smoked almonds. And, honestly, it never occurred to me that three of them were chock-full of anthrax until we returned to Freehold and saw the sad news. I have to be honest; it really bothered me to realize I'd inadvertently unleashed a cloud of deadly spores throughout downtown Des Moines. That means we're going to be three canisters short now when we show Jesus' love to Planned Parenthood in Ames next weekend."

NOTICE TO ROMPING HARLOTS
Mrs. Harry "Heather" Hardwick has posted all of the digital photos she took at Satan's Retreat on Landover's website. Ladies, please take a moment before you move out of state to let her know if she misspelled your name—or if it is someone else's vagina.

Jesus Hates "Jesus Loves" Christians

A SPECIAL MESSAGE BY AMERICA'S BEST CHRISTIAN,
MRS. BETTY BOWERS

Whatever happened to the powerful and wrathful God of the Bible? I've looked for Him, but a cuddly, weepy wimp of an imposter—*the Oprah Jesus*—has replaced Him. Apparently, an angry, judgmental God was "testing negative" in an America that prefers to act upon its cherished self-esteem with neither judgment nor consequence. After all, what place does the concept of adultery have in a country that has exchanged the immorality of the act of cheating with the victimhood of the "disease" of sex addiction?

A hundred years ago, if you succumbed to immorality, you provoked God's anger. Now, you simply hurt His easily bruised feelings. New Age "Jesus Is Love" Hallmark Greeting Card Christians run around talking about a God who never asks the inconvenient questions. Instead, He's taken to crying while saying "I love you so much!" like your worst codependent nightmare.

You see, through the resourcefulness of American marketing (and our singular ingenuity for making everything *all* about us), God has suddenly become helplessly obsessed with His love for us, as if He spent the past decades having His power and morality bludgeoned out of Him by incessant sensitivity training and anger management by some touchy-feely homosexual Jewish psychiatrist. So, if you do something evil, instead of calling you into account and sending you to Hell, He meekly sits back and cries like a drunken drama queen watching *Terms of Endearment*. With a languid, resigned flip of His lustrous dark-ash-blond hair, Jesus simply, and timidly, dabs his Nordic-blue eyes and watches you drown your children and set fire to your trailer, hoping you will get around to loving Him so He can give you all the neat stuff you want in the Hereafter!

Well, I have news for you: The *real* Jesus and I are absolutely sick of these lying heretics who have embraced their New Age brand of Painless Christianity. Frankly, they make Jesus vomit.

Mrs. Betty Bowers, righteously stoning a harlot of lesser faith as she leaves her so-called "church"

Attorney General Authorizes CIA to Begin Intercepting Prayers

"If folks are on their knees asking for box cutters, plutonium or condoms, we can't sit around waiting for the Lord to give it to them!"

New Biblical Criminal Code Promises Every Unsaved American in Jail by 2010

S tate Senator Hugo White, a 20-year Landover Platinum Level tither, introduced a bill last month to revamp the Iowa criminal code to incorporate penalties for crimes mandated by the Holy Bible. The bill was the product of three months of intense prayer circles and work sessions involving White and other Republican members of the legislature. "Some of the issues were fairly straight-forward," noted the senator. "If you speak to your parents with unsavory language, you're beaten to death. If you worship a God other than the Christian one, you are executed. If you eat or drink too much, your life ends. Simple enough. However, some of the proscriptions had to be modified to better suit contemporary times. After all, there isn't a lot of sacrificing of animals at the altars these days, so the verses ordering the bloody demise of those who sacrifice beasts with a blemish or without hooves had to be adapted to more modern customs, such as outdoor barbecuing. In today's world, a comparable act would be serving your guests USDA select, instead of choice or prime, steaks. Believe me, if the law was as God ordered, none of us would have to worry about biting into a

Bible Quiz:
God's Favorite Ways to Kill

When a community's sins really irritate the Lord, how does He find comfort?

A. By slaughtering every third person He runs into with a sword.

B. By killing a third of the Zip Code with plagues and famine.

C. By whispering into the ear of people from surrounding areas that it would be a great idea to start a war and kill off a third of the sinners who got under the Lord's thin skin.

D. All of the above.

Answer: D. "'Wherefore, as I live, saith the Lord God; Surely, because thou hast defiled my sanctuary with all thy detestable things, and with all thine abominations, therefore will I also diminish thee; neither shall mine eye spare, neither will I have any pity. A third part of thee shall die with the pestilence, and with famine shall they be consumed in the midst of thee: and a third part shall fall by the sword round about thee; and I will scatter a third part into all the winds, and I will draw out a sword after them. Thus shall mine anger be accomplished, and I will cause my fury to rest upon them, and I will be comforted." (Ezekiel 5:11–13).

chewy piece of tough flank steak on some cheap neighbor's patio ever again!"

Unfortunately, Senator White's bill has yet to pass committee. Aside from whining about so-called "fairness" (an outrageously superfluous concept and popular red herring with liberals), Democrats have expressed concern that the bill will be found to be so-called "unconstitutional." Republicans have expressed the only legitimate concern over passage: whether it will be financially feasible to implement the Old Testament penalties and to provide adequate facilities for the disposal of transgressors' bodies. Testifying in response to the latter consideration was longtime Landover pastor Brother Harry Hardwick. "Plagues, disease and pestilence aren't nearly as difficult as you might think," said Brother Hardwick. "We can easily inject wrongdoers with a myriad of viruses which have been stored by our military for experimental use in enticing brown and yellow people to acquiesce to Jesus' unwavering demand for flattery. Frankly, swarms of locusts aren't that difficult to muster, if you have enough honey and Mexicans. We can whip up a whole mess of them on farms in Freehold, Iowa. Granted, swarms of locusts aren't known for their pinpoint accuracy, so we can expect some collateral damage. But we mustn't worry about so-called 'innocent victims' who are accidentally eaten alive by an industrious swarm of locusts just because they are careless enough to live in the same town as a targeted sinner."

Landover Baptist Asks Local Congressman to Put American Judicial System on eBay.

President George W. Bush Joins Pastor in Celebrating the Release of the New, Improved Republican American Bible. Finally, Jesus Rides into Jerusalem on an Elephant.

If I'd known that the temple undies included a push-up bra, I would have become a Mormon a LONG time ago!

Greetings from Salt Lake City

[handwritten: Shame on you! This is FILTH] *[handwritten: F]*

Truman Vidal
September 1, 2006

Mrs. Ida Mae Jenkins
Landover Christian Academy for the Saved
Baptist Creative Writing 401

THE PASSION THAT KNEW NO BOUNDS

Though 30 years old, as a devout Christian, Jesse's son, David, had remained celibate all his life, recognizing that the only people who will enter Heaven are the 144,000 men who never had sexual relations during their mortal lives.[1] But he ached with desire. He had awoken many a night, to discover that his passion had contaminated his bed sheets, compelling him to leave home for brief periods.[2] He could barely control the erections that sprang as he examined the sagging bosoms of the African natives in his father's National Geographic magazines. But the underwear models in the family's Sears & Roebuck catalogues forced him to unzip, simply to reduce the pain. What was most surprising, though, was his inexplicable need to enter his parents' bedroom late at night, to examine his father's naked anatomy.[3] He could finally control the desire no further.

[handwritten: SATAN!]

It happened first when the family's maid brought her underage daughter to assist with her work. The girl was a beautiful damsel David suspected was a virgin[4] even though she was dressed in a revealing, skin-tight outfit one might expect on a prostitute.[5] Her low-cut blouse revealed breasts so huge, they were like towers.[6] Yet, they were shapely and gorgeous, like two baby twin fawns.[7] He knew he had to have his way with her. But that would be risky. If, despite her young age, she was engaged, he would have to silence her cries as he forced himself upon her, so that both would be spared death.[8] If she were neither married nor engaged, and they were caught, he would have to pay her father $50 and propose.[9] Despite the risks, he couldn't resist.

[handwritten: yes!]

During her break, he invited her to his bedroom to examine his sketches. He immediately disrobed and danced around her naked, explaining he was doing so to honor the Lord.[10] She was mesmerized by his manhood, that featured an appendage the size of a donkey's.[11] She thought to herself, "Let him kiss me with the kisses of his mouth: for thy love is better than wine."[12] He grabbed her, ripping off her blouse and planting his lips on her nipples, telling her, "Thy breasts shall be as clusters of the vine."[13] Her bosom thoroughly satisfied him.[14] She thought to herself, "He shall lie all night betwixt my breasts."[15] He had the green light to proceed after removing her panties and seeing she was not suffering from her period of uncleanness.[16] His hand moved down her body, and he vigorously fondled her opening. She soon came, gushing all over his fingers.[17] They had wild, passionate sex until morning.[18]

[handwritten: Unwise choice of words!]

[handwritten: this is pornography that knows no bounds!]

She arose before him and, remembering the advice of her mother-in-law, moved her way down his torso to his manliness, which she devoured like a starving peasant consuming knockwurst.[19] She was enraptured with delight, for his organ "was sweet to [her] taste."[20] As he approached fruition, he awoke, startled, and shot his wad onto the floor. Recognizing this was an unforgivable sin,[21] he fled the room in horror, and she quickly dressed and went home.

[handwritten: You are in serious trouble young man! See me After class!]

[handwritten: unwise choice of words]

choose another word

remove these paragraphs

Ashamed of his premature mistake, he flung on a bathrobe and walked onto the back patio. That was when he saw the muscular son of the family's gardener. Unable to forget the image of his father, he approached Jonathan, who was obviously as interested as he. Jonathan immediately stripped,[22] then fondled David's testicles,[23] as "they kissed one another.[24] They made love for hours. Afterward, David turned to Jonathan and said, "Very pleasant hast thou been unto me: thy love to me was wonderful, passing the love of women."[25] ①

Suddenly, the gardener entered the yard and, discovering his son's inclination, exclaimed: "Thou son of the perverse rebellious woman, do not I know that thou hast chosen the son of Jesse to thine own confusion, and unto the confusion of thy mother's nakedness?"[26] David fled in terror, knowing Jonathan's homophobic father was determined to have him killed.[27] ②

use the word, "GODLY" here

A terrified and confused David who, 24 hours earlier, had never known man nor woman, had now left the realm of the celibate few who could enter Heaven. Desperate to find a way to save his soul, David rushed into the kitchen, pulled a steak knife from the utensil drawer, and, in one fell swoop, sliced his mammoth genitals from his body. The excruciating pain caused him to lose consciousness immediately, and the loss of blood killed him within the hour, but David died knowing that, by making himself a eunuch, he had restored the possibility of his eventual ascension into Heaven.[28]

yes

Good!

[1] Revelation 19:12
[2] Deuteronomy 23:10
[3] Genesis 9:20-25
[4] Genesis 24:16
[5] Genesis 38:27-28
[6] Song of Solomon 8:8-10
[7] Song of Solomon 4:5
[8] Deuteronomy 22:23-24
[9] Deuteronomy 22:28
[10] 2 Samuel 6:14, 20-22; Isaiah 20:2-5
[11] Zezkiel 23:20
[12] Song of Solomon 1:2
[13] Song of Solomon 7:6-8
[14] Proverbs 5:18
[15] Song of Solomon 1:13
[16] 2 Samuel 11:2-5
[17] Song of Solomon 5:4
[18] Proverbs 7:18
[19] Ruth 3:3-14
[20] Song of Solomon 2:3
[21] Genesis 38:8-10
[22] 1 Samuel 18:4
[23] Genesis 24:2, 9
[24] 1 Samuel 20:41
[25] 1 Samuel 1:26
[26] 1 Samuel 20:30
[27] 1 Samuel 20:31
[28] Matthew 19:12

A+

(I AM sorry! I didn't see your footnotes.)

Very Well Done!

THE GOOD NEWS

Pastor Opens Fire in Lingerie Section of Local Wal-Mart

Last Saturday, Brother Harry Hardwick and Pastor Deacon Fred made a trip to the Wal-Mart on Rural Road 44 to fill the back of Pastor's BMW SUV with handguns for the Landover Junior High for the Saved's Annual "Who Would Jesus Blow to Bits?" jamboree. By the time Pastor had pulled into the store's parking lot, he had damned just about everything in plain view to Hell. After settling for a parking spot in the periphery of the lot, Pastor noticed a teenage boy pull into a handicapped spot. "Why do those dang cripples get to park so close to the entrance?" asked Pastor, as they walked toward the boy's Jetta. "They're like those cotton-picking homosexuals, always wanting special rights. Jesus must have His reasons for leaving that gimp lame—and I'm sure it wasn't so he could get the best parking spot in the whole darn lot!" According to Brother Harry, Pastor's irritation turned to fury when he witnessed the allegedly handicapped driver get out of his car and gracefully stroll toward the store. It was then that Pastor pulled out his concealed weapon and shot the able-bodied boy twice, once behind each kneecap, yelling, "I'm just making an honest man out of you, Mr. 'I'm a Dang Cripple So I Get a Better Parking Spot Than You'!"

"Pastor, losing interest in the screaming boy, turned to me and asked me if I saw something funny in the giant red Wal-Mart logo over our heads," recounted Brother Hardwick. "When I said no, he just lit into me, Pastor said, 'You can't see a damned penis in there, brother? There are two of them! Hidden as plain as day in the two lines in the L letter! One of them is long and thick like mine. The other, at the bottom laying sideways, is short and squatty like yours! I feel like I'm in handicap heaven around here with that boy who can't walk—and you who can't see! Now, let's get in there and get us some guns because I'm fixing to get angry."

By this time, a crowd had pooled around the wounded boy, who was writhing in pain on the hot, gooey asphalt. "Damn

What's Hapening Today in Heaven?

Murdered Children to Be Reunited with Their Born-Again Killer

rubberneckers, blocking the doorway," grumbled Pastor as he elbowed his way through the growing crowd. Stepping over the boy and into the store, Brother Harry eventually guided the agitated Pastor to the gun section. "All Hell broke loose about three minutes later," said Brother Harry. "Tin Level tither Bruce Taylor, the gun clerk, gave Pastor several clips and loaded up a .357 snub-nosed pistol. I turned my head for a second and Pastor was gone. It wasn't until I heard gunshots in the lingerie section and Pastor's voice yelling: 'Well, at least now I know where all the town whores shop!' that I knew where to find him."

Brother Harry was so distraught that he immediately took Pastor to the Landover Baptist Hospital for the Saved, commandeering an ambulance that had arrived for someone injured in the parking lot. A blood test and casual observation revealed that Pastor's bloodstream had been possessed by demons that had soaked their little bodies full of alcohol, to the tune of a 0.32 blood alcohol level. Pastor was ordered to stay at the hospital overnight and was released the following morning to preach. He had no recollection of the incident. Wal-Mart claimed that $93,000 of merchandise, fluorescent light fixtures, floor tiles, display racks and employee uniforms had been destroyed by Pastor during his eight-minute outburst.

Featured Sinner of the Month

NAME: Reginald F. Whittaker
VIOLATION: Caught being a sissy playing with dolls
VERDICT: Felony sin of wanting to lie with man (Leviticus 18:22) plea bargained to the misdemeanor sin of idolatry (Deuteronomy 5:8)

God Ignores the Cries of Little Girl Trapped in Wishing Well

Residents of Freehold conducted an around-the-clock vigil last week as seven-year-old Nancy Austin lay trapped in the bottom of a new wishing well behind her family's tobacco drying shed. Over 120 people from Consuming Holiness Pentecostal (Tongues, No Snakes) Church gathered around the well and beseeched God in Heaven to save the frightened child.

"She was the sweetest girl," said Ruby Johnson, "not an evil bone in her little body. Our faith is so strong that we told the rescue workers to leave because they were just wasting their time. Jesus was going to save her. Besides, their annoying machinery was drowning out our prayer circles. We knew where to place our faith. When those miners were saved years ago in Kentucky, everyone knew who to give all the credit. Not to the silly rescue workers, but the Lord Jesus, that's who! And I just knew the Lord would send a band of angels to swoop down and save little Nancy Austin at any minute. But, after four days of praise and worship, it became clear to all of us that He had decided to go ahead and kill her."

Bible Quiz

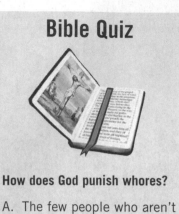

How does God punish whores?

A. The few people who aren't whores of some sort are eagerly awaiting Judgment Day to find out!

B. By refusing to tip.

C. He pulls up their skirts and exposes their nakedness, thereby increasing their whoredom.

D. He strikes them with a plague and makes them appear like middle-age skeletons, so that they lose any customer without an Ann Coulter fetish.

Answer: C. "Therefore will I discover thy skirts upon thy face, that thy shame may appear. I have seen thine adulteries, and thy neighing, the lewdness of thy whoredom, and thine abominations on the hills in the fields" (Jeremiah 13:26–27).

The entire tithe from the Sunday morning service had been set aside to pay for these repairs. Once $378,450 in tithes was collected, however, cooler heads prevailed.

Mrs. Betty Bowers remarked, "I think someone is exaggerating rather wildly. Surely, if one decimated their entire stock, from car tarps to frocks, if indeed there is a difference, one could do no more than $9,000 of damage at a Wal-Mart. If I gambled, I'd bet that $9,000 is a darn sight more than they pay a whole village of Oriental urchins to sew, 'We Support Our Troops' T-shirts every year." Mrs. Bowers then scooped out two fistfuls of cash and coins from the buckets, declaring: "As God is my witness, this is rather a lot of money for those sort of people. Let's consider this unsavory matter closed. Never to be spoken of again."

AMERICA TESTS THE POWER OF PRAYER

Next week, all Americans west of the Mississippi will pray to a placebo god. We will then compare which side of the country wound up with the coolest stuff.

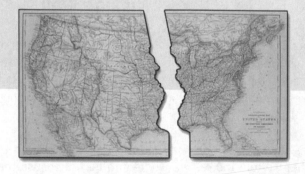

PASTOR'S MOTHER'S DAY SERMON

A Biblical Approach to Mother's Day

Mother's Day is really no different than any other pagan holiday. Its object is to get you to the mall and then trick you into worshipping someone other than Jesus. As True Christians™, we must come to terms with the full knowledge that Satan's *burping whore of Babylon*, the Catholic Church, is behind every shameless secular holiday to venerate mothers. With Mother's Day, the foul stench of papal involvement couldn't be more obvious. The ring-kissing, altar-boy-buggerers have made a history of whipping their psychosexual cravings for Jesus' mother into such a fever pitch, they spend all their time worrying about what went into her Holy Vagina, leaving no time to worship what came out of it—the Baby Jesus!

Do You Hate Your Mother as Much as Jesus Hated His?

Hell-bound Catholics (as if there are any other kind) would have you believe that Jesus loved his mother. But the Holy Bible tells us differently. Jesus said, "If any man come to me, and hate not his father, and mother . . . he cannot be my disciple" (Luke 14:26). So it is perfectly clear from Scripture that we are called upon by Christ to hate our parents. Fortunately, as sweet Jenna and Barbara Bush have found, this isn't a very onerous request. We may spend our entire lives doing our best to emulate the Lord Jesus, but rest assured, we will never match the utter contempt and intolerable scorn that He had for His own mother. And that's not even getting into how Jesus felt about His daddy! (Just imagine what you would feel like if you knew your father was out to kill you only to make Himself look more forgiving to others!)

Even for a Jewish mother, Mary was clearly a pest. To underscore how tiresome Jesus found her company, one time, when he

Last Week's Favorite Hymn:

"Rock of Ages, Preferably from Tiffany"

A Bible Based Mother's Day Card

A vase of tight roses
    a box of bad candy
These are the gifts
    this day used to reveal
A day to keep a florist
    or your dentist handy
And a secular card
    to hide how I feel

I used to buy what the
    unsaved might choose
Without asking first,
    "What would Jesus do?"
And remembering when His
    Mom brayed for booze
He spat: "Woman, what've
    I to do with YOU?"

So, this year no flowers
    shall I buy or send
Washed in the Blood, only
    Jesus' needs I sate
For He has asked,
    even if it does offend
To look at you only with
    eyes filled with hate

was drinking with friends, his needy mother came to bother him. Jesus had so successfully drummed that woman from His mind that, when told his stalker/mother was standing outside, cooling her sandals and waiting for Him, He asked, "Who is my mother?" He then gleefully ignored her (Mark 3:33). Scripture also reveals that Mary was an insufferable leech when she reached the bottom of a wineglass. Once, when Jesus was attending a poorly catered wedding party in Cana, His mother started pestering Him to perform one of His magic tricks when the hosts ran out of wine. Jesus, who was drinking unfermented grape juice, turned to her and said, "Woman, what have I to do with thee?" (John 2:4). He was so fed up with His mother's incessant nagging that He turned six vessels of water into that Manischewitz-style wine his boozer of a mother loved. She slurped it until she was forcefully asked to leave by an exasperated bride's mother, causing Mary to resort to language that the editors of the Gospels wisely refused to transcribe.

Even while Jesus was hanging up on the cross, being barbecued in the hot sun for the sins of mankind, He was still able to muster enough strength to look down at His mother (who was playing poker with Roman centurions) and scream, "Woman, behold thy son!" (John 19:26). This was the Judaic equivalent of "Well, I hope you're satisfied!" Jesus' words betrayed the smug satisfaction, even in His pain and suffering, that He would never again be subjected to a life of having to impress His mother's friends at Jerusalem tea parties by bringing their relatives back from the dead or making His head spin 360 degrees.

So we encourage you to make this Mother's Day Bible-friendly by sending your mother a little card to remind her of how much you and Jesus loathe her. By doing so, you will ensure that, come Judgment Day, you will join Jesus in a knee-slapping, big old belly laugh as both of you watch your mothers slide down a greased chute toward the unquenchable fires of an everlasting, mother-welcoming Hell.

To Play It Safe, Church Orders Sterilization of Demon-Possessed Infants

Annual Spring Bible Crawl—"The first thing we do," Pastor Deacon Fred explains, "is put a giant-print, leather-bound King James Bible on a golden pedestal near the ground— something that no one with Jesus in his heart could resist a flip-through. What happens next can be the most important moment in any tyke's little life. You see, each precious baby is given almost five minutes to decide whether he is on the Lord's team or he is going to suit up for Satan. If the baby crawls away from the Bible, he signals his choice and immediately becomes a candidate for sterilization. The possessed child is then placed in a crib with a reasonably clean piglet, as Jesus taught us that pigs are like fly paper to demons (Mark 5: 11–13). We then take the pig to Lake Walk-on-This to see if it drowns itself in accordance with Scripture. If the pig drowns, the child may stay with its Christian parents. That's the thing about genuine salvation: There is always a death involved somewhere. But if the pig does not kill itself, then we know that the demon is still in the infant. That means the child must be wrapped in Bible pages and shipped off to the Landover Home for the Demonically Possessed in North Dakota. It can sometimes take 20 years until it is safe to return the little *demon hotel* to its mother—but that gives her plenty of time to explain what a demon was doing in her womb in the first place."

True Christian™ TV Guide

"I don't care what kind of fansy-shmancy dish you have: If the program isn't on this list, you ain't watching it!"

—Pastor Deacon Fred

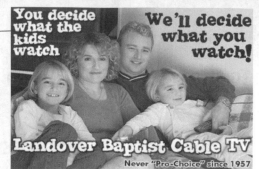

	Landover Baptist Satellite Network	Freehold Clear Channel
9:00 A.M.	**Landover's Most Embarrassing Videos:** Former Landover members caught in church doing what they oughtn't by 186 eagle-eyed security cameras.	**The Christian Chef:** Sister Edith Twiddle shows homemakers how they can get closer to recreating the miracle of Jesus' famous "Loaves and Fish" recipe by simply substituting more bread and tuna.
10:00 A.M.		**Good News!** Brit Hume talks about how wonderfully things are going in Iraq.
11:00 A.M.		
12:00 P.M.	**HWJI?** In "How Would Jesus Invest?", Pastor Deacon Fred, Jerry Falwell and Pat Robertson discuss what Jesus would have done if God had blessed Him with as much money as He lavished on the panel.	**Missionary Mechanic:** Is it a faulty starter or do you have demons under the hood?
12:30 P.M.		**News You Can Choose!** Video-on-demand allows you pick the type of news you want to hear. Very Conservative: #234; Even More Conservative: #235; Fascist: #236; Southern Baptist: #236.
1:00 P.M.	**Keeping a Satan-Free Home:** Rev. Mitch Walker demonstrates his hardware store's new demon-sensitive motion detectors from Korea (only $350 to first 450 callers!).	**Are You Sure You're Saved?** Theological experts goad Christian contestants into questioning their very salvation.
2:00 P.M.	**All My Catholic Children:** Christian soap opera about a family of garish drunks with vague ties to the Mafia.	**Founding Fathers Forum:** Panel of Republicans vociferously debate whether Bill Clinton ranks 42nd or 43rd in the list of "God's Favorite Presidents."
3:00 P.M.	**After-School Special:** Martha says a curse word and gets leukemia.	**GAME SHOW: Godly Homo-Hater or Just Another Closet Case?** Rick Santorum and Ralph Reed try to stump the panel of experts from Focus on the Family.
4:00 P.M.	**EDUCATIONAL: The Creation Science Hour** with Dr. Jonathan Edwards. "How fast do angels have to run to carry sunlight?" (repeat)	**Gardening in Eden:** How to create fabulous flowerbeds for the nice Christian lady who's paying you $2/hour. (Broadcast in Mexican.)

	Landover Baptist Satellite Network	Freehold Clear Channel
5:00 P.M.	**Fairly Unbalanced Evangelical News:** An unbiased look at what those stupid liberals got up to today!	**All White Girl News:** If she's missing or killed—and she's white—she's news. Host: Nancy Grace.
6:00 P.M.		**Imprecatory Prayer Hour:** With your host, Brother Harry Hardwick. Today's target: people who worship the god Yoga.
7:00 P.M.	**REALITY TV: Amos 'n Andy:** Amos lies to a police officer and leers at his betters. (repeat)	
7:30 P.M.	**REALITY TV: Father Knows Best:** Princess learns that no matter what happened to her after school, decent people don't use the "rape" word at dinner.	**Local High School Football:** Replays of games only when the Lord doesn't get all mixed up and answers the prayers of the *other* team.
8:00 P.M.	**REALITY TV: Leave It to [Censored]:** Wally and Eddie return from a long weekend in Key West, claiming that they dislike Beaver.	
9:00 P.M.		**SITCOM: There Goes the Neighborhood!** Flora finally says something her Mormon neighbor doesn't believe!
10:00 P.M.	**The No-Sin Zone:** Host Betty Bowers welcomes friend, First Lady Laura Bush. (Tonight's sacramental wine drinking game word: "teacher.")	**Gone Gay!** Shepard Smith tells you about America's most dangerous homosexuals—and the best hours to reach them.
10:30 P.M.	**Say Your Prayers, Boy!** Mandatory viewing for all current church members. ($200 tithe per view)	**ADD Shouting:** Fox News pundits jump to conclusions in 15 seconds or less, *guaranteed.*
11:00 P.M.	**Sin Patrol:** HDTV closed-circuit surveillance of random members' bedrooms. (Premium tithe per view—*see Pastor*)	**Holy Hannity!** Fox's *Hannity & Colmes* with all the "Colmes" edited out (the normally hour program now runs a brisk, commie-free 57 minutes).
11:30 P.M.	**TPRL:** Total Prayer Requests Live	
12:00 A.M.	**Off Air** Outdoor activity curfew: **10:30 P.M.** Television Curfew: **12:00 A.M.** Indoor activity curfew: **12:10 A.M.**	**Off Air:** Broadcast resumes at the stroke of the sixth chapel bell (6:00 A.M.)

OUR NUCLEAR WINTER FORECASTS ARE 60% SUNNIER!

PENTAGON TV

If You Allow One Person to Be a Homo, Soon Everyone Will Want to Be One!

SERMON BY BROTHER HARRY HARDWICK

Now, friends, I'm going to have to ask your patience during today's sermon. Wives, get ready to give your dozing hubby a sharp smack across the knees with a hymnal. Because secular laws are not something we Christians normally give a hoot about. But each time those numskulls on the United States Supreme Court have found a new privacy right in so-called "personal" behavior, the end result has been a society more tolerant of that conduct. It has therefore always been left to industrious Christians like us to torment and mock those who try to exercise this newfangled right, as has been the case in the vile wake of *Roe v. Wade*.

For example, in the 1965 *Griswold v. Connecticut* decision, the Court struck down a state law prohibiting married couples from purchasing contraceptive devices on the ground the law violated sex-crazy married folks' so-called "privacy" rights. Now, friends, this just shows you how detached from reality these liberal activists on the Court are, to think that Americans have *any* "privacy" rights. Because we all know that the only thing that stopped our Founding Fathers from foreseeing a president sitting in the Oval Office and listening in on everyone's calls was their inability to foresee the telephone! At any rate, as a result of the decision, over time, more and more couples began using birth control (much to the annoyance of the last person on earth who would ever want to even look at a vagina, much less enter one, the homo-to-beat-all-homos in Vatican City). The result is that whereas in the 1960s, husbands and wives copulated annually—*folks, don't look so shocked; that means every year!*—knowing that any such encounter could result in yet another mouth to feed, today, married couples have sex at will, sometimes two, three or even four times a year. Having a Supreme Court packed with a bunch of pandering pimps has turned every bedroom in America into a nonstop amusement park full of naked calisthenics and harlotry.

Similarly, in *Loving v. Virginia*, the Court struck down a state law prohibiting interracial marriage on the ground it violated the so-called "privacy" rights of couples, apparently forgetting that those Deuteronomy-flouting miscegenationists rarely keep their outrageous conduct private! As a result of that decision, mixed marriages, and sometimes even mixed dating, has gained shocking acceptance outside of Bob Jones University.

Now it is the homosexuals' turn to get a green light to sodomize everything in sight by our nation's highest—and don't doubt for a moment they don't pass around the beer-bong during deliberations—court. Pansies used to limit their association to deviant acts in out-of-the-way Texaco restrooms and the places in Catholic churches so synonymous with rectal intercourse they are simply called "rectories." But in 1969, a few flamers became flame throwers when police righteously announced "last call!" through bullhorns at Stonewall Sodomy Bar in New York City.

As if to throw a pitcher of pink cosmopolitans on the fire, several years ago, the U.S. Supreme Court decided to become cheerleaders for our nation's always frisky homosexuals. In *Lawrence v. Texas,* the Court struck down a sensible Texas law that made various sex acts perfectly legal when committed by normal folks but criminal when committed without a vagina in the room.

What *Loving* did to segregation, *Lawrence* will undoubtedly do to hatred of homos, if we aren't vigilant. If we don't raise our voices in Christian anger, we may one day live in a society that concerns itself with neither color differences nor sexuality distinctions, ignoring people's private lives altogether. If that happens, what will folks have to talk about? It falls on the shoulders of America's conservative Christians to make sure that sad day never arrives! Everyone who hears the fury in my voice today: Consider yourself conscripted!

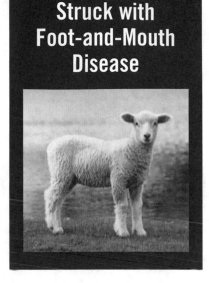

Lamb of God Struck with Foot-and-Mouth Disease

$20.00 Off Prayer Request

Submit Request, Tithe Account and Coupon to Church Secretary

Expires: January 30, 2010

Only Valid For One Monthly $175 Mandatory Pastoral Prayer Request

3,000 Horses That Refused to Trust God and Fly Are now Dead

"Them boy-bonking Greeks had flying horses like we have mosquitos," noted one respected Christian scholar. "As Christians, we know that all of their crazy stories about gods who impregnated human virgins are outrageous, improbable lies, but the stuff about that Pegasus breed of horses was the Gospel truth."

While most Christians turn on their TVs each morning, eager for welcome news of cataclysmic carnage in the Middle East, the folks at Landover Baptist know there is a much more reliable sign that the return of the Lord is at hand. "Revelation, Chapter Six teaches us to be on the lookout for horses that sprout wings and fly," warns Pastor Deacon Fred. "That might happen this very afternoon, so most True Christians™ are worried about these emormous four-legged creatures having enough time to learn how to fly. You know, they are sort of heavy."

Believers familiar with the Bible, however, know that equine flight is possible, since horses have flown before. Second Kings 2:11 teaches that one of God's favorite modes of transportation was to light a few horse butts on fire, attach them to a chariot, place some of his favorite people inside and fly them to Heaven in blazing glory.

Nevertheless, there is concern in Christian circles that after centuries of galloping about, horses may have forgotten how to fly. Whether through laziness or lack of willpower, these earthbound nags may end up derailing the whole Second Coming by refusing to fulfill prophesy. A report on Operation Fly in the Anointment released to church members in 1972 is particularly troubling to those looking out their windows in hopes of seeing Seabiscuit flapping across the sky. In the report, Landover Baptist's Rev. Dr. Jonathan Edwards concluded that after 14 years, 2,984 horses, 420 gallons of kerosene and 18 books of matches, all that was left was glue to fix his loafers and enough dog food to feed all of Mexico for about 12 minutes. "The highest we got a horse to fly was about four feet during a steeplechase," said Edwards, "and while he got the taking-off part of flying right, he was a real disappointment in the staying-up-in-the-air part of flying. Frankly, we didn't find one single horse with the gumption to do any serious flying. Even the ones we dropped off the side of the barn never got the hang of it."

ATTENTION CHURCH MEMBERS!

Please leave seat 21 in row K, Orchestra Center, vacant. Jesus will be sitting in it this whole month. Thank you.

Bible Fear Factor Promises to Have Television Audiences Soiling Themselves

This fall, the Christian Reality Network will broadcast the most talked-about, Bible-based reality program since a cast of 12 died in the very first episode of *Jonah's Real World: The Whale. Bible Fear Factor,* a show too gruesome for network television, will feature six participants testing their mettle against the Lord's uncanny knack for thinking of outlandishly cruel things to do to the humans He loves.

BIBLE FEAR FACTOR

1. THE FIRST CHALLENGE: COLLECT 200 FORESKINS

Each contestant will have eight hours to collect 200 foreskins with nothing more than a toenail clipper, a Mason jar and three bus tokens.

> Wherefore David arose and went, he and his men, and slew of the Philistines two hundred men; and David brought their foreskins, and they gave them in full tale to the king, that he might be the king's son in law. And Saul gave him Michal his daughter to wife (1 Samuel 18:27).

2. THE SECOND CHALLENGE: GORGE AT THE LOCUST, POOP AND URINE BUFFET!

Each contestant will vie to be the quickest to gobble up John the Baptist's favorite meal: a big, crunchy bowl of live locusts, followed by the Lord's oven-fresh treats made with human excrement. Each contestant who survives such Biblical fare without unsightly vomiting will move on to the next round after chugging a warm, foamy quart of his own urine.

> And the same John had his raiment of camel's hair, and a leathern girdle about his loins; and his meat was locusts and wild honey (Matthew 3:4).

And thou shalt eat it as barley cakes, and thou shalt bake it with dung that cometh out of man, in their sight (Ezekiel 4:12).

But Rabshakeh said, Hath my master sent me to thy master and to thee to speak these words? Hath he not sent me to the men that sit upon the wall, that they may eat their own dung, and drink their own piss with you? (Isaiah 36:12).

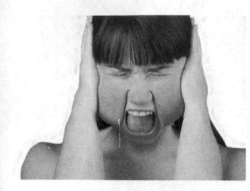

3. The Third Challenge: Surviving the Vicious Pranks of an Angry Lord

The remaining contestants will go sandal-to-sandal with the Lord as they are burned, shot with arrows, made hungry, burned again, subject to gnawing by wild beasts and exposed to poisonous snakes—all before finally scrambling before a cheering crowd at Landover Christian Coliseum as the Lord pulls out even crueler torments from His endless bag of tricks.

For a fire is kindled in mine anger, and shall burn unto the lowest hell, and shall consume the earth with her increase, and set on fire the foundations of the mountains. I will heap mischiefs upon them; I will spend mine arrows upon them. They shall be burnt with hunger, and devoured with burning heat, and with bitter destruction: I will also send the teeth of beasts upon them, with the poison of serpents of the dust. The sword without, and terror within, shall destroy both the young man and the virgin, the suckling also with the man of gray hairs (Deuteronomy 32:22–25).

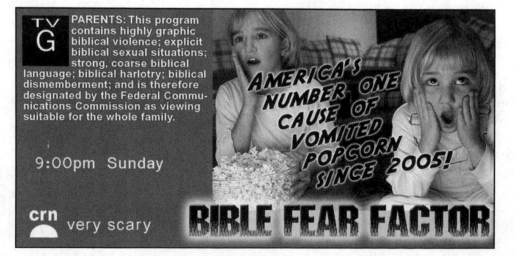

TV G

PARENTS: This program contains highly graphic biblical violence; explicit biblical sexual situations; strong, coarse biblical language; biblical harlotry; biblical dismemberment; and is therefore designated by the Federal Communications Commission as viewing suitable for the whole family.

9:00pm Sunday

crn very scary

AMERICA'S NUMBER ONE CAUSE OF VOMITED POPCORN SINCE 2005!

BIBLE FEAR FACTOR

4. THE FOURTH CHALLENGE: MAKING A LIORSE

Each contestant will be given a match, a lion, a horse, a penknife, a bag of sulfur briquettes and a Swingline stapler. They must stuff the lion's head with burning sulfur, and then attach it to the horse's body without killing the horse—or being bitten by the lion.

> The heads of the horses were as the heads of lions; and out of their mouths issued fire and smoke and brimstone (Revelation 9:17).

5. THE FINAL ELIMINATION ROUND (AVAILABLE ONLY ON PAY-PER-VIEW)

All remaining contestants, beginning at the toes and working their way up (assiduously avoiding naughty places), will try to eat each other until only one is left alive and sated.

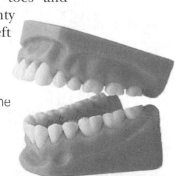

> I will cause them to eat the flesh of their sons and the flesh of their daughters, and they shall eat every one the flesh of his friend (Jeremiah 19:9).

CHANGE YOUR CHANNEL BY 9:10 OR YOU'LL BE CHANGING YOUR UNDIES BY 9:15!

crn
very scary

BIBLE FEAR FACTOR

My Imaginary Friend Just Told Me His Name Is Jesus!

In last Sunday's sermon, Pastor Deacon Fred recalled a conversation he had with an unsaved cashier at a Safeway in Des Moines. "This feller was just yapping to himself, and mumbling," said Pastor. "So I asked him, who in tarnation are you talking to? To which he replied, 'My 2,000-year-old invisible flying friend.' I told him that part of being an adult is living in the real world and not clinging to made-up stories and imaginary friends, no matter how comforting. Then he happened to mention that his friend was called Jesus. I told him, Well, why didn't you say so? That's a different kettle of fish entirely, my friend!"

Landover Baptist Creation Scientist Dr. Jonathan Edwards gives candid advice to True Christians™ who have unsaved family members with invisible or so-called "imaginary" friends. "When does a friend stop becoming imaginary?" asks Dr. Edwards. "Well, most Christian psychologists believe it is when your imaginary friend tells you his name is Jesus," says Edwards. "And I believe that to be true in almost every case. You see, when a person finally becomes a True Christian™, all imagination ceases to exist. So if a person is saying that his imaginary friend just told him or her that its name is Jesus, it is reasonable that the friend is no longer imaginary. To put it in simple terms, their friend is the living Son of God who sits on a golden throne in Heaven up on a cloud and hears and watches everything that every single person on Earth does, each and every

Bible Quiz

After a zillion years, poop and pee-pee still give God the giggles! It is little wonder that the Lord took to *demanding* praise, rather than sitting around waiting for it, as He has always indulged in various off-putting obsessions. One of His least endearing hobbies is an infatuation with excrement, both human and animal.

Why did God require His early followers to attach a paddle to their weapons?

A. So they could play a relaxing game of post-slaughter cricket.

B. So they could cover up the human poop lying around their camp, in case God happened to walk through the camp wearing sandals.

C. So they could scoop fat out of the carcasses of animals they killed for sacrifice and consumption.

D. None of the above.

Answer: B. "And thou shalt have a paddle upon thy weapon; and it shall be, when thou wilt ease thyself abroad, thou shalt dig therewith, and shalt turn back and cover that which cometh from thee: For the Lord thy God walketh in the midst of thy camp" (Deuteronomy 23:13–14).

Even Chickens Can Get Demons!

Earlier this week, 78-year-old farmer Hank Rollins told Landover security officers that "howling noises" coming from his backyard woke him up at four on Monday morning. "It sounded like a whole pack of coyotes was a gettin' after my chickens," he said. By the time he got outside, he suspected the very worst. Satan's little calling card was the stench of mutilated chicken coming from the henhouse. When Hank and the officers got to the henhouse, they found that the chickens had been so filled with demons, they turned on each other in a bloody rampage. There were more chicken pieces on the floor than at an NAACP picnic. "It was so horrible," recounts farmer Rollins, "that only moments before, I had seen a coyote running out of the henhouse—no doubt in horror over what them demons had been doing." Occult detective Mitch Walker (who was on the scene) informed everyone to "just sit tight." He explained, "more n'likely, we got ourselves a flock of demon-possessed chickens." As the Lord's sun was rising overhead, the eggs in the henhouse glowed red a bit. Detective Mitch later said that "it was God's way of letting us know that there was a whole pack of new demons in them eggs waiting to be hatched. We made ourselves a demon omelet right there on that wooden floor. Praise God!"

hour—and that includes having to watch millions of sinners masturbate every single day!"

Landover Baptist youth ministers are professionally trained to spot young children with imaginary friends. "We start as early as nursery school," says Youth Pastor Christian Wright. Landover Nursery School for the Yet-to-Be Saved teachers encourage young pre-Christians who appear to have imaginary friends to develop a speaking relationship with their friend. "It is important that we find out if their imaginary friend is Jesus, the Holy Ghost or a demon, as quickly as possible," notes Wright. "I don't think we have to explain why. Let's just say it's no fun telling a Christian parent that their two-year-old has just been shipped off in a chicken cage to the Landover Home for the Demonically Possessed in North Dakota."

At Landover Baptist, our church members are blessed enough to have pastors who make it a priority to stop imagination long before it becomes dangerous. "That's usually at the age of three, as we understand it," says Pastor Deacon Fred. "I believe the angels in Heaven throw a party and the demons in Hell pound the sandy shores of the lake of fire in anger each time a young pre-Christian tells his nursery school teacher 'My invisible friend just told me his name is Jesus!' And what a joy it is also to hear the same thing from unsaved adults on their deathbeds, two seconds before they take their last breath as their imaginary friend kills them."

What to Bring to Bible Gun Camp?	What to Leave at Home?
• King James Bible (1611 version)	• Notebook, Pens and Pencils
• Highlighter	• Secular Music
• Semiautomatic Pistol	• Sleeping Bag
• Revolver with Telescopic Lens	• PJs
• Plenty of Ammunition	• Soap and Shampoo
• Knives Suitable for Skinning	• Swimsuit
• Cell Phone and Walkie-Talkie	• Night-light
• Fireworks	• Camera and Film
• Tape Recorder	• Stuffed Animals
• Handcuffs	• Sunscreen
• One Change of Clothes	• Insect Repellant
• Money for Offering Plate	• Rain Gear
• Rope	• Sissy Friends

"The lesson we learned from Columbine is that guns don't kill people, unsaved children do!"
—Pastor Deacon Fred

Send Your nancy-Boy to Vacation Bible Gun Camp

What can I do to help my child have a great camp experience?

Fathers, before your little nancy-boy leaves for Bible Gun Camp, privately discuss the importance of your church family's reputation. Make sure he is fully aware that if he does anything to embarrass you or the Lord this summer, Jesus will tell on him and you will beat his little bare behind with a rusty buckle that will have him wishing he'd been shipped off to a Cambodian orphanage when he gets home.

How do I handle homesickness?

Mothers, if you receive a call from the camp pastor telling you that your child is acting like a little mincing prisspot and crying about how much he misses his mommy, resist the temptation to "rescue" your child—because we won't let you. You will not be permitted to communicate with your child for the entire four weeks he is away at camp. Please understand that we are doing everything in our power to make a man out of your 12-year-old boy. We own him for a month. Any calls you receive from the camp pastor are just to get our unsaved lawyers off of our back.

What is the policy on sleep mates?

Sleeping assignments are carefully orchestrated by the Bible Gun Camp staff. Counselors observe each boy through closed-circuit cameras as he is left to fend for himself alone in the wilderness for the first two days. During this time, we watch your child to see if we can detect any outward manifestations of possible homosexual tendencies, such as weeping, admiring nature and excessive wiping with leaves after defecation. We utilize our findings to avoid placing two molly-coddlers within reach of each other's privates for the next several weeks.

Do I send food with my child?

Please do not send food to camp with your child. Jesus set out for forty days in a desert without remembering to pack any food. We assume that your child is not so sinful that he expects better planning and provisions than Jesus. Other than that, understand that your child is attending Bible Gun Camp to learn post-apocalyptic techniques on how to hunt, stalk and kill his own food or starve to death. No meals are served during the first two weeks. All boys (except the offspring of Platinum Level tithers) will be forced to eat what is scooped onto their tin plates. Camp is no place for finicky eaters or silly claims about allergies. Platinum Level tithers are encouraged to get special dietary requests to room service three weeks before departure.

Only Five Children Die in First Week of Landover Vacation Bible School

"It is always sad to see little tykes leave us—especially before they have had an opportunity to make a 'WWJD?' potholder for their mommies to remember them by," said Pastor Deacon Fred. "But the fact is that every year some folks have got to be the Muslims if we are going to be able to perform our annual Crusades reenactment. I send out my sincere condolences, but remind all parents that, regardless of the circumstance, Vacation Bible School tuition is not refundable or prorated through the time of impalement."

The Golden Rules of Gun Safety

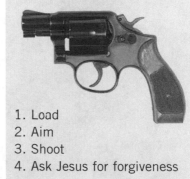

1. Load
2. Aim
3. Shoot
4. Ask Jesus for forgiveness

How much money should my child take to camp?
Your child should take 30 $20 bills. An offering will be taken up after morning services each day. Enabling your youngster to place a $20 bill in the collection plate will ensure he learns the importance of giving money to people who matter most to the Lord. Any child who fails to put $20 into the offering plate will be taught a valuable lesson about peer pressure and mob dynamics. The child will then be locked in a bat-infested cave for the duration of the summer where he can more carefully contemplate his selfishness.

What is there to do?
Apocalyptic wilderness survival training, Bible reading, Scripture memory contests, marksmanship competitions, Old Testament wild deer and boar sacrifices, gun care and cleaning, manly fellowship, Bible skits and evening super-surprise game competitions where children use tranquilizer guns to hunt unsaved vagrants who are dropped into the mountains by helicopter.

What if my child is caught with drugs or alcohol on the camp property?
Drugs and alcohol will be confiscated by the camp pastor. Your child will be stripped naked and a full cavity search will be mechanically performed. The child will then be forced to endure the next 30 days of Vacation Bible Gun Camp without clothes or company.

Tongue-Tied Pastor Accidentally Damns Himself to Hell

Pastor Gary Simpkins's pronounced stutter got the best of him during Wednesday's sermon when he accidentally blasphemed the Holy Spirit, thereby committing the only unforgivable sin. "I came in late and Pastor Simpkins started crying so much," observed Inez Watkins. "Mercy sakes alive, with all that blubbering going on, I thought Jimmy Swaggart was up there again after spending the weekend shacked up in a motel room with a Bible-bong and a pack of streetwalkers!"

Landover Baptist Church
Official Permission Slip
VACATION BIBLE GUN CAMP

I, the undersigned True Christian™, do hereby grant my saved child, _____, permission to attend Landover Baptist Vacation Bible Gun Camp for the duration of the summer, July 1, _____, through September 1, _____. I understand that over 3,000 Landover youth will attend camp and that deacons, pastors and teachers from the Landover Baptist Academy for the Saved will be granted parental rights over my child for the duration of the summer. These rights include, but are not limited to, righteous punishment as abetted by the Lord that may or may not result in sundry bruising and/or, in rare circumstances, a discontinuation of pulmonary functions.

I also understand that the purpose of this retreat is to introduce wicked, sissified young boys to the lashing love of Jesus Christ by any and all means necessary. I am fully aware that my child will be equipped with a semiautomatic handgun and will be involved in constructing, carrying and/or lighting dangerous explosives. In addition, I understand that my child may be deprived of food and water for extended periods of time and will be subject to ridicule and public humiliation by his peers. I am aware that my child may be requested to remove his clothes and complete the duration of the summer wearing nothing but a maple leaf.

I agree to indemnify (including attorneys' fees) and hold harmless Landover Baptist Church and all of its many subsidiaries for any causes of action resulting directly or indirectly from any death, injury or property damage, especially those resulting from gross negligence.

I have enclosed $3,500 in cash or ready funds to cover the costs of ammo, U-Haul rental and fertilizer.

PLEASE CHECK ALL BOXES BELOW THAT APPLY TO YOUR CHILD:

☐ This is a Platinum Level tither's child and he will require a special diet and sleeping arrangements. Enter your Platinum Level tither's account number here for verification: _____.

☐ My child will supply his own firearm(s).

☐ My child has already carried a stick of dynamite in his teeth.

☐ My child has killed for food or retribution before.

☐ My child does not have permission to miss more than three consecutive dinners due to incarceration ($1,000 bail money enclosed).

Father's Signature: _____   Date:_____

Experts Conclude:
Women Probably Don't Have Souls

This week, Landover Baptist Creation Scientist Dr. Jonathan Edwards announced findings related to his research into the nonexistence of the female soul. "The absence of salvation for women finds extensive support in the Word of God," he reported." The New Testament teaches us that the sole reason God created women in the first place was to provide companionship and service to men (1 Corinthians 11:9). God determined that men would be lonely or turn to buggery living without a convenient vagina nearby, so he created women purely to keep men company and serve their libidinous needs (Genesis 2:18–22). It stands to reason, though, that once men enter the Kingdom of Heaven, they will be one with God, and will no longer be lonely and in need of mortal companionship. The reason behind having women will no longer exist, as the Lord is not about to allow any recreational copulation between dead people. Women, like four-legged members of the animal kingdom, having served their purpose, will fall by the wayside."

Dr. Edwards went on to say, "Once men reunite with their Maker, they will no longer be burdened with the care of women. After all, women were disappointing creations from the start. Women are self-indulgent (Isaiah 32:9–11), silly (2 Timothy 3:6), dishonest (Proverbs 7:10; Ecclesiastes 7:26). They cause men to be sinful, idolatrous and blasphemous (Jeremiah 7:18; Ezekiel 13:17, 23; Numbers 31:15–16; 1 Kings 21:25; Nehemiah 13:26). It was the inherent weakness of women that led them to be deceived by Satan, who finds men more of a sporting challenge (Genesis 3:1–6; 2 Corinthians 11:3; 1 Timothy 2:14). Consequently, before the Lord could turn around after creating, He was cursing women (Genesis 3:16). There is simply no room in Heaven for such flawed and inadequate beings."

GUEST LECTURE NOW ON DVD

"Quizzical Supermodels Debate Intelligent Design." "Okay, so we were created in God's image, right?" begins moderator Naomi Campbell. "So, like, who do all them ugly blokes look like?"

Pastor Orders Over 300 Chatterbox Wives: "Go Wait in the Car!

Pastor Deacon Fred had some comforting words for the Ladies of Landover: "I personally want to assure all female members of this church that until we have finished praying over Dr. Edwards's research, all of you little gals should proceed on the assumption that you have souls, perhaps only pint-size little demi-souls—whether they are actually in there or not—until you are told otherwise. Mark my words, our team of Bible experts will find some way to tippy-toe around these Scriptures. After all, we're American Christians, and if there is one thing we know how to do well, it's nimbly step around Scriptures that make us feel uncomfortable or pose an inconvenience." Some of the women present to hear Dr. Edwards' findings were visibly shaken. A teary-eyed Sister Hortence Magillicuddy said, through choked sobs, "I've heard of Negresses not having souls, but me? NO! This is outrageous! I won't stand for it!" Once she was backhanded into respectful silence by her husband, the meeting was adjourned.

Faith-Healing SWAT Team Called in Response to Crisis of Faith After Mrs. Doris "Elmer" Jordon Cracked Open a Lunchtime Fortune Cookie Informing Her: "You Will Die Sad and Soon."

SEARCH

LEVI the DANCING COCKROACH

a book for Christian children by Pat Robertson

Levi, The Dancing Cockroach

by Reverend Pat Robertson

List Price: ~~$112.97~~

Our Price: $112.97

You Save: Your sullied soul

Availability: Usually ships in less time than it took Jesus to rise from the dead. Overnight shipping probably ensures delivery before the Rapture.

Summary: A delightful children's book for Christian youngsters age 5–10 wishing to learn about other, false faiths. *Levi, the Dancing Cockroach* teaches kids about Jewish behavior, traditions and culture in a fun and easy-to-remember way. The story follows greedy little Levi, a dancing cockroach, on the adventure of a lifetime! Journey with the dirtiest little critter on earth through the sewers of New York City to the altar of the First Baptist Church in Montgomery, Alabama.

Kids will learn about Jewish traditions and visit the inside of a tiny little synagogue in a shoebox where Levi and his fellow insects sillily think they are actually praying to a God who listens to people who killed his Son. Youngsters will learn about nature and the insect world as they meet different characters through the severely myopic eyes of Levi the Cockroach.

Your children will fall in love with Levi the Cockroach as he dances in a flea circus with his relatives on the back of a mangy Irish wolfhound. He eats the dollar bills that are thrown at him every day until one day a nice Christian man throws Levi a paper with a New Testament verse on it. Levi giddily swallows the Scripture, but he gets very ill and almost dies. While he is sick, he vomits up the fragments of the Bible tract and begins to read it.

Miraculously, he decides to give his little cockroach life to Jesus Christ. His parents get very upset with him. "Levi!" they scold. "You know that cockroaches don't believe in Jesus!" But Jesus swats them off the back of the dog, touching Levi's little hand and heart, thereby turning him into a lovely little blond boy.

Trade paperback 1st edition (March 1978)
Christian Children's Books; ISBN: 011983402: Dimension (in Godly inches): 0.1 x 5 x 7.5
Amazon.com Sales Rank: 2,445,719
Average Customer Ranting: ★★☆☆☆
Number of Reviews That Don't Violate Hate Crimes Legislation: 4

Spotlight Reviews

3 of 17,890 people found the following review helpful:
★★★★★ *What a treat to find this little book still in print!*

Reviewer: **Pastor Deacon Fred, Landover Baptist Church,** September 1, 2006

I was jumping for Jesus when I saw this book on Brother Falwell's Listmania. Rumor in my prayer circles had it that every single copy of this Disney-like take on the Lord's formerly chosen had been retrieved and destroyed by Brother Pat's new PR firm (the one that had so ably assisted Sister-in-Christ Lynne Cheney in removing *Sisters*, her hot, steamy take on prairie lesbo fiction, from circulation). That would've been a pity, as I've never seen a book that combines fun and learning in such an expert, subtle way. Children will remember Jewish characters from the Bible and associate them with precious members of the insect world. I use the same method to remember the names of Jewish folks I meet when our church visits the Holy Land each year.

Annual All-You-Can-Eat Endangered Species Dinner

This Year's Theme: Genesis 9:3: "Every moving thing that liveth, shall be meat for you."

This year's Endangered Species Dinner will be held around the church's newly constructed Olympic-size outdoor baptism pool on July 15. Diners should assemble at 6:00 P.M. (sharp) at the Landover Petting Zoo to select their choice of entrées. "It will sort of be like those fancy restaurants in Des Moines that have aquariums with lobsters in them," said Pastor Deacon Fred. "Bring a rifle because we are going to have some mighty fine rare birds up in the trees so folks can pick off the ones that look tasty. You just can't get spotted owl fresher than that."

Landover Baptist began this wildly successful shindig back in the Dark Ages of the Hillary and Bill Clinton administration as a convivial way to annoy all those alarmist pinkos that have conniptions every time Uruguay is down to its last redspotted wharf rat. The dinner has raised over $2 million to promote the Biblically sound message that the Lord has graciously given us all the animals of the Earth, and whether there be a million of them or just one little, bitty one hiding, scared out of his wits, in a tree somewhere, they are ours to smack over the head and barbecue.

"As a Baptist, I don't need a tree-fondling zoologist to tell me the ideal population for our planet's almost 200 species," said Mrs. Betty Bowers, America's Best Christian. "Genesis settled that question just after all the animals were created about 6,000 years ago. As you will recall, the Lord specifically told Noah all you need is two of each. The rest is gravy. Literally."

M E N U

Before Dinner Drink
Nectar of the Haleakala volcano flower in commemorative native-carved ivory cups (limit of 24 per family).

Appetizer
Black-Footed Ferret Bisque with Spotted Owl Egg Confetti Garni

Salad
Seared Breast of Whooping Crane Roulade with Haricots Verts and Sun-Dried Grapes. Served with Oil of Baby Dolphin Lips Dressing on the side.

Entree
Roasted Florida Panther, Baby Sea Turtle fins and White Tiger Meat Cassoulet, served with purple Bali Cabbage Chiffonnade, Fumet of Rare Mushrooms and A-1 Steak Sauce.

Dessert
Sweetened Rhinoceros Crème Brûlée or Caramelized Vancouver Island Marmot Soufflé with Crème Anglaise.

After-Dinner Drink
Panda Juice with or without pulp, served in a decorative take-home hollowed-out Panda Paw.

Sorry, Little Billy, I Don't Care What Your Mamma Told You: Your Kitty Is in Hell

Only dogs go to Glory. Cats are the accoutrement of witches and the alacritous minions of the Great Deceiver.

INTELLIGENT DESIGN FACTOID

When the Lord designs an animal at His Holy Drafting Table, the die is cast for that species. This is why every cocker spaniel is exactly 25 inches long and weighs precisely 25 pounds, without any variation. Glory!

The Only Limit on This Year's Liberal Hunting Season Will Be the Supply of Ammo

Landover Deacons Join Hunt for Liberal Bargain Prescription Pill Junkies Crossing Canadian Border

After being quickly deputized by longtime Silver Level tither John Brown, regional INS director sitting in Des Moines, 75 Landover Baptist Church deacons took up posts along the U.S.-Canadian border less than three weeks ago. "We are not about to let none of them rich, over-educated, weak-kneed, Blue State liberals leave this country until they've paid enough taxes to cover Red State highways and crop subsidies," reported Pastor Jim Hawkins, as he raised the scope on his high-powered AR-15 assault rifle from his post on the periphery of the Richard B. Cheney National Strip-Mining Park in North Dakota. "Last week, I unloaded a half-pound of lead into the shiny white heinies of two long-haired, dope-smokin' varmints running through the woods like a pair of drugged-out deer. It wasn't until I got within two feet of them and saw their flannel undies that I realized they were just a pair of Canadian farm women—or lesbians—if there's a difference."

The pastors were reacting to reports of a mass exodus of anti-Bush (a/k/a anti-American, anti-Jesus) citizens across the Canadian border. With Canada's immigration service overwhelmed by applications of Americans seeking asylum ever since November 2, 2004, many traitors have attempted to covertly slip into the country. "So long as I have one index finger that can squeeze a trigger, no communist New Yorker is gittin' by me," railed Pastor Aubrey Coleman, perched from his post on a hill in northern Minnesota.

Unofficial reports cite at least 55 foiled unauthorized border crossings in the brief period that the church was so enthusiastic to assist the immigration agency that it didn't wait to be asked. Rev. Bill Shortland set up an informal roadblock on Interstate 75 in Michigan using 24 cow carcasses and a rusted-out Whirlpool ice maker. "A few questions usually reveal whether these folks are legitimate tourists or just horny liberals out to score some heavily discounted Viagra in Ontario. I intercepted one family last week in a fancy BMW with their radio unapologetically tuned to NPR. The parents were drinking from Starbucks cups and both teenagers in the back, doped to the gills on primo Seattle caffeine, were reading books, neither of which had 'Holy' or 'Bible' imprinted anywhere on the cover, as far as I could tell. I wasn't going to let those liberal rascals within 10 feet of that frozen Land of Homosexual Marriage to our north without full body cavity searches and a bracing baptism in the frigid waters of Lake Michigan. Talk about some holy shrinkage!"

Not all church members support the deacons' actions. "I think it is a colossal waste of time," observed Brother Harry Hardwick, chair of the Board of Deacons. "They may be most of the rich folks, but we don't need their money. President Bush has shown his commitment to maintaining all the pork programs, while massively expanding military spending and still creating the miracle of tax breaks. Since the federal deficit is already higher than ever, what difference will a few trillion additional dollars make? We'll just borrow it from the Chinamen. Besides, as any Republican poll-watcher can attest, it takes a lot of effort to suppress the Democrat vote. And having them actually disappear from the country, instead of just the voter registration files, will make winning elections even easier."

NOTICE FROM PASTOR

Gentlemen, do not expect to avail yourself of the convenience of dropping your family off under the canopy on rainy Sundays if your car does not prominently sport a "W still the President" decal. Violators will find up to two of their tires and/or headrests riddled with gunshot. Consider yourself warned.

INTELLIGENT DESIGN IN THE NEWS

Creation Scientists are going gaga over what the Lord is showing in flagellum proteins this season. Notes a giddy Professor Henri François Welch, "We're seeing some surprisingly kicky new looks for bacteria on the go from the Lord for the fall."

Landover Baptist Academy for the Saved
Creation Science 101: Final Exam

1. Why are there clouds in the sky?

A. Clouds form when rising air, through expansion, cools to the point that some of the water vapor molecules clump together faster than they are torn apart by their thermal energy. Some of that (invisible) water vapor condenses to form (visible) cloud droplets or ice crystals.

B. Clouds are God's footprints in Heaven and are made up of the dust from His feet.

2. What causes thunder and lightning?

A. God's will. Thunder is the sound of His bellowing voice. Lightning is a deadly force He deliberately hurls at various places.

B. Lightning is the result of a significant difference between positive and negative electrical charges in a cloud or between clouds. Lightning causes air to heat and expand, thereby resulting in sound waves that make up thunder.

3. Why do we sometimes see rainbows?

A. Rainbows occur when sunlight is refracted (bent) through millions of raindrops.

B. God puts rainbows in the sky to remind Him, periodically, that He has promised not to brutally kill all the men, women, children and unborn children of the Earth again (although, technically, He only meant by flood).

4. What causes tornadoes to form?

A. Tornadoes are spawned by unusually violent thunderstorms forming in warm and humid conditions in which wind direction is changing and wind speed is increasing in the lower atmosphere.

B. God creates tornadoes to kill sinners when He wants a quick result, as opposed to the somewhat slower means of plagues and pestilence.

5. What causes earthquakes?

A. Earthquakes are caused by faulting, that is, a sudden lateral or vertical movement of rock along a rupture (break) surface in the Earth.

B. God creates earthquakes to inflict pain and fear on sinners when He is really angry.

6. Why do rivers sometimes dry up?

A. Quite simply, this is the product of the sin of those nearby.

B. The condensation of moisture from bodies of water into the atmosphere outstrips the amount of rain or ground water needed to replenish the bodies.

7. Why do certain areas of the world experience drought?

A. There is an imbalance between water evaporation and rainfall, often caused by a lack of proximity to substantial bodies of water or changing wind patterns.

B. This is one of God's many punishments for sin.

8. What causes some goats to be striped or spotted?

A. An unusual pigmentation of their coats.

B. Placing striped or spotted tree limbs in goats' watering troughs causes their babies to be born striped or spotted.

9. Why are we able to see the stars in the sky?

A. Stars are tiny objects of light—so small that every star in the universe will eventually fall onto the ground of the Earth.

B. Even though stars are many times the size of Earth, they are so far away that they appear as little dots in the sky.

10. Why are we able to walk on the Earth without floating around or falling off?

A. Gravity keeps us pinned to the rotating Earth.

B. The Earth is flat, with four corners.

Creation Science 101: Final Exam Answers

1(B) " The Lord hath his way in the whirlwind and in the storm, and the clouds are the dust of his feet" (Nahum 1:3).

2(A) "Hear attentively the noise of his voice, and the sound that goeth out of his mouth. He directeth it under the whole heaven, and his lightning unto the ends of the earth" (Job 37:2-3).

3(B) "I do set my bow in the cloud; and it shall be a token of a covenant between me and the earth . . . . And I will remember my covenant, which is between you and me and every living creature of all flesh; and the waters shall no more become a flood to destroy all flesh" (Genesis 9:13-15).

4(B) "Behold, the whirlwind of the Lord goeth forth with fury, a continuing whirlwind: it shall fall with pain upon the head of the wicked" (Jeremiah 30:23). "And he shall also blow upon them, and they shall wither, and the whirlwind shall take them away as stubble" (Isaiah 40:24).

5(B) "Therefore I will shake the heavens, and the earth shall remove out of her place, in the wrath of the Lord of hosts, and in the day of his fierce anger" (Isaiah 13:13).

6(A) "He turneth the rivers into a wilderness, and the watersprings into dry ground; A fruitful land into barrenness, for the wickedness of them that dwell therein" (Psalms 107:33-34).

7(B) "The Lord shall make the rain of thy land powder and dust: from heaven shall it come down upon thee, until thou be destroyed" (Deuteronomy 28:24).

8(B) "And Jacob took him rods of green poplar, and of the hazel and chesnut tree; and pilled white stakes in them, and made the white appear which was in the rods. And he set the rods which he had pilled before the flocks in the gutters in the watering troughs when the flocks came to drink, that they should conceive when they came to drink. And the flocks conceived before the rods, and brought forth cattle ringstraked, speckled, and spotted" (Genesis 30:37-39).

9(A) "And the stars of heaven fell unto the earth, even as a fig tree casteth her untimely figs, when she is shaken of a mighty wind" (Revelation 6:13).

10(B) "And after these things I saw four angels standing on the four corners of the earth" (Isaiah 11:12).

Suspiciously Lenient Salvation Evaluation Committee Expels Only 1,404 Church Members this Year

Dear Unsaved Trash:

Settle up your tithes and find a church that doesn't give a rats patootie about offending Jesus!

Salvation Evaluation Committee

FINAL

EXPELLED MEMBER	REASON FOR EXPULSION	SCRIPTURAL SUPPORT
Jack Michaelson (X)*	Diagnosed with testicular cancer on November 14, 2002	"He that is wounded in the stones, or hath his privy member cut off, shall not enter into the congregation of the Lord" (Deuteronomy 23:2).
Marcus Morgan (X)	Neutered by wife when packet of Sweet 'n' Low turned out to be methamphetamine	
John Smith (X) (the one at 256 Hosea Heights Boulevard)	Married Hu Nan Tran	"One of the children of Israel came and brought unto his brethren a Midianitish woman. . . . And when Phineas . . . saw it, he rose up from among the congregation, and took a javelin in his hand; And he went after the man of Israel into the tent, and thrust both of them through, the man of Israel, and the woman through her belly. So the plague was stayed from the children of Israel" (Numbers 25:6–8).
Joseph O'Brien (X) (the one at 1495 Zephaniah Circle)	Married LaShanquita "Hollaback" Washington	
Patrick Donaldson (X) (the one at 34 Malachi Meadows Way)	Married Obidiah el Refghaniluk	
Adrian Wisenstock (X) (the one at 87925 Leviticus Acres Drive)	Married Maria del estanto la en Sangrato di Chimichanga	
Matthew Martin (X) (the one at 7859874 N. Retribution Road, Unit #5)	Married Frau Greta Heinenstopf	

*KEY: P = Platinum Level tither; G = Gold Level tither; S = Silver Level tither; T = Tin Level tither; X = Tither in arrears

EXPELLED MEMBER	REASON FOR EXPULSION	SCRIPTURAL SUPPORT
James Alton (X)	Parents married several minutes after his birth	"A bastard shall not enter into the congregation of the Lord, even to his tenth generation shall he not enter into the congregation of the Lord" (Deuteronomy 23:2).
Jonathan Wilson (X)	Recent audit of family tree reveals his great-great-great-grandmother never married	
388 members whose names are posted outside Pastor's office. You know who you are (X).	Their mothers were married before their current "marriages" to the children's fathers, thus making them vile, illegitimate offspring	"But I say unto you, That whosoever shall put away his wife, saving for the cause of fornication, causeth her to commit adultery: and whosoever shall marry her that is divorced committeth adultery" (Matthew 5:32).
Andrew Allen (X)	Herniated disc in lower back at L4-L5 level	"And the Lord spake unto Moses, saying, Speak unto Aaron, saying, Whosoever he be of thy seed in their generations that hath any blemish, let him not approach to offer the bread of his God. For whatsoever man he be that hath a blemish, he shall not approach: a blind man, or a lame, or he that hath a flat nose, or any thing superfluous. Or a man that is brokenfooted, or brokenhanded, Or crookbackt, or a dwarf, or that hath a blemish in his eye, or be scurvy, or scabbed, or hath his stones broken" (Leviticus 21:16–20).
David Myers (X)	Nose smashed in during senior year as Landover Academy for the Saved quarterback, 1992–93	
Randall Doyal (X)	Recently developed polio and is confined to a wheelchair	
Christopher Wright (X)	Suffers from occasional pink eye	

EXPELLED MEMBER	REASON FOR EXPULSION	SCRIPTURAL SUPPORT
Phillip Rodgers (X)	At least one of his ancestors lived in a gated community in Ammon	"An Ammonite or Moabite shall not enter into the congregation of the Lord; even to their tenth generation shall they not enter into the congregation of the Lord for ever" (Deuteronomy 23:3).
Carl Moore (X)	At least one of his ancestors had a studio tent in Moab	
Donald Rumathan (the one on Route 444) (X)	During his college years, he once met John Ashcroft and assisted the then attorney general with mixing his proprietary blend of anointing oil, made of equal parts Crisco and Old Spice	"And thou shalt speak unto the children of Israel, saying, This shall be an holy anointing oil unto me throughout your generations. Upon man's flesh shall it not be poured, neither shall ye make any other like it, after the composition of it: it is holy, and it shall be holy unto you. Whosoever compoundeth any like it, or whosoever putteth any of it upon a stranger, shall even be cut off from his people" (Exodus 30:31–33).

Youths Jailed for Mocking President Bush

Funeral services for Kenny Jenkins, 14, Billy Gordon, 17, and Rick Williams, 16, will be held this Sunday in the tractor shed. They had been apprehended on Tuesday for making unsavory remarks about President Bush. All three died in Landover Baptist Jail for the Unsaved at approximately five minutes after midnight on Wednesday of natural causes and were immediately cremated.

EZ Slide Tithe™ Credit Card Offering Plates

Earlier this year, Landover Baptist Church authorities directed Pretty Secure Technologies, a Christian manufacturer of monetary transaction and information products, to work with church officials to balance the burden of the recent rise in mandatory tithes from 10 percent to 18.2 percent with the convenience of new state-of-the-art offering technology. The company's efforts resulted in a revolutionary new offering plate design that we are sure you will be extremely excited about. It's called the EZ Slide Tithe™. It takes all the guesswork out of showing the Lord how much you love Him!

These beautiful gold offering plates are equipped with credit card slide and approval-on-demand slots. Church members who do not have cash on hand will now be offered the option of using any major credit card (other than Discover) right at their pews. Simply slide the card through the slot at the top of the offering plate and sit back and smile because EZ Slide Tithe™ has just told Jesus what He wanted to hear! In a miracle of seconds, the EZ Slide Tithe™ pulls your weekly gross salary from the church's server and then instantly acquires authorization for payment of 18.2 percent of that amount (plus 0.5 percent if using American Express). Gone are the days of fumbling through hundred-dollar bills in church to make things right with the Lord!

$12.00 Off Pastoral Visit

Valid Only For Mandatory $500 Annual Visit

Present Coupon to Church Secretary 1 Month Before Scheduled Visitation

Expires: January 30, 2010

Mrs. Harry "Heather" Hardwick exercises her patience before treating herself to a lovely side of beef.

Heather's Guide to Bible-Based Physical Activity

"For bodily exercise profiteth little: but godliness is profitable unto all things" *(1 Timothy 4:8).*

Gals, if you insist on waisting (wink!) your time exercising, you won't have to slip into a harloty flank-flashing aerobic G-string to perform these godly routines:

Stone throwing—With so much sin around, a lady should always be prepared to satisfy the Lord's whim of imposing some good old-fashioned Biblical retribution. When guided by the Lord's hand to exact His will, stone throwing becomes both a wonderful triceps toner and way to curry favor with an angry Lord. Start with repetitions of light sedimentary rocks, working your way up to the satisfaction that comes only from the deeper indentations made by igneous missiles of rebuke.

Muscles Worked: *Biceps, triceps, hips, thighs, lower back. Also may provide cardiovascular conditioning (heart muscles), depending upon the number of sinners involved.*

Bible toting—The Bible's not just for church anymore, gals. A True Christian™ lady always has her KJV 1611 in hand. For instance, if stuck in line at the bank, remember how our Lord Jesus showed His displeasure with slow service from money changers! Wave your heavy, leather-bound Bible to clear a path of righteousness to the next available teller, using a 1-2-3 motion to carefully step over anyone the Lord's fury has just sent face-first into the carpeting. Then, resourcefully whip open your Bible to rebuke those behind you while the inept money changer fumbles her way though your change.

Muscles Worked: *Triceps, wrists, fingers, mouth and jaw muscles, hamstrings.*

Abortion clinic protesting—Whether you're carrying a purse full of Ziploc bags filled with cow's blood, wielding a few jars of rotting pig fetuses in formaldehyde, or simply screaming at a young teen harlot about how she'll sizzle like bacon on Satan's griddle until she cries, you're sure to get a great aerobic workout.

Muscles Worked: *Cardio; lungs, neck muscles, mouth muscles, lower jaw, forearms and fingers (during unzipping motion).*

Being moved in the Spirit—Thrusting your body parts around to a Jane Fonda tape like some mentally retarded call girl is never acceptable conduct for a lady. But if done in church, you can always claim you were filled by the Holy Spirit and had no control over your actions (or stains in the carpeting).

Muscles Worked: *Cardio; hips, groin muscles, knees, lower back, tushie and, unfortunately, bladder and sphincter muscles.*

American Christianity's Most Common Crisis of Faith Questions

1. Why does God allow decent Christians who make over six figures to suffer?
2. Why does the Lord give you 100 extra dollars with one hand, only to give you 100 extra pounds with the other?

PASTOR'S PULPIT

Hating Your Family: It's Not Only Easy—It's Required!

SERMON BY BROTHER HARRY HARDWICK

Friends, the End Times are finally upon us! We have a great deal of preparation ahead of us, if we wish to be among the chosen few men the Lord picks to spend eternity with Him in Heaven. The first thing we must do is to divorce ourselves from our mortal families and get used to not having them around because we will no longer have a need for them in Heaven. Understand that God allowed us to have these families only because we are imperfect beings and would have sinned like the dickens without them. We must also understand that while those most worthy of God are, of course, men, they are *only* the men who never contaminated themselves by touching the more sinful, lesser gender. As John told us when describing Jesus' revelation to him about the Rapture:

And they sung as it were a new song before the throne, and before the four beasts, and the elders: and no man could learn that song but the hundred and forty and four thousand, which were redeemed from the earth. These are they which were not defiled with women; for they are virgins. These are they which follow the Lamb whithersoever he goeth. These were redeemed from among men, being the firstfruits unto God and to the Lamb (Revelation 14:3–4).

So we see that the most Christ-like among us are those who devoted their lives to Jesus and never got sidetracked by figuring out ways to stick their willies in women. The rest of us were allowed to marry only so we wouldn't sin. As Paul wrote: "Now concerning the things whereof ye wrote unto me: It is good for a man not to touch a woman. Nevertheless, to avoid fornication, let every man have his own wife" (1 Corinthians 7:1–2). The most worthy of God's children are the eunuchs, men who never defiled themselves with fleshly contact (Matthew 19:10–12). Friends, the rest of us are weak, and since we are weak, we must marry, for if we cannot remain virgins, "it is better to marry than to burn," which gives you some idea of the low regard the unmarried Apostle Paul had for so-called "connubial bliss"! (1 Corinthians 7:9).

Not only did Jesus want us to refrain from marriage on Earth, He expressly told us we will have no families in Heaven. The Pharisees once asked Jesus about seven brothers, each of whom had married his older brother's wife when the brother had died. They asked to whom the woman would be married in Heaven. Jesus replied: "When they shall rise from the dead, they neither marry, nor are given in marriage; but are as the angels which are in heaven" (Mark 12:25; see also Matthew 22:29). We won't even know or recognize our wives in Heaven. It will be like *Monday Night Football,* 24/7. Pinch me, Jesus! You certainly know how to throw a nag-free party!

So, it's best to rid ourselves now of our "honey-pies" and "sweethearts" whom we have known and who have cooked our meals, swished out our commodes and dutifully Wisked-away our skid marks for so long. As Jesus told us: "Every one that hath forsaken houses, or brethren, or sisters, or father, or mother, or wife, or children, or lands, for my name's sake, shall receive an hundredfold, and shall inherit everlasting life" (Matthew 19:29). My goodness, friends! It is not even enough for us to separate ourselves from our relatives; Jesus wants us to outright reject them, slap them across the face, delete their numbers from our cell phones and send them on their way. Jesus said: "I am come to set a man at variance against his father, and the daughter against her mother, and the daughter in law against her mother in law. And a man's foes shall be they of his own household" (Matthew 10:36).

Until you get it through your thick, God-fearing skulls that your love of family hinders your love of an acutely jealous Christ, you might as well get used to the fact that you won't be invited to sit in the VIC (Very Important Christian) section when you get to Glory. Let me put it this way: Why bother continuing to love those whom you will not know in Heaven anyway? Face it: They are only dragging you down. It is best to rid yourself of the family albatross now before you have to go to the time-consuming trouble of killing them. Jesus admonished: "The brother shall deliver up the brother to death, and the father the child: and the children shall rise up against their parents, and cause them to be put to death" (Matthew 10:21). Whether motivated by the promise of Heaven or the threat of patricide, the time for family values is over!

Last Week's Favorite Hymn:

"Praise God from Whom All Crude Oil Flows"

Pastor Forbids Glancing at Bobbing Breasts and Penises During 2008 Olympics

For those of you who missed sunrise services last Sunday (you should have already received notification of a penalty for truancy through your Direct-Withdrawal Tithe® account), Pastor is prohibiting all True Christians™ from watching anything other than hands, heads (the one above the shoulder, covered in noncoarse hair—except in the case of colored athletes) and feet during televised broadcasts of the upcoming Beijing Olympics. "I think if folks Scotch-Tape construction paper over the middle third of their HDTV screens, they'll find they're protected from almost 70 percent of sexually suggestive material incurred in normal viewing," instructed Pastor. "Let's face facts: The Olympics have always been a showcase for a particular body part best left unseen outside of a sideways glance at a urinal. And it is no coincidence that the Olympics are being held in that godless country with more unsaved people per square inch than Hell itself," noted Pastor.

Aretha Franklin's Christian Charity Met with Rudeness

Last week, visiting Detroit singer Aretha Franklin kindly volunteered to stop by a local Churchs Fried Chicken to pick up dinner for all of the gals at Mrs. Betty Bowers's Christian Crack Whore Ministry. Miss Franklin ordered 103 buckets of (mixed) fried chicken, 13 buckets of wings, 18 pounds of mashed potatoes and 145 honey-butter biscuits. The impertinent person behind the counter asked, "Miss Franklin, is that for here or to go?"

Pastor Deacon Fred's words came on the heels of his participation in a two-month investigation conducted by TRASH (Traditional-families Raging Against Sluts and Homos). Hundreds of hours of footage of the past six Olympic Games were analyzed, paying particularly close attention to the undulation of the more generously sized penises, bottoms, breasts and testicles of athletes engaged in physical activities that require them to wear tight-fitting attire such as spandex. "After watching the Atlanta Games with all that clingy Lycra, there can be no question in anyone's mind regarding whether Michael Johnson lives up to his lewd surname," observed Mrs. Betty Bowers, president of TRASH. "The Olympic Village became indistinguishable from a teeming nudist colony by the time the games inevitably returned to Greece, the birthplace of buggery, in 2004. The outlines of breasts, penises and buttocks were in plain view under clothing that was stretched tighter than even the most competent housewife can manipulate a piece of Saran." Pastor Deacon Fred supported Mrs. Bowers's concerns: "It is a well-known fact that in the original Olympics, all the Greek homos used to oil up each other's bodies and prance around as naked as on the day they were born straight. Yes, friends, the entire original Olympics were shamelessly done in birthday suits. And one look at the diving competition reveals that little has changed."

New Focus on the Family Study Reveals Passive-Aggressive Christians' Favorite Ways to Proselytize from Behind a Cash Register

"Would you like to Super-Size your lonely Judaic God for a Trinity?"

"You know when this immodest little bikini will come in handy? When you're in Hell for wearing it."

"I have a feeling that if you just asked yourself 'What Would Jesus Do?' you'd walk out of here with a matching Burberry golf umbrella!"

"You know, I could have filled this here contraceptive prescription, giving you free license to run about town like the penis-addicted whore you no doubt are, if the Lord Jesus hadn't just asked me to tear it into itty-bitty little pieces. Have a blessed day."

Self-Castration Epidemic Leaves Town Full of Eunuchs

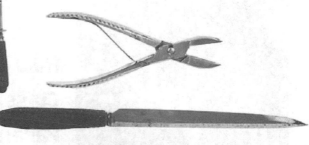

Last Sunday, 1,087 men returned home from Landover Baptist Church's 8:00 A.M. service and, using various crude mechanisms, hacked off their testicles. "Billy Ray was in a funk after service and went out to his toolshed for a spell," recalled Mrs. Suzzanna Beth Simpkins. "I was in the kitchen when I heard him screaming something awful. When I'd finished putting sprinkles on the cupcakes I was making, I went out to the shed. Lord have mercy! He had used a pair of pliers to pull off his balls!"

Such spontaneous outbursts of self-castration occurred throughout town in response to a rousing sermon by Pastor Harry Hardwick. Rev. Hardwick had spoken of the need for men to taint neither their souls nor bodies with frail, conniving women during these precious final days before the Lord Jesus returns to destroy, judge and kill. During the sermon, Pastor Hardwick reminded the men gathered of Heaven's stringent discretionary door policy: The males who have the best shot at entrance are those who have not even allowed a sinful woman to touch their tallywhackers. (Revelation 14:3–4). In lieu of such Godly willpower, Jesus taught that men should become eunuchs for the Lord by removing their testicles (Matthew 19:10–12).

Upon hearing that roughly one-tenth of the town's men were suddenly without testicles, church secretary Helen Floribunda immediately went into action. Mrs. Floribunda, famed in 14 counties for being able to preserve everything from peaches to pig's feet, quickly drafted the help of the Ladies of Landover Auxiliary to carefully place matching sets of testicles in Mason jars with formaldehyde.

"I carefully marked each jar with a snapshot of each owner that I took with my digital camera," said Mrs. Floribunda, "so that our menfolk wouldn't end up with each other's, well, uh, things. I told them to keep them jars with them at all times—even at work or out at restaurants. You never know when the Lord will return and no one wants to be in God's Glory missing stuff. That's why I always sleep in my best wig."

KEWL KIDZ 4 CHRIST

How to Trick Your Little Foreign Classmates into Renouncing Their Parents' Phony God!

The following 10 tips are designed to assist Christian children in utilizing the Pledge of Allegiance as a tool for rescuing their Hell-bound classmates from false religions:

Pray the Pledge 10-Step Checklist:

1. If you are not assigned seats in your class, use your nose ("Is that garlic I smell?") and eyes ("My, her skin is darker than even buttermilk!") to root out classmates of foreign extraction who have probably been raised to loathe your holy playmate, Jesus.

2. Before the pledge begins, if your little classmates haven't noticed that you have your hands folded in prayer, not over your heart, bring it to their attention. If you are bold enough, right before the class gets ready to say the Pledge of Allegiance—shout, "Dear Lord Jesus . . ." and then continue with the rest of the class in unison.

3. After the pledge is over, thank one or more of your odd-looking (see Step 1) classmates for joining you in public prayer. This should raise their childlike curiosity.

4. Ask your little friends how it feels to be an honest-to-goodness Christian. When they admit that they are not Christians, try to look as puzzled as you possibly can. Cry if you can. Ask them directly why they just falsely stated during the Pledge of Allegiance that they are under your Christian God, but just now admitted that they are not. Tell them you don't appreciate liars and neither will the principal when he gets your note.

5. More often than not, they will probably respond by saying some

deceitful secular nonsense about the word "God" not being the proper name of our God, but simply a noun to refer to a deity. If they add, "What kind of stupid, unimaginative name for a god is God anyway? It's like calling your dog, Dog!", place your fingers in your ears and say "la la la la la" until they have stopped moving their mouths. Now take the opportunity to give them a much needed history lesson. Remind them that there were no Muslims, Hindus, Atheists or Jews among the Pilgrims or Founding Fathers. In fact, the Pilgrims were forced to turn on each other to have someone to hate until they met the heathen, naked, alcoholic Injuns.

6. At this point, understand that you have planted a seed of faith, and it should be harvested immediately! Be careful though! Avoid getting too excited. Don't spill the beans and tell them that they're going straight to Hell. Although this is true, we suggest you break it to them gently by reaching into your desk and slowly pulling out your Bible. Do not break eye contact with your potential converts even if you have to grab a tuft of their filthy, unwashed hair to hold them in place!

7. Refer to your Bible as "your magical, mystical Holy Book" and when you touch it, act like it gave you a powerful electric shock. Most foreign trash is very superstitious and will probably become bug-eyed, and possibly soil their drawers, in the face of your new, mysterious powers. Tell them that this Holy Book says that only stupid people worship an invisible man who lives in the sky. Except for yours.

8. At this point, tell the students that you will be highly offended and consider it a hate crime against your religion if they do not do you the courtesy of bowing their heads, shutting their eyes and repeating after you. Wield your electroshock Bible like a Taser gun if they exercise their free will to disobey you.

9. Here is your window of opportunity—before anyone has a chance to open his mouth, start this prayer and refuse to be interrupted: "My God, the one we are all under *whether we like it or not*, I'm not naming any names but if any of us standing here is unsaved, we ask Jesus Christ to come into our hearts and stomp out the multi-armed demons of Hindu, the suicide-bombing demons of Allah, the fat little demons of Buddha, and if we are Jewish, we ask you to forgive us for killing your Son and for Barbra Streisand. A-men."

10. If your classmates just prayed that prayer, it means they're saved. Scribble down their names and addresses immediately. March right out of your class and find a pay phone. Call your pastor so that arrangements can be made to spare your little friends from the indignity of being a Christian living amongst unsaved trash.

Take the Annoying Guesswork Out of Voting!

The Christian Coalition, always working to make voting as pleasantly predictable as possible, has decided to remove the confusing use of candidate names on all future Voter Guides. From now on, the Voter Guides will simply state: "Vote for the Republican or wind up in Hell." This streamlining has allowed them to preprint Voter Guides for the next 125 presidential elections. Copies are now available in the lobby for purchase.

Pastor's Pansy Patrol

Baptist Scientists Link Faggotry to "Something Somewhere in the Air Somehow"

Adrian Coleman had been a model student and respected Landover member throughout his young life. "He was the finest of boys," his mother, Mrs. Coleman, told Brother Harry Hardwick. "He was caring and sensitive, and would never harm another living creature. He never got into fights at school because I taught him that Jesus told us to turn the other cheek. Adrian let the bullies pick on him, sometimes even beat him severely, but he never retaliated. He was every teacher's pet, valedictorian of Landover Baptist University for the Saved and president of the Thespian Club." Adrian was perhaps best known for running Freehold's top interior design firm with his roommate and dear friend, Christopher Stouffer, with whom Adrian had been best friends since they shared a tent at Vacation Bible Gun Camp when they were in junior high. All in all, Adrian appeared to be the most Christ-like young man to grow up in Freehold, Iowa.

That all changed, however, after a fateful move to another country called "California." Within mere weeks of being exposed to the invisible something causing homosexuality that fills the air around San Francisco Bay like an unseen ticker tape parade, this exemplary lad brought disgrace to his family by announcing, out of the blue, the shocking news that not only had he rashly chosen to become a homosexual overnight, but he had gone a mile further down the crooked road to Hell by engaging in a sacrilegious so-called "wedding ceremony" with Stouffer. "It all started when Adrian came to me and announced that he and Christopher had decided to move to that dreadful San Francisco," sobbed Mrs. Coleman. "We've all heard Pastor tell us countless times that that place is just *not* for Christians. I was foolish enough to believe the boys were strong enough in Christ to bring the Lord's healing word to a city full of sinners. Well, I was wrong. I should have listened to my pastor. I received the phone call that destroyed my life forever right after my boy moved into Satan's lair. Something in that horrible, foreign country and the city of Sin Fransissyco turned my sweet little baby boy to a life of debauchery, and I demand to know what it is!"

Yearbook photo of Adrian Coleman singing "I Enjoy Being a Girl" in Landover Baptist's Boys Glee Club production of "Flower Drum Song."

Under contract with Mrs. Betty Bowers's ministry, Baptists Are Saving Homosexuals (BASH), Brother Harry Hardwick commissioned an in-depth, three-year investigation into the question of why so many promising Landover youths suddenly become as queer as an Ikea store on Super Bowl Sunday when they wind up in cities with more than four traffic lights. It took Brother Hardwick less than a week to reach the scientific conclusion he announced at a press conference last week: "The answer is so simple, you are gonna laugh when I tell you. Folks don't go gay overnight because of genetics or Jewish mothers. No, being a homo is caused by something floating somewhere in the air somehow sometimes someway. It's like anthrax. Only stronger. And probably comes in 400 shades of taupe. It may be in the water or strictly airborne, but either way, when you get off the plane at an airport in any major American city, chances are good, by the time your cab arrives at your hotel, you'll be prancing to the registration desk like a little limp-wristed homo."

Bible Quiz

What does God say is the surest way to determine if your wife is cheating on you?

A. Accuse her. The Lord will strike her lame if she hems and haws.

B. Have the priest give her holy water mixed with dirt to drink. If she's an adulteress, her belly will swell and her thigh will rot.

C. Pray to the Lord, who will have been watching while she fornicated and be able to regale you with the details.

D. None of the above.

Answer: B. "If any man's wife go aside, and commit a trespass against him, and a man lie with her carnally . . . then the man shall bring his wife unto the priest . . . and the priest shall take holy water in an earthen vessel. . . . And when he hath made her to drink the water, then it shall come to pass, that if she be defiled, and have done trespass against her husband, that the water that caused the curse shall enter into her, and become bitter, and her belly shall swell, and her thigh shall rot" (Numbers 5:12–27).

Pastor's Demonstration of the Fires of Hell Leaves First Four Pews without Eyebrows

THE GOOD NEWS

Baptist Ladies Give Churchful of Pentecostals Involuntary Makeovers

"Before"

"After"

Almost everyone in our Godly congregation has complained at one time or another about the visual pollution of plain, unsightly Pentecostal women walking into our field of vision when we're shopping in town. Outside of the occasional spirited remonstration, however, no one seemed willing to raise a finger to do anything to help these ghastly frumps. That indolence came to a glorious end last Friday evening. After years of having their polite heckling-for-Christ ignored at the grocery store, the Ladies of Landover were called by the Lord to make the world a prettier place. Several members, accompanied by six certified cosmetologists and 17 .22-caliber rifles, blew the locks off the doors of Freehold's notoriously dowdy Pentecostal Holiness Church, startling a roomful of drab housewives, purportedly busy in prayer. The Godly group from Landover immediately wrestled the surprised Pentecostal women to the floor and proceeded to give each of them a vigorous comb-out and a depilatory beauty treatment in a last-ditch effort to make the women more pleasing to the Lord.

"These Pentecostal nuts have it in their heads that the Bible tells them not to shave any hair on their body," said Helen Floribunda, who was placed in charge of the critical "Mustache-Bleaching" operation. "One of those gals looked like an overfed Yellowstone grizzly bear in a caftan. We could have bought these folks a decent- looking church by selling her to the Moscow Circus. Now, I have as much respect for other folks' religious beliefs as any Baptist. I'll support these crazies' right to believe whatever they want 1000 percent—unless they conflict with my beliefs. But doing this whole 'look like a Mexican man for Jesus' thing is just thumbing their hairy noses at the Lord."

"It's like I always say," remarked the chic Mrs. Betty Bowers, overseeing an impromptu Botox triage, "since we are created in God's image, if we don't look good, *He* doesn't look good. Only Jesus can save those dreary tongue-talkers from Hell, but at least we can save them from *looking like Hell* in the meantime. True, the Lord said that long hair is a glory for women. But, I ask you, since when would any sane woman take hairstyling tips from someone who isn't a practicing homosexual?"

"I brought an Epilady, a dozen rolls of duct tape and a diesel Toro weed whacker I borrowed from the yard help," noted Mrs. Heather Hardwick. "To be honest, we should have brought a dog groomer and a machete because I ruined 18 Lady Bics trying to hack through legs that looked like Robin Williams's back." The makeovers began around 7:00 P.M., when the Baptist ladies burst into the meeting hall wearing pink gas masks and the Pentecostals were enveloped in a cloud of animal tranquilizer gas. "My job was to sit right on the chest area of any Amazon woman who came to while Sister Inez and the folks from the spa did their magic on the lower regions," noted Mrs. Hardwick. "One of the girls I pinned down fought me so fiercely to get free that I think I still have rope burns on my derriere from her hairy arms."

Mrs. Floribunda quickly ferried between the lucky ladies, applying hot wax and tape to sideburns, mustaches and unsightly unibrows in the vain hope of tearing them off before the anesthetic faded. "I used enough wax on one of those Bigfoots to keep a Catholic cathedral in candles for a year!" laughed Mrs. Floribunda, sharpening her sheers on a heavy whetstone that had been used to keep one of the more restless Pentecostals in place. "She kept screaming, 'I'm Charismatic, I'm Charismatic!' I said, 'Honey, maybe you will be when we get through with you, but right now you're enough to make Bill Clinton celibate.'"

THE GOOD NEWS

Like the Lord, Landover Homeowners Association Destroys All That Displeaseth

The Donald Herron family returned from a relative's funeral in Boise only to discover they no longer had a house. Instead, the lot that had just two days earlier contained their stucco home, a lovely half-scale model of the Alamo, featuring a Davy Crockett floor plan with an optional four-vehicle carport, now sported fresh sod and a bill for demolition. As soon as she saw that the Herrons' Lexus had pulled up, Mrs. Ginger Kravitz, secretary of the Leviticus Acres Homeowners Association, ran out from her lovely quarter-scale Biltmore Estate mansion across the street to rebuke the family. "Just like the lawless fools who danced to golden Baal, drunk in their disobedience before Moses' holy tablets," Mrs. Kravitz bellowed, ignoring a carful of questions, "you thought there would be no consequence for flouting the homeowners association's commandments!"

As the Herrons were well aware, the association, governing the most devout suburb in town, famous for its historic replica homes, recently amended its bylaws: "Every homeowner in Leviticus Acres must display the full text of the Ten Commandments on their (a) mailbox in at least 24-point Arial font gold relief lettering of no less than 14 karats; (b) garage door(s) such that every "shalt not" shall be legible from a passing car going no more than 45 mph; and (c) driveways, with each letter, in red or blue fluorescent paint, sized so that the Lord's words can be read from Pastor's helicopter when flying just above the decorative spruce tree cell phone towers."

While the Herrons had complied with the rules regarding their mailbox and driveway, they refused to paint the Lord's solemn edicts on their garage door, using the suspiciously convenient excuse that carports don't have doors. A week later, the homeowners association unanimously ruled, "Well, get some." Witnesses reported that several members of the neighborhood Christian Watch team had used 14 gallons of Roundup to write "Devil-Worshippers!" in dead fescue grass on the Herrons' front lawn seven days before the demolition. This was in strict accordance with the written-notice provisions of the bylaws that must be followed before the homeowners association can resort to the use of any bulldozers or firearms in the enforcement of a covenant.

With a look of courteously tempered triumph as she glanced down at the Herrons' children crying in the back seat of the car, Mrs. Kravitz spoke the words that all members of Landover Baptist fear most (well, next to a son saying "Pop, I'm going to devote my life to musical theater!"): "Like Adam and his fruit-snacking harlot, you are cast out!" With that verbal rebuke, given pursuant to homeowner bylaws, out of the way, Mrs. Kravitz served the family with a formal "Get Thee Hence" bumper sticker, as required by Subsection ii(a) to Homeowners Commandment No. 2,349. With her official duties as secretary of the association out of the way, Mrs. Kravitz, an avid jogger, then voluntarily hectored and rebuked the Herrons as she ran beside their car. She and her two barking Dobermans kept up with the vehicle until the godless family was almost in sight of the three 50-foot brass crosses that mark the entrance to the exclusive subdivision they had once called home.

Solid Gold Calf Removed from Sanctuary

Church decorator promises it will work better in the Prayer Foyer.

Christian Tourists Rave: A Visit to Landover Baptist Is Like Being Born Again, Again!

"It'a just like I imagined Heaven—only without free refills on your soda and ice tea."

This Week's Children's Sermon:

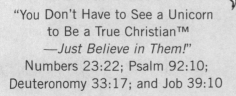

"You Don't Have to See a Unicorn to Be a True Christian™ —*Just Believe in Them!*" Numbers 23:22; Psalm 92:10; Deuteronomy 33:17; and Job 39:10

A Christian Parent's Handy Guide to Proper Biblical Terminology

From the *Landover Baptist Bible Reference Library* (2006 edition)

Concept	Sinful, secular terminology	Godly, proper words	Biblical support for Godly words
The process of discharging the monthly flow of blood from the uterus	menstruation period	uncleanness sickness filthiness	Leviticus 18:19 Leviticus 20:18 Zephaniah 3:1
An individual whose sexual orientation is toward people of the same gender	homosexual gay	dog sodomite	Deuteronomy 23:18 Deuteronomy 23:17; 1 Kings 14:24; 15:12; 22:46; 2 Kings 23:7
The act of excreting a liquid beverage from the body	urinate or urinating	piss or pisseth	1 Samuel 25:22; 34; 1 Kings 14:10; 16:11; 21:21; 2 Kings 9:8; 18:27; Isaiah 36:12
A woman who has had more than one sexual partner	sexually active female	whore	Leviticus 19:29, 21:7, 9; Deuteronomy 22:21; 23:17, 18; Judges 19:2; Proverbs 23:27; Isaiah 57:3; Jeremiah 3:2; Hosea 4:14; Revelation 17:1, 15, 16; 19:2

Concept	Sinful, secular terminology	Godly, proper words	Biblical support for Godly words
A woman who has had more than one sexual partner	popular	harlot	Genesis 34:31; 38:15, 21, 22, 24: Leviticus 21:14; Joshua 2:1; 6:17, 22, 25; Judges 11:1; 16:1; 1 Kings 3:16; Proverbs 7:10; 29:3; Isaiah 1:21, 23:15, 16; Jeremiah 2:20, 3:1, 6, 8, 5:7; Ezekiel 16:15, 16, 28, 31, 35, 41; 23:5, 19; 44; Hosea 2:5; Matthew 21:31, 32; Luke 15:30; 1 Corinthians 6:15, 16; Hebrews 11:31; Revelation 17:5
The two protuberances of the chest through which uncivilized women who live in areas where milk and infant formula are not available reputedly feed their infants	nipples	teats	Isaiah 32:12; Ezekiel 23:3, 21
People who question your religious views	intellectuals philosophers critics	fools hypocrites serpents vipers	Matthew 23:17–37
Descendants of the Israelites who believe Jesus was a good man but not the Son of God	Jews	Sons of the Devil Unruly liars	John 8:44 Titus 1:10–11
The offspring of two people who aren't married	illegitimate child fatherless child	bastard	Deuteronomy 23:2; Zechariah 9:6; Hebrews 12:8
Someone who does not believe in God	atheist	Antichrist	1 John 2:22

THE GOOD NEWS

Foot-and-Mouth Epidemic Forces Scottish Farmers to Return to Their Wives

The Lord recently reached into His bag of tricks and pulled out an old standby—pestilence—to save Christian marriages throughout Scotland. After tearful goodbyes to sheep incinerated as a result of the latest foot-and-mouth epidemic, farmers throughout the Scottish Highlands returned to sodomizing their previously neglected wives for the first time since the last outbreak of this pernicious livestock malady. Women who had all but given up on ever feeling the connubial touch of their spouses responded with relief after decades of neglect. As an elated Gladys McHaggis of Inverness told the missionaries from America's wealthiest church, Landover Baptist: "I said to my Ewan, 'It's either me or ewe.' But all the ultimatums in the world wouldn't get him to drop his kilt and come down from that bloody paddock. That cheap little tart—strutting about the pasture like a sheep half her age. Mutton dressed as lamb, I tell you! Truly, it was the Lord who took pity on my broken heart and killed that little four-legged minx. But, in truth, He was just a week ahead of me. It's not so easy getting your hands on a gun in these parts. Not like you lot in your America. Around here, when we say we enjoy a round of shots, we mean whisky."

Landover Baptist missionaries immediately responded to the Lord's widespread killing of cattle throughout the United

Last Week's Favorite Hymn:

"Cometh O Lord, Thine Heart Aches for Cataclysmic Destruction!"

Kingdom with relief. As Pastor Deacon Fred told the BBC: "When the Lord gets it into His head to start doing a lot of smiting, I always get a little nervous and back up out of the way to see how it will all pan out. I was very relieved to see that He limited His latest killing spree to cheap little seductresses who should have been turned into car-seat covers a long time ago. There are thousands of randy farmers in Scotland today who should be very relieved to know that the lamb died for their sins."

This Wednesday's Encore Sermon:

Rebuking Homosexuals May Have Slipped Jesus' Mind, but Not Ours!

Bible Quiz:
And on the Eighth Day God Started Killing

What is God's prescribed punishment for bestiality (sex with an animal)?

A. None. God forgives all sins, especially those committed in rural farming communities such as Freehold, Iowa, and He would recognize the need for disinfecting and counseling in this situation.

B. Death of the victimized man.

C. Death of the wanton animal.

D. B and C.

Answer: D. "Whosoever lieth with a beast shall surely be put to death" (Exodus 22:19). "And if a man lie with a beast, he shall surely be put to death: and ye shall slay the beast" (Leviticus 20:15).

To Mark the 42nd Anniversary of the Civil Rights Act, Church Relaxes Negro Admittance Policy

In 1962, in bald violation of states' rights and simple etiquette, a surprise raid by U.S. marshals forced Landover members finally to free their heartbroken slaves. In righteous retaliation, the church added Negroes and government agents to the lengthy list of people we are allowed to discriminate against because of our Christianity. This past Wednesday evening, however, marked a radical turning point in the church's always reluctant dealings with the unfortunately pigmented. After a meeting with Mr. Karl Rove, Pastor Deacon Fred sent elderly church members into a tizzy of profane catcalls when he announced that Landover Baptist would be admitting Negroes into the main sanctuary for the first time in history. He assuaged their fears by confiding that people of color would have limited access to the general congregation and would be restricted to hidden areas. "We've got to face it, my friends," he said. "The only way we are going to be able to keep sodomites from getting civil rights is to dole out a few more rights to the coloreds. Friends, I know what you are thinking, because I feel the same way, but it's not the same world anymore. There are colored folks in this town who make more money than some of our Tin Level tithers, and cash doesn't discriminate based on color. It's all green to Jesus and He doesn't care if it comes out of a white man's wallet, or a Negro's shoe . Just as long as it ends up in our offering plates on Sunday morning. Besides, we need to be doing more to trick these impressionable souls into voting for rich, white Republicans."

Landover Baptist will utilize a traditional screening process invented by wealthy, educated men of color. "We know that colored people with money are just as leery of other Negroes whose ancestors apparently include females so hideously unattractive that no obese, drunken white man could even bring himself to rape them," said Pastor Deacon Fred. "We understand that this is a very exciting time for local Negroes—for many, it's their first opportunity to worship in a real church, with a floor that doesn't turn to mud when it rains, and to be among people who don't wave their hands around like they are trying to dry their nails all service and who righteously shut their stony mouths, allowing the preacher to be the center of attention."

Prospective colored church members' annual household income must exceed $148,000 (in legitimate income not involving selling narcotics or renting genitals, as verified by Jewish accountants) to qualify for the following admittance tests:

1. Brown Paper Bag Test

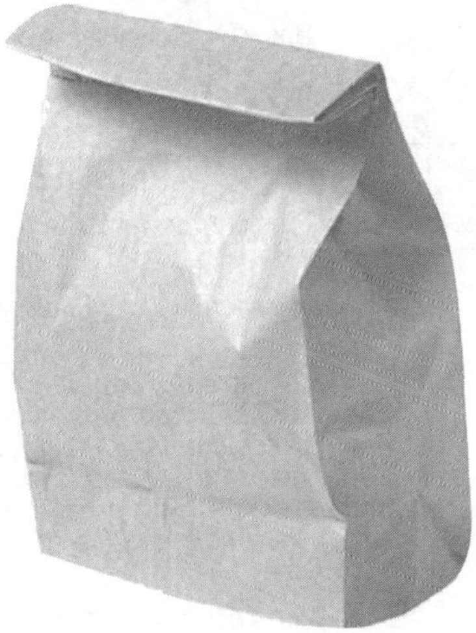

A brown paper bag will be placed next to the face of each candidate. If the skin of the candidate is darker than the bag, the candidate will not be admitted into the church. If a qualifying person is unable to tap-dance or engage in any other harmless talent to the delight of the families making their way from the reserved parking decks, the talentless light-darky will be immediately escorted by Pastor Sergeant Connor into the next county.

2. Pronunciation Test

Candidates will be given a series of simple English sentences to memorize and recite. Example: "I say, don't you rather think that this pish-posh about it being dreadfully inclement was balderdash, as it appears that it shall be most agreeably lovely—just absolutely, gloriously brilliant—for well into the next fortnight, no?" If the candidate forgets or mispronounces any of the words, or if the pastor doing the testing is not comfortable with his quarrelsome or uppity inflection, he will not be admitted to the main sanctuary, but will be allowed to join us in worship from the parking lot or from behind the one-way mirror above the center balcony.

SEARCH

Banned Book Block™ is active (check with your pastor about deselecting this option)

Welcome to Books!
Click here to explore more.

Books you recently looked at include:

Guide to Abstinence: Saving the Hole in Front for Marriage
by Barbara Bush

Hillbilly Heroin Cookbook: Baking with OxyContin
by Rush Limbaugh

...STER Scalia's Bitch
Clarence Thomas

Donkeys Can Talk, People Can Fly, and a Man Named Jesus Lives Up in the Sky

Creation Science for Teens—by Rev. Joseph Whipple

Special Offer: $57.99 (plus $40 fuel surcharge for Landover Baptist's fleet of ministry Gulfstream jets)

Summary: *Donkeys Can Talk* is a Bible-based textbook designed to reclaim America's children from the corrosive influences of today's fact-obsessed secular culture, which prizes the poisonous grays of logic and reason over what's plainly written in black and white right there in the Bible. With President Bush's help and encouragement, this invaluable classroom guide will soon replace all suspicious and/or heretical high school science textbooks (that is, those written in the last 175 years).

The book opens with an unforgettable Bible truth in the form of a poem:

Donkeys can talk, people can fly
There's a God-man named Jesus who lives in the sky
Secular science is just Christ-hating bunk
So listen to Jesus, not Isaac Newton's junk!
Because God has a great gravity lesson to tell
When he drops you like an apple straight into Hell.

This painstakingly typed book will inculcate impressionable youngsters with colorful stories, yarns that have proven to be far easier to remember than any artless scientific theorems and theories. Children will discover that people once lived to be almost 900 years old and that donkeys and snakes can not only have conversations with humans, but can also be surprisingly condescending while doing so. Furthermore, your students will be excited to learn that the Earth has four corners, that bats are really birds, that man is made of mud, that the first woman was made from a rib bone, that the world was made in six days, that God drowned everyone on Earth because He was upset that fallen angels were having sex with humans and creating dinosaurs, and much, much more!

Hardcover 1st edition (November 1823)
Scholastic Children's Books; ISBN: 00000000004: Dimension (in Godly inches): 8.47 x 9.5 x 12
Amazon.com Sales Rank: 7
Average Customer Ranting: ★★★★☆
Number of Correct Reviews: 3,306,127 (have PayPal Auto-Tithe account number ready in order for your review to post)

Pastor Deacon Fred
If children were reading factual books like *Donkeys Can Talk* by Rev. Whipple and *Jesus Had Short Blond Hair* by Dr. Jack Hyles, instead of ridiculous secular fairy tales about "biology" and "math," we wouldn't be in the position we are today, having to deprogram our kids to remove ideas about untested, speculative theories like evolution and gravity to make way for more fabulous Bible stories!

PASTOR'S PULPIT

He May Have Worn a White Gown,
but Jesus Was No Sashaying Sissy!

SERMON BY BROTHER HARRY HARDWICK

I've tried again and again to make it perfectly clear to annoying liberal Christians that God has historically hated sinners and almost always been more than happy to condemn them to painful deaths. Do you know what these pseudo-Christians have the audacity to say in reply? That Jesus supposedly "took all that away," like God's whole set of rules for mankind was just a stinking bag of garbage waiting by the curb for Jesus to toss out. Well, that is utter blasphemy, my friends! The very idea that an Omnipotent Father would stand for His only Son telling everyone "Just ignore what the Old Man said" is outrageous on its face. Do you think a Father who spent so much time talking about killing disobedient children would allow His upstart Son to pretend Daddy had never spoken? I don't think so. If Jesus had even tried to do this, God would have yanked Him back to Heaven and given Him a good whupping with a rod that crossed several lifeless galaxies.

Jesus, fortunately, never shared such liberal delusions. He admitted that he is subordinate to the Father who rules over Him (1 Corinthians 11:3). Jesus told the Apostles that He had not come to destroy the law of the prophets of old; rather, He had come to fulfill that law (Matthew 5:17). In fact, the Apostle Paul became enraged by the people who knew Jesus when He was alive because they all still followed the Jewish laws after Jesus' death. Jesus approved of His Father's command that children who curse their parents are to be put to death (Matthew 15:3–4). Jesus chastised the Pharisees for failing to kill those children who defied their parents' commands (Mark 7:9–13). Jesus never contradicted His Father's word, and I'm sorry, but anyone who suggests otherwise is going straight to Hell. And not a moment too soon!

Jesus certainly wasn't averse to malicious, virulent punishments to those who didn't accept even His most careless word as Gospel. For example, Jesus told the disciples to bring before Him any man who didn't believe in Him, and to violently slaughter the nonbeliever while Jesus watched (Luke 19:27).

*"I believe that true love waits. I also
believe that opportunistic lust is
somewhat less patient."*
—Mindy Abernathy, age 15

And if folks questioned the price Jesus placed on fawning, He took care of them good. Jesus killed one man by having the fellow's body eaten by a swarm of worms because the man failed to give Jesus His due (Acts 12:23). Jesus struck a Jew blind for thwarting His teachings (Acts 13:8–11). Jesus struck a man dumb for failing to listen well (Luke 1:20). Jesus took the lives of a husband and wife by scaring them to death for not forking over all the money they made on a real estate transaction (Acts 5:1–10). During one particularly temperamental time when He was hungry, Jesus even killed a fig tree for failing to bear figs, even though Jesus knew figs weren't in season (Mark 11:12–14). My friends, the Bible is clear: Jesus means business!

The Bible teaches us that, come Judgment Day, Jesus will gather together all the sinners who ever lived and hurl them into a furnace of fire where there will be uncontrollable wailing and gnashing of teeth (Matthew 13:41–42, 50). Entire cities of people who don't believe in Jesus will suffer a fate worse than that of Sodom and Gomorrah (Mark 6:11). Jesus told us that God, who we already knew is subject to violent mood swings, will take "vengeance on them that know not God" by burning them forever "in flaming fire" (2 Thessalonians 1:7–9).

As Roosevelt did to Nagasaki, Jesus will use every weapon at His disposal to torture sinners. He will send an earthquake to kill 7,000 people (Revelation 11:13). And to add just a bit more drama, He will exercise His wrath by inflicting bodily sores, turning the seas and rivers to blood, scorching everyone with fire, causing people to consume their own tongues in pain, and causing horrendous storms that will strike dead the now speechless (though sated) sinners (Revelation 16:1–21).

So you see, Jesus is far from a Mr. Lovey-Dovey, turn-the-other-cheek, Goodie-Two-Shoes like all these demonic liberals say He is. Countless New Testament passages show Jesus was just as vengeful, vexatious and violent as His Father, perhaps more so. Of course, if you ignore these hundreds of Bible passages and just focus on the one—John 3:16—you can live in a fantasy world believing you are going to Heaven even though 587 other verses say you'll burn for eternity in Hell. Like a silly little Hell-bound Pollyanna, the liberals go skipping about, looking up into the sky and admiring the pretty sunset, refusing to notice the face of Jesus glowering back at them in rage.

LANDOVER BAPTIST CHURCH
"A Bulldozer to the Wall between Church and State since 1788"

AUGUST NEWSLETTER

Oral Sex: A Dangerous New Way to Speak in Tongues!

Intelligent Design teaches us that a thousand years to human beings is like a casual belch to the Lord. So, it isn't any wonder that God is just now finding out that His most sinful creatures (humans) have become very keen on slithering their tongues like a serpent of Satan into disgusting places on other folks' bodies that those folks can't reach on their own (not for lack of trying). Creation Scientists are beginning to believe that the talk around the ambrosia coolers in Heaven

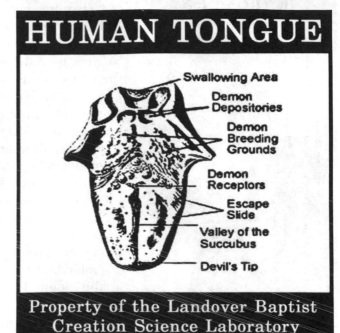

HUMAN TONGUE

- Swallowing Area
- Demon Depositories
- Demon Breeding Grounds
- Demon Receptors
- Escape Slide
- Valley of the Succubus
- Devil's Tip

Property of the Landover Baptist Creation Science Laboratory

Bible Quiz
The Lord's Pet Peeves

What is God's prescribed punishment for couples, married or otherwise, who have sex during a woman's monthly curse?

A. None. Consensual sexual relations between a husband and wife are unrestricted by anything other than agility.

B. They must use myrrh oil (the Biblical equivalent of club soda) to clean all areas of their cot and bodies that the woman's foul "issue" might have touched.

C. They are banished from society and not permitted to interact with civilized people.

D. They may invite no one into their home for at least two full days unless they generously spritz all rooms with equal parts sandalwood and lavender.

Answer: C. "And if a man shall lie with a woman having her sickness, and shall uncover her nakedness; he hath discovered her fountain, and she hath uncovered the fountain of her blood; and both of them shall be cut off from among their people" (Leviticus 29:18).

INTELLIGENT DESIGN IN THE NEWS

National Conclave of Faith-Healing Anthropologists unanimously voted male nipples as God's Least Intelligent Design.

INTELLIGENT DESIGN FACTOID

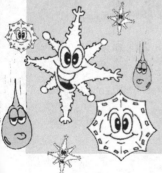

Because the Lord is kept so busy designing the billions of unique snowflakes it takes to cause an avalanche, there is never time to yell, "Look out below!"

is that God's creatures on Earth are using their mouths for a lot more than simply eating food and preaching the Gospel.

Recent studies in Creation Science show us that oral sex can be more dangerous than riding in a taxi in Thailand. (For those of you young people who have not yet been to Bible College "oral sex" means *the placement of a coochie, heinie or tallywhacker into a human mouth*.) Christian researchers have proven that Satan is using the human tongue to infiltrate the soul by way of the vagina, anus and hole in the tip of the penis (enormous penises have bigger holes, allowing for a greater number of demons to gain entrance, which is why black men commit so much crime). Creation Scientists have not yet determined exactly how thousands of tiny little demons lift their tiny feet out from the sticky goo of human semen and vaginal secretions, but they are convinced that once they reach the human tongue, they celebrate with wild abandon. "It is on the palette where the Devil's minions spawn and reproduce like swarms of tiny red maggots," teaches Landover Baptist Creation Scientist Dr. Jonathan Edwards. "Once enough of them are bred, an army is assembled. They exit the nesting area and enter the throat. It is at this point that you are infected, and the battle for your internal organs and, finally, your soul begins."

Landover Baptist's research on oral sex was started about a year ago when Pastor Lewis Morris of Freehold, Iowa, through means his son is now reconciled with, once acquired some of his son's own semen in the middle of the night, and used a tongue-depressor and a large eye-dropper to splash torrents of the gooey liquid down a helpful bullfrog's gullet. The frog died instantly. As a follow-up experiment, Dr. Edwards tried the same thing on a cat, using a sample of coagulated secretions he found inside his mother's vagina. The pussy died within fifteen minutes. Our researchers have come a long way since those first two experiments, but these results alone should be enough to raise the hair on the back of your tallywacker and make you think twice about committing oral sex. Oral sex is like playing Russian roulette, only this time the gun is made of skin and there are almost always bullets in the chamber, if you lick hard enough.

Die Already!

Annual Pope's Death Celebration Rescheduled: Hoping for Worse Health Next Year

The Roman Catholic tradition of choosing a new pope from cardinals too old to still molest altar boys keeps Landover Baptist hostesses perennially on their toes. "We know this latest, and I must say *homliest,* incarnation is going to be called to Hell anytime, but we are just not sure which month, much less day," remarked Mrs. John "Ernestine" Mercer, manager of Freehold Iowa's Smith & Wesson Convention Center. "That makes planning a celebration difficult," she added while flipping the pages of her monthly calendar, which seemed to bleed with the sanguine markings of upcoming events. "As soon as the pope dies, everyone—except those Mary-worshipping Guineas—will want to have a huge party to celebrate. I mean, even the loss of your garden-variety Catholic is reason enough to cheer. But our main room is booked for the rest of the year with huge True Christian™ banquets. I just checked our bookings this morning and only December 14 is free. Landover Baptist just canceled its Feed and Clothe the Homeless charity dinner that night due to lack of ticket sales. So, in order for this to work, that old pansy in Rome needs to kick no sooner than December 7, but no later than December 10. Otherwise, Landover will lose its deposit. I've already talked to Pastor and there will be no exceptions."

"When Pope John Paul I was killed by God after just a month, it caught us totally by surprise," lamented Mrs. Betty Bowers, America's Best Christian. "We had to scramble. Everyone wants the celebration of the Lord killing a pope to be a special occasion, since it happens all too infrequently. For example, the food and music for John XXIII's death were absolutely legendary. Sammy Davis, Jr,. did a fabulous, if slightly off-colored—oh, dear, can you even use that expression with those people?—number called 'Papal Bull' that had everyone in stitches. So there is a glorious legacy to which

Investigators Locate Priest with No Sodomy Past

A team of Vatican investigators reported last week that they have located a U.S. priest who has never been accused of sodomizing any parishioners. Father Francis O'Leer of Phenix City, Alabama, has presided over his seven-person parish for 37 years with no proven complaint of sexual abuse other than sundry molestations. Protestant analysts were quick to note that this may be due to the fact that Father Francis was born without genitals.

Church Member Spotlight

Elbridge Gerry, 92, was expelled from church earlier this week for praying to the ruby and ivory sculpture of Moses in the East Hall rotunda. Admonished Pastor: "I don't care how expensive that statue looks, the only dead Jew that answers prayers around here is Jesus!"

this year's party will inevitably be compared. You just *know* when something is thrown together at the last minute—like an NBC sitcom. I can always tell if someone available on short notice has done the flowers. It just winds up looking like a black funeral."

In addition to planning to fete True Christians™ celebrating a world with one fewer Catholic, the death of a pope provides a wonderful opportunity to use a moment of vulnerability to proselytize to people who have embraced a faith that guarantees a certain descent to Hell. "We need to be ready this time," said Pastor Harry Hardwick. "Whenever a pope dies, tens of thousands of priests become depressed and turn to booze. Since almost all priests are Irish, this means a lot of mean drunks. They are dangerous to be around, but we are really trying to reach out to Catholic priests, so we have to go to them regardless of the risks to the personal safety of the people we hire. This means having hourly employees witness for the one True Faith— Southern Baptist—at all the places Catholic priests tend to frequent in times of grief, whether it is at gay bars, gay bathhouses, gay public sodomy locales or Madonna concerts."

"Of course, those buggering priests' reactions may be a tad different to the passing of this pope, since he has spoken against homosexuality—well, the kind that goes on *outside* the Catholic Church," cautioned Mrs. Helen Floribunda, Landover's diplomatic envoy to the Vatican. "While some may think the pope's condemnation a little timid, we applaud the courage that even that meek message must have taken. I mean, a pope speaking out against homos is like Nelson Mandela condemning Negroes. You just don't expect folks to turn on their own kind like that."

Pastor Hires Unsaved Security Guards to Protect Church Property After the Rapture

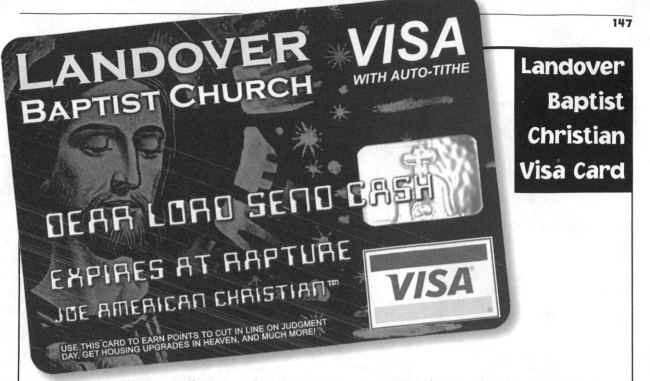

Finally, a credit card that announces to every cashier and waiter: *I'm a better Christian than you!* With a Landover Baptist Visa card, you can shop with the security of knowing that you will never again have to ask yourself, "What Would Jesus Buy?" Any attempted purchase of an item our pastors think you have no business owning is instantly blocked and automatically flagged for itemized rebukes at only $10 per sin. Embossed with a handsome hologram of your Savior rendered in counterfeit-proof Idaho lamb's blood, if the card is reported stolen, a Bluetooth signal will cause the plastic-explosive card to detonate with the force of almost two sticks of dynamite in the thief's hand or back pocket.

Features:

Low Introductory Rate Pegged to Temple Money Changers!

Auto Tithe—Donates 10 percent (minimum) of the price of every purchase (including returns) directly to an offshore account of Landover Baptist Christian Holdings Grand Cayman LLC.

EZ Slide Tithe™ Compatible—The Landover VISA is compatible with our EZ Slide Tithe™ offering plates. You can use them from the comfort of your own reserved pew seat, when the state-of-the-art, sophisticated, electronic collection plate comes around.

Satan Guard—For $6.95 per month, Satan Guard will automatically refuse payment for purchases of liberal or otherwise indecent materials or any item that has a sales price that includes three consecutive sixes. This optional embarrassment of having your Jesus card declined in public will make you a more careful Christian shopper, realizing that the only savings that matter involve souls.

Advanced Satan Guard—For $29.99 per month, Advanced Satan Guard includes everything in the original Satan Guard but extends the decimal points out to nine digits! Imagine avoiding fractional Marks of the Beast, previously invisible to the naked eye! Demonic vendors will be shocked to discover that they can't reject your card, but it can reject them!

Special Discounts! Get background check waivers and a special NRA discount when purchasing Chinese firearms and ammo for your home or militia! Special discounts when used at certified "Mistress-Free" Christian Motels® and Sizzler restaurants. "Cash to Christ Bonus" automatically rounds tithes to the next dollar so you don't have to! Specially reduced rates on Rapture Insurance when traveling, to avoid penalties for not returning vehicles to pickup locations.

Bible Quiz

To God's trained eye, who has greater market value: men or women?

A. Neither. God values all His children equally as long as they don't rub Him the wrong way.

B. God has expressly said men are worth more, providing actual monetary amounts.

C. Women are worth more because they can bear and feed children.

D. Women are worth more because they have an extra rib and operating nipples.

Answer: B. "And thy estimation shall be of the male from twenty years old even unto sixty years old, even thy estimation shall be fifty shekels of silver, after the shekel of the sanctuary. And if it be a female, then thy estimation shall be thirty shekels. And if it be from a month old even unto five years old, then thy estimation shall be of the male five shekels of silver, and for the female thy estimation shall be three shekels of silver. And if it be from sixty years old and above, if it be a male, then thy estimation shall be fifteen shekels, and for the female, ten shekels" (Leviticus 27:3–5).

THE GOOD NEWS

Farmers Use Menstruating Women to Fertilize Crops

The Biblical Conformance Commission's Edict 5,876,112, which requires that any toilet used by a menstruating woman be wrenched from the floor and smashed into dust after each use, has sent many of Landover's homeowners into debt trying to bring their homes up to Biblical code. "I understand that the Lord isn't all that crazy about women anyway, and that He thinks they are particularly filthy when going through their monthly curse," said Sid Bellows. "But a Kohler commode can run you around $1,000 apiece. So, we're talking about $10,000 each month just so the Missus can take a dump." Mr. Bellows joined many husbands and fathers in asking Pastor for suggestions about more economical ways to bring their homes into compliance with Leviticus 15:20 ("And every thing that she lieth upon in her separation shall be unclean: every thing also that she sitteth upon shall be unclean").

Everyone (except a few carping, PMS-riddled females) was pleased to find that the solution was surprisingly economical.

"Fellows, you don't want these dirty gals in your house at all when they are manifesting the sins of Eve," said Pastor Deacon Fred. "As you all know, the Lord, like many of our wives, abhors a vacuum. When blood drains from a woman's clammy places, something must go in to replace it. Well, that 'something' is, of course, *demons*. That is why menstruating women are so bloated, fidgety and cranky. They're chock full of demons! Creation Scientists will vouch for the fact that during this time of the month, a woman's uterus is a little Hyatt Hotel for conventioning demons.

"During urination," Pastor continued, "some of the more clumsy demons slip on urine and wind up under the rim of your potty bowl. If you check a can of Lysol, you'll see the manufacturer's lawyers have obviously told them that it would be a lie to claim that it kills demons, 'cause they make no such claim. In fact, they are real careful to claim only 99.9 percent effectiveness. Well, my friend, that remaining 0.1 percent they can't kill is *demons*. As such, all those toilets would need to be destroyed after each use even if Leviticus didn't tell us that the Lord holds his nose in disgust every time womenfolk flush a toilet. So, really, the best thing is to get those bleeding gals on out of the house altogether.

"At first, we were going to just let these females loose in the woods behind Mrs. Hawthorne's farm. Since it was the first woman's frail faith in the Lord that got them into this mess in the first place, it is only fair that they be the ones who have to worry about finding a place to squat down and go to the bathroom. But the Holy Spirit led the Board of Deacons to the novel solution of renting these leaking ladies out during their times of uncleanness to local farmers to help fertilize their cornfields. And that way, you fellows can take a poop safe in the knowledge that some lady demons aren't going to hop off the toilet seat and climb aboard your dangling man business."

Pastor Orders Widow to Release Her Husband's Soul from Mason Jar

It was discovered this week that Widow Wankin parlayed her vigil at her husband's deathbed into an opportunity to catch his soul in an empty Mason jar. Mrs. Wankin told friends: "At the very moment Elmer passed, I grabbed that jar and scooped up his little soul just as it rose from his dead body. That rubber flange was squished tight before that dear, lovely soul knew what had happened to it. You should have seen the look on its little soul-face. It's all I have left of my wonderful Elmer." A spokesman for the Iowa State Fair commented: "That is a woman who knows how to put up some preserves. If she pickled his soul, you can bet it's not going anywhere."

Worried Baptist homemakers ask:

"Who will be cleaning our mansions of gold in Heaven if all the unsaved Mexicans will be in Hell?"

Food for Ethiopia Fund Airlifts Emergency Snacks to Peckish Missionaries

The continuing famine in Ethiopia this year almost caused Landover Baptist's 345 missionaries there to check out of their four-star safari-themed resort and return home. Several of the Platinum Level Tithers claimed that the country's inability to come up with any actual food, much less appealing garnishes, meant that their meal service fell disappointingly short of the lovely four-color pictures in the missionary recruitment brochures, and was certainly not commensurate with the $23,450 room and board charged per traveler by the church for the trip. After Methuselah Christianson watched in horror as an entire village of unsaved Ethiopians noisily converged like voracious piranha on a can of Diet Dr Pepper he had slung through the window of his speeding Range Rover, he was moved to tears, concerned that the snack foods and carbonated beverages he so much enjoyed might not be readily available locally. With the entire trip in peril, Pastor Deacon Fred called upon all church members, right down to the parsimonious Tin Level Tithers, to contribute to a specially organized Emergency Food for Ethiopia Fund.

Proving that Christian generosity knows no bounds when there are those in need, $2 million was raised within four days, ensuring that those called by God to a spot on the globe not fabled for its cuisine would be feted in a style worthy of the Lord's magnificence. In a letter to the missionaries, Pastor Deacon Fred reassured them: "We are not ignoring the food shortage in Ethiopia, friends. As you go about the Lord's work,

American Christians Tell Abortion Clinics:
"Don't Confuse the Anthrax We Send with the Stuff Sent by Foreign Religious Fanatics."

"We are very concerned," said anti-abortion group Lambs of the Lethal Lord representative Mrs. Charles Pennyworth, "that clinics that we send pestilence to will give all the credit to that phony-baloney god Allah. I can guarantee that these spores are coming straight from the *real* God. We've been at this terrorist game a might bit longer than those Islamic crazies and it chaps my hide that those Johnny-come-latelies now get all the credit."

you're going to be surrounded by so many Hot Pockets and Entenmanns's raspberry crumb cakes, you won't even know you left Iowa."

News of the emergency airlift was greeted with relief and enterprise by Landover's missionaries. "When I first came here, I naturally assumed that everyone in town either had an eating disorder or a reliable source for methamphetamine—like Hollywood," said Mrs. Betty Bowers, America's Best Christian, in a cam conference with deacons from Debra-zeit. "But as soon as I noticed that the men weren't overweight, I knew something very non-Hollywood was afoot! These poor, dreadful people are willing to sell any possession for food! So, naturally, having extra food on hand will create marvelous investment opportunities. Why, just last year, when they weren't even as desperate as they are now, I picked up a lovely coffee plantation for a packet of Lifesavers!"

Ernestine Mercer, a VIC (Very Important Christian) who enjoys afternoons sipping tea at the Kook'a'choo sidewalk café in downtown Addis Ababa, was also pleased to know that an Air Force cargo plane is on its way with the type of delicious snacks that are made especially for folks who aren't even hungry. Oftentimes, she is called to read from Gospel tracts to the illiterate, starving and unfortunate children who gather like panting stray dogs on the other side of her portable electric fence. "Witnessing is hard work," said Ernestine, "especially when you don't have so much as a Snickers bar to nibble on between those awful buffet meals back at the hotel."

Bible Quiz

God v. Allah: Which god ordered the cruelest, most sadistic warfare practices?

A. Neither god encourages cruelty in warfare.

B. Obviously, the Muslim god, since the Christian God never endorsed warfare, especially against fiction authors like Salman Rushdie.

C. The Muslim god, because he ordered his followers to imprison and enslave their enemies temporarily.

D. The Christian God, because He is wont to order His followers to kill all the men in the towns they invaded, enslaving only the women and children (who sometimes were to be slaughtered as well, along with every other living thing in sight, including unborn babies).

Answer: D. "So when you meet in battle those who disbelieve, then smite the necks until when you have overcome them, then make (them) prisoners, and afterwards either set them free as a favor or let them ransom (themselves) until the war terminates" (Koran 47:4). "And when the Lord thy God hath delivered [a city] into thine hands, thou shalt smite every male thereof with the edge of the sword: But the women, and the little ones . . . shalt thou take unto thyself. . . . But of the cities of these people, which the Lord thy God doth give thee for an inheritance, thou shalt save alive nothing that breatheth" (Deuteronomy 20:13–16).

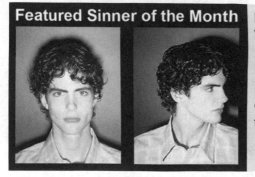

Featured Sinner of the Month

NAME: John Osella
VIOLATION: Being a straight-A student who reads Marcel Proust in the original French
VERDICT: Guilty of the sin of pride. Bonus reprimand for having pretensions that exceed even minimum entry requirements to join the intellectual elite.

Jesus' SMACKDOWN on Sodomy Starts with the WWE!

Sweaty men in tight women's underwear who can't keep their hands off each other—in a non-Olympic year, no less—may be fooling the unsaved world, but they're not fooling Jesus. For nearly 50 years, Satan's World Wrestling Entertainment has convinced unsuspecting, naive Southerners to gawk at nearly naked men fondling and groping each other. Before lustful, screaming, unsaved rednecks, depraved sissies on steroids flirt with each other, taunt each other, play hard to get, and ultimately allow themselves to be touched in places Christian men don't even allow their wives to caress. Anti-Christian Ted Turner has been more than happy to use his pornographic cable empire to soil the living rooms of Red State Americans with the sight of prancing homosexuals acting out their shameless fantasies of performing S&M, dress-up and heavy petting before a live audience of shameless sexual voyeurs. Everyone living within five miles of a trailer park is buying into the outrageous notion that men wearing nothing more than spandex bikini briefs should be cheered, instead of driven out of town at gunpoint. A recent study by the Family Research Council of longtime fans of Capitol Wrestling concluded that "except for a widow in Memphis, all WWE fans studied reveal learned homosexual traits. These latent nellies fantasize about being "pile-driven" (wink, wink) with a "stiff clothesline" (wink, wink) administered after a "belly-to-belly press."

Landover Baptist Church has declared the WWE and all of its affiliates "A Stronger Magnet for Homosexuals than a Cher

Poorly Worded Prayer Leads to Accidental Rape

Pastor explained, "This is all very regrettable and everything, but it certainly isn't the Lord's fault that there was a slight miscommunication. Sometimes, when a girl prays 'no' she means 'yes' (believe me, my wife has done this many times), so it is often hard for the Lord Jesus to understand her true intent. And when secular ghetto lingo has our young people confused to the point where 'bad' means 'good' and 'phat' means 'thin,' you can hardly expect the Lord to make heads or tails of what these teenagers are going on about when they are praying for stuff!"

Farewell Tour." At a press conference last week, Pastor Deacon Fred called on Christians everywhere to "take up the cross of Jesus and smack a 400-pound homo in the head with it. Because when they get knocked down, they'll finally know that they are down for the count when God Almighty steps into the ring."

Reliable Christian sources tell us that the WWE is already complying with a petition to remove controversial "holds" or "wrestling moves." The "stones lick," "heinie hapdazzler," "prostate flapwizzer" and "foreskin roll" are the first four of 10 "moves" to be banned. Nevertheless, "this is going to be a long, hard road," Pastor Deacon Fred noted. "These demon-possessed men can sometimes reach heights of over seven feet. Some of them weigh over 500 pounds! The Bible tells us that none of this matters. Remember what happened to that over-sized homosexual predator Goliath? The Lord would not allow him to turn little David into his catamite, so David cracked Goliath's skull open like a hen's egg (before returning to Jonathan, with whom his relations were not broadcast to hill-billies 24/7). To God, these wrestlers are nothing more than gigantic sissies. The bigger the man, the more of a sissy he is. You remember that, when you get ready to rumble for Jesus!"

Middle East to Be Bulldozed for New Christian Theme Park

Landover Baptist Offshore Holdings LLC, in a joint venture with Pat Robertson Productions Inc. and Halliburton Inc., has been awarded a no-bid contract to

convert the unsightly, but Biblically significant, areas of the Middle East into a new amusement park to be called Six Flags Over Jesus.

"One visit to the Middle East, a dreadful preview of Hell if there ever was one, makes it abundantly clear that Jesus had a far higher tolerance for foreign food, accommodations and, well let's not mince words, *people* than the average, more particular, American Christian," dryly observed Mrs. Betty Bowers while swabbing a plastic 55-story high-rise with a Lysol Mountain Spring sanitary wipe, as she and Pat Robertson unveiled an enormous model of the 1,500-square-mile Six Flags Over Jesus to the secular press. "Americans have always wished to walk in Jesus' footprints—but only as long as it didn't involve unnecessary inconvenience. And this is true both figuratively regarding His rather quixotic, anti-materialistic teachings—as well as literally regarding the austere, dusty places He traipsed around while on Earth. Honestly, I challenge any one of you to spend just one week at a hotel in Judea and then question the reasonableness of Jesus' willingness to climb up on a cross and have done with it!"

The Middle East's dearth of five-star accommodations will change next month when Halliburton dynamites the unattractive mosque that currently clutters the Temple Mount, making way for a glorious new Four Seasons Resort hotel. Also in the works is a proposal to turn the very hill upon which Jesus was killed into a spotless, crucifix-themed restaurant serving generous portions of Applebee's food. After their meals, American diners will be able to retrace the steps of their Savior's last moments on Earth by riding the new Vertical Drop to Golgotha Log Flume.

"Since Revelation tells us that Jesus won't swoop down and start killing with gusto until the Jews are back in the Holy Land, we are going to man all the money-changing kiosks throughout the park with Hebrews," explained Pat Robertson. "That way, not only will the park provide a spic-and-span view of Jesus' high school, its construction will also be the thing that finally triggers the Apocalypse." Indeed, stateside Ticketmaster outlets have already been inundated by requests for seats in Armageddon Stadium in Megiddo, which will be the centerpiece of Six Flags Over Jesus when it is built. Modeled after the Circus Maximus in

Pastor Discovers Detained Terrorists in Church Basement Are Actually Mexicans

Last week, Pastor ordered the release of three of the 21 Freehold convenience store clerks rounded up and detained on September 12, 2001. In light of President Bush's renewed resolve to pander to voters who speak Mexican, Pastor agreed to investigate President Vicente Fox's claims that the unabashedly swarthy men shackled to the church's hot water pipes are supposedly Mexican nationals, rather than what they otherwise show all signs of being—Arab terrorists who love tacos. "I don't know how finding out they are Catholics instead of Muslims will make our congregation—particularly the more comely young boys—feel any safer," observed Pastor, "but as a gesture of goodwill, they will be set free—just as soon as they settle up for room and board and renounce Mary in a language saved folks can understand."

This Week's Sermon:

"'Allah!' May Be Something You Scream When a Stick of Dynamite Goes Off in Your Arab Undies, but It Is Not a Name the Real God Answers To!"
—Pastor Deacon Fred

Rome, the 300,000-seat stadium will allow lucky spectators to sit back, enjoy a lovely cold beverage and watch Jesus harvest the grapes of wrath, turning all the local Jews and other non-believers into an enormous river of blood. "Now that's a halftime show that beats Janet Jackson's old black boobies any day," declared Pat Robertson.

Last Week's Favorite Hymn:

"We'll Rest Our Weary Heads on Pillows Stuffed with Disinfected Angel Feathers"

Demons Fill Pastor's Pocket with Penis Enlargement Pills

"I found a half-used bottle of Cockzilla Professional Penile Pro-traction Pills in the right pocket of my husband's best preaching jacket when I took it to the cleaners," a still shaken Mrs. Harry Hardwick told Pastor Deacon Fred. "It is scary to think that horrid demons have run their hands through my wonderful husband's lined clothing like a grabby pack of streetwalkers and left something so disgusting. I'm telling you, I haven't felt such revulsion since I reached into Sister Dora Denkins's purse at church for a Lifesaver and ended up sliding my finger into the open end of an enormous used condom."

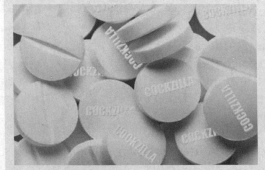

Mrs. Hardwick quickly discounted the fact that the pills may have been ordered by her husband. "With his blessings of abun-dance in his waist, Harry hasn't seen his unmentionable area in years, so why would he worry about how big it is? Goodness knows, I don't. Besides, he knows the Lord Jesus doesn't go for all that crotch-medicine like Viagra. When Jesus said his Peter was a rock, he was talking about a person, not a tallywacker! But, frankly, I shouldn't have been surprised to find something to make a willy bigger turn up in a laundry chock-full of Chinamen!"

Have Trouble Taking the Holy Bible Seriously?
This Pill Can Help.
SALVACIL
S
The Salvation Medication.
Four out of five Christian doctors in Jesusland prescribe Salvacil to born-again patients who suffer from faith-related problems. Whether they be doubts about one's eternal security, panic attacks regarding Biblical inerrancy, or post-traumatic depression over the loss of an unsaved loved one who is being roasted alive by a smiling, loving God over a spit in a literal lake of fire, there's hope, help, and a little boost of faith with Salvacil.
POSSIBLE SIDE EFFECTS:
Some Christian patients have reported unpleasant sexual side effects such as erections, tingling between the legs, willingness to try new things, and even mild orgasms during intercourse. If any of these symptoms occur, cease taking Salvacil immediately and consult your Christian faith healer.
FDA WARNING: Patients reading road signs and menus or engaged in any other activity when the meaning of words might have actual consequence, should not take Salvacil.
Pfizer

LANDOVER BAPTIST CHURCH

"Gossiping Out Of Christian Concern For Over 350 Years!"

from the spirit-filled desk of
Suzzanna Beth Simpkins

Gals in Christ:

I'm crying as I type. I have come to the conclution that schools our no place for childrens. Just yesterday my little Hunter came home and told me that his teacher had teached the <u>theory</u> of a president called Trueman—like it was some sort of proven fact or some thing! And that is just the tip of the icepick. Hunter was told that America went through depression in the 1930s! Whats next? That the Statute of Liberty wasn't made in America? Honest Lee, I just cant believe all the unchristian, America-hating hooey that is been rammed down are babys precious little throwts. Big time!!! Did you all no that a teacher is allowed to talk about ungodly folks like Einstein (a Jew) and Darwin (a liar) but our not allowed to spend the hole day reading Bible storys two are youngsters? Don't laugh—its true!

That is why I started Landover's "Homeskooling Are Children" project. To protect are youngins from dangerous secular humaniacist garbage been teached in public schools—like physics and chemistry. As durn every Christian nos, the noledge we keep <u>out</u> of are babys heads is even more important than the noledge we allow in! The Bible says somewheres that noledge puffeth uppeth and even childrens don't need to be carrying that pudgy extra water waite. I no I don't! Frank Lee, a lack of noledge is the most important gift a Christian parent can give—next to a right sharp smack across the neykid fanny when they show up to breakfast looking like Paris Hilton or a Negro.

The Lord Jesus Christ <u>Hisself</u> called me out of Junior High to deliver my darling baby Billy Ray Junior—just to spare me from being poisoned by a pubic education. Instead, He in His mercy spared me from witch-crafty subjects like foreigner tongues (like the stuff folks say in Paris, Germany) and occult frog sacrifices (so-called "Biology").

I is encouraging all of you alls to help us teach are precious babies Christain reding and Christain writting. Our you real good at something??? I'm gone to be teaching Advanced English Compositioning and Faith

Saved Children Crossin

Four Christian Children Remain in Critical Condition After Suffering Third Degree Brimstone Burns During Backyard Sodom and Gomorrah Reenactment

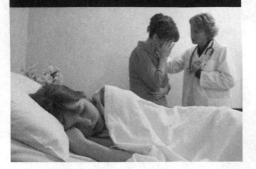

Heeling 101 (still looking for a corpse or something). But we our currently looking for someone to teach Christain Calculust (which proves that the world is bout 6,000 years old if you add up all the begets in the Bible, divide by the number of Philistine foreskins in First Samuel, and multiply by the number of Solomon's concubines) and Christain Logic (if you can talk reel fast, the job is yours!!!).

One thing I can promise you—their WILL be prayer in ARE school! We starts evrury day with prayer requests! ALL the times!! And NO black trenchcoats, harlotty make-up or things pierced that ain't hangin' on a cross! An are children will learn to RIGHT WRITE!!!! Hallalewya!!!!!"

You'res in Christ,

Mrs. (Suzzanna Beth) Billy Ray Simpkins
President, Bringing Integrity To Christian Homemakers,
Freehold Chapter

MEMBER SPOTLIGHT:
Billy Ray and Suzzanna Beth Simpkins

Mr. and Mrs. Billy Ray Simpkins joined Landover Baptist three years ago. Billy Ray used to be a male escort in West Hollywood, California, until he met his future wife, Suzzanna Beth, at the tattoo parlor on Venice Beach where she worked when AWOL from her junior high school in Chino. When the meth wore off, Billy Ray recalled that Suzzanna Beth had introduced him to her Savior Jesus. Having the phone number for *Globe* magazine in her purse, the couple were able to negotiate a lucrative out-of-court arrangement with one of Billy Ray's more famous former celebrity clients, thereby blessing them with the financial means to join Landover Baptist.

Since moving to Iowa, Suzzanna Beth has become local president of Bringing Integrity To Christian Homemakers and is a majorette in the Ladies of Landover's Rebuking Squadron. Her husband works nights. On Wednesdays, they both go to the Southern Baptist faith healer Trudy Tomlin, who has promised that their many vulgar and pointedly obscene tattoos will be healed before God comes to judge in Glory.

Harry Potter vs. Bible Tracts: Is Satan More Savvy at Marketing than Jesus?

S atan has stocked every secular bookstore in Jesusland with tens of millions of thick, glossy Harry Potter books. Meanwhile, Jesus is left to leaving a flimsy two-color pamphlet on a urinal or subway seat. By comparison, Jesus' ad campaign might seem a bit underwhelming—especially when He begins each cold call by telling the potential customer that, without His product, they face eternity in Hell. That is certainly not the sales pitch that made Mary Kay a household name! Are we about to be defeated by Christianity's worst enemy: more ingeniously packaged superstitions?

Make no mistake: The assault is on. Satan is coming after the hearts of our precious children with tales of mystical powers even more appealing than those in the Bible (like Jesus' parlor game of making dead people walk across your living room). In a cagey attempt to go after the coveted 8–18 market, Satan is using his Harry Potter books to teach children that they—not unemployed adults like Jesus—have all the power. In the world of Harry Potter, children wave 11-inch rods to cast spells and routinely back-talk adults. In the Old Testament, adults brandish 11-inch rods to cast out the demons of impudence from the bare backsides of children (Proverbs 13:24)—and stone them to death if they dare back-talk (Deuteronomy 21:18–21). Clearly, Satan has a defter touch than our Lord when it comes to writing a book that children will kneel before at their beds at night and pray is true.

Harry Potter signals that Satan is clearly going after the most reliable demographic Christian churches normally count on for tithes—people gullible enough to believe that spells and hexes are real. Truly, there is no gratitude in this god-eat-god world of supernatural marketing. Indeed, if it weren't for us Christians,

This Month's Sermon Series

"The Holy Trinity: The Miracle of Having Three Gods and Still Not Being a Polytheist Pagan"

3 HEADS ARE BETTER THAN 1

In response to the recent building boom in the Bible Belt, Landover Baptist has commissioned architect Santiago Calatrava to add an 850-foot steeple with an observation deck to the main sanctuary so that the church may recapture bragging rights as "The Closest Church to God."

there would be no satanic witchcraft. After all, we were the ones who invented Satan in the first place (as a vehicle for explaining all the horrible stuff that occurs on God's watch). If you don't believe in the Bible, then you don't believe in Satan. It's that simple! Indeed, Satanism is little more than an embarrassing by-product of Christianity—like head cheese is to pork chops. Satanism's followers believe all the same stuff we do about the power of blood, demons and magic; they just pick the wrong character in this story to emphasize. (As such, they are virtually indistinguishable from the Mary-worshipping Catholics.) Clearly, it takes a Christian to imbue an air of authenticity to a concept that nonbelievers might otherwise be inclined simply to dismiss as harmless, far-fetched fiction. Magic tricks like walking on water that can later be turned into a sea of oaky chardonnay? *That was us!* We therefore deserve all of the credit for making otherwise intelligent adults regard wildly outlandish tales as real. And what is the gratitude we get? Satan uses this carefully nurtured credulity to trot out an even slicker story than the erstwhile greatest one ever sold—Harry Potter!

Department of Justice Action Alert: Report Demonic Activity in Your Home with the "Little Ears Ministry"

Report Your Unsaved Parents to the Federal Government!

Kids, thanks to our anointed president, George W. Bush, and the Patriot Act, it is now easier than ever for Christian children like you to turn your unsaved parents in to federal authorities. You've seen the road signs, "Report Suspicious Behavior," and you've heard your Mommy and Daddy whispering about how nervous that makes them. Well, now you can do something about it!

Signs That Your Parents Are Engaging in Suspicious Thoughts or Activities

- Your parents mention people or foreign countries whose names you cannot pronounce.
- Your parents show an abnormal interest in gathering intelligence—like reading sensationalistic anti-American propaganda such as the *New York Times* and the *Washington Post*.
- Your parents are out too late at night, and when you ask them where they were, they just laugh or tell you to mind your own business.
- Your parents don't allow you to play certain video games, claiming they are "too violent," which is their sinful way of mocking most of the Holy Bible.
- When you tell your parents that anyone who doesn't believe that Jesus is the Son of God is going to burn in Hell, they tell you to be more "tolerant" of other religions. This is VERY suspicious! "Tolerant" is code for turning Christ-loving children like you into godless (people who spit in Jesus' eye) homosexual (people who put your pee-pee into their heinies) communists (people who put your blessings into their pockets).
- Your parents try to get you to read Harry Potter books. This is VERY suspicious! Your parents are trying to get you to learn how to be a witch. This is an almost certain sign that they are witches—and since many witch spells call for parts of little children, you (or parts of you) are in peril.
- Your parents laugh when President Bush slurs his words after two glasses of his unfermented beverage, or gets defensive or snippy, or says something they call a "malapropism" on television.
- Your parents use words like "no," "not found," "where," "what," "whose" or "America's" when they talk about "weapons of mass destruction." This is VERY suspicious!
- You find a copy of the Koran (sometimes called the Quo'ran—or "The Satanic Bible") in your house. Oh boy, is this ever suspicious!

Pastor Alerts Congregation:

"Friends, recharge your Tasers! Jehovah's Witnesses were spotted in Des Moines and they're headed this way!"

$3.00 Off Creation Science Museum Visit

Landover Baptist Center for Creation Research and Designs for Intelligence
18 Soulwinner's Lane
Freehold, Iowa

Expires: January 30, 2010

Is the World of Star Trek Helping Americans Understand Muslims and Their Alien Culture of Terror?

True Christian™ *Star Trek* fan and Sunday School teacher Geoffrey Mullins thinks so. Most fans of the popular television series *Star Trek* are already aware through the always-reliable Christian grapevine that the show's creator, Gene Roddenberry, gathered ideas for his fictional Klingon species during a trip to the Holy Land in the late 1960s. After only a cursory viewing of an early episode of *Star Trek*, Landover Baptist pastors were shocked at how closely Roddenberry's Klingon characters resembled Arabs, in both their features and mannerisms. "I'm not a big fan of Mr. Roddenberry," says Landover Baptist Pastor Deacon Fred. "But our opinions are very similar when it comes to them Muslim fellows. Being a Jew, Mr. Roddenberry knew firsthand what it was like to be persecuted by the shocking prejudices of such a filthy, backward race of warmongers. My guess is that he couldn't come right out and say what he felt in public, so he used the television series *Star Trek* to get his views across. I'm telling you, you'd have to be almost as stupid as one of those Mormons not to see how obvious it is that *Star Trek*'s Klingons are actually Arabs in disguise. I understand it gets harder and harder to tell with each new series, because they started to get politically correct and had to change the blackface makeup so it wasn't so obvious. Well, as a True Christian™, I think the new makeup does an even better job of bringing out the demonic nature and character of those unnecessarily swarthy Arab types."

Sunday School teacher Geoffrey Mullins has incorporated several Klingon-filled *Star Trek* episodes into an eight-week Bible-based media study on Muslim culture and behavior. Landover Baptist is the first church to use Mullins's study in its

🧍 Muslims Riot Over Accusations of Violence

An Islamic spokesperson appearing on al-Jazeera television responded to riots that had erupted earlier this week after a Baptist pastor told the media that he believes that Islam is a religion of violence. "We are a religion of love and peace," stated the Islamic spokesperson. "And all 14 hostages will be beheaded unless an apology for accusations that we are otherwise is issued immediately by the American Baptist infidel."

senior high school's Lesser Cultures studies. "Our Christian children are getting most of their information about Arabs and Muslims from the media," says Mullins, "and the media is biased toward Muslims. What we like about *Star Trek* is that they just tell it like it is. The show's writers don't tiptoe around the negative facts about Muslim crazy-as-coons behavior. They don't even try to hide how silly the Muslim religion is, or how Arab people, with maybe one or, at most, three exceptions, are nothing more than a pack of bloodthirsty dogs, hell-bent on destruction. *Star Trek* even accurately depicts the Arab language as something that sounds more like a discombobulated hyena trying to hack up a glob of phlegm the size of a softball than it does someone trying to communicate using words."

Martha Stewart Opens An Eye for an Eye Spare Body Parts Store

(Reprinted from the *Wall Street Journal* with permission asked, but ungraciously declined.) With the perennial news of lackluster sales at retailer Kmart, marketing doyenne Martha Stewart announced that she is abandoning ship. "Frankly," said Ms. Stewart, while firing one of her whisk designers for having an odd air about him, "We've done market studies and there just aren't enough Pentecostals in this country to have a big enough market for the cheap plastic crap Kmart sells. While I'm willing to attach my name to successful garbage if the price is right, as a businesswoman, I can't afford to be associated with unsuccessful garbage!"

Within hours of admitting her long-speculated-about departure from Kmart, Ms. Stewart announced that she would be focusing her attention on the flagship store of her new retail chain An Eye for an Eye at Landover Baptist Christian Mall. An Eye for an Eye will specialize in selling sinless plastic body parts to Christians who have been betrayed by their own flesh. True Christians™ are told by the Lord Jesus that if any body part might cause them to sin, it is best that they cut it off (Mark 9:43–47; see also Matthew 18:8–9; Luke 20:46–47).

Ms. Stewart saw a golden marketing opportunity in the recent spate of Baptists removing naughty body parts to get ready for Judgment Day, when they will appear before the White Throne of Judgment. "That throne will be

After Asking Himself "What Would Jesus Do?" Pastor Daniels Shows Up Dead on a Cross in Widow Hanover's Rose Garden

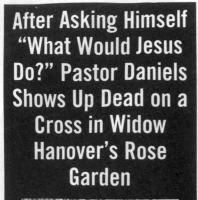

perfect because white goes with everything—except bone—which has really freed us up to do lots of kicky things with color! Whereas God uses a rather staid palette, I'm offering shoppers an opportunity to be more expressive with complementary hues. For example, why not finish off a new vulva in putty with a pair of labias in raspberry?" asked Ms. Stewart. "It's all so exciting! While I'm not a born-again Christian, it's like my dear, dear friend Barbra Streisand told me when she made her last Christmas CD: You don't have to be Christian to make a buck off them!"

Typical of An Eye for an Eye's patrons was an unmarried couple excitedly ogling the halogen-lit display cases for items to replace body parts they had recently removed. They were ecstatic to have such handsome and affordable body parts at a store conveniently located between the Quaker and Shaker Modest Couture dress shop and the Samson's World of Wigs store in the mall. "After you have cut something off, it's nice to have a place to go with such a wonderful assortment of replacement parts," noted Bobby Lee Williams as he longingly fingered his way through a case of artificial testicles outside of his price range. Bobby Lee's girlfriend was unable to express her opinion, as she had yet to receive the prosthetic tongue she recently ordered.

America's Best Christian, Mrs. Betty Bowers, was not so sanguine about the new store. In a press release, she stated: "I don't think that when the Lord Jesus invited people to remove offending body parts, He intended for them to trade *up*! I don't pretend to have a breadth of knowledge of such things, unlike Dora Denkins, but surely three 12-inch penises in 'Octoroon' should have lasted Martha at least a week! And I would think that a 14-inch uncut penis in 'Caucasian' should be a special order item of exceeding rarity. But according to my spies, Martha is selling both items like hotcakes, while the 6-, 7- and 8-inch penises gather dust. As any white Christian housewife can tell you, these male customers should be ordering tongues, too, because they are clearly lying when they order replacements!"

MEMBER SPOTLIGHT

Eunice Ramsbottom, who devoted her life to counting sins on reality television programs, is dead. She willed her Excel spreadsheet containing 2,340,871 verified transgressions against the Lord to the Landover Foundation for Promoting Moral Decency and Legal Tax Shelters.

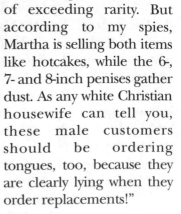

HEATHER'S HOLY HABITS

How to REAR a Child

Mrs. Harry "Heather" Hardwick

What more important topic is there to a lady's mental health than effective child rearing? Nothing can spoil a lady's disposition, not to mention a quiet prayer breakfast on the lanai, than a bunch of unpleasant brats, rudely screaming for food and attention. My time-tested helpful hints can save you from the inconvenience of diverting your quality time with either Savior or shopping cart to tend to intrusive children.

Before we begin, let me emphasize that every Christian lady must endure the unfortunate hardship of raising these little people. Because Eve ate that darn apple, the Lord, who knows no match when it comes to nursing a grudge, has cursed all women throughout time for Eve's overreaching diet. Our only hope for salvation? Bear a passel of children! The Apostle Paul, Jesus' posthumous publicist, tells us this in First Timothy 2:11–15:

> Let the woman learn in silence with all subjection. But I suffer not a woman to teach, nor to usurp authority over the man, but to be in silence. For Adam was first formed, then Eve. And Adam was not deceived, but the woman being deceived was in the transgression. Notwithstanding she shall be *saved in childbearing,* if they continue in faith and charity and holiness with sobriety.

These verses certainly don't bode well for ladies like Ima Jean Tanner, a Platinum Level tither and diabetic. Ima Jean has tried to carry a child to term on seven separate occasions, only to be rebuffed by the Lord each time. We had high hopes when the last of her unborn children reached the onset of the third trimester, but alas, it willfully croaked shortly thereafter, spoiling any hope of her unlikely salvation. The Ladies of Landover maintain vigilant prayer sessions in which we beg the Lord to let Ima Jean make it to the delivery room so that her baby at least exits the womb and cries before it perishes. It's just another of the countless paradoxes of our faith that the difference between spending eternity in bliss and forever in flames is the seemingly subtle difference between SIDS and miscarriage. But it appears that God, too, is in the details.

INTELLIGENT DESIGN IN THE NEWS

Orangutan uses tree branch and rock to make a sundial that is right twice a day.

Once the baby is born, you are not only allowed but required to send it to its Maker if it turns out to be unruly (Deuteronomy 21:21), curses you (Exodus 21:17) or, Heaven forbid, is foul-tempered enough to strike you (Exodus 21:15). Harry and I were committed to having 12 children, all boys, so we could have an entire family of youngsters named after the disciples. (As Harry says, a real man shoots only Ys.) What a shame it took 14 deliveries (and an episiotomy that included two Zip Codes) for us to maintain such a clan. But there will always be one or two rotten apples in a barrel. You sometimes just have to thin the herd.

I don't recommend following the verses that tell us to eat unruly children (Ezekiel 5:10; Deuteronomy 28:53, 57). One needn't follow Weight Watchers to recognize how much excess saturated fat you'd add onto your waistline after digesting a few naughty, well-marbled children. Nevertheless, you can put the fear of God in your offspring by reciting these verses to them whenever they misbehave. Our oldest son, Matthew, didn't open his troublesome mouth for a week after the night I slowly turned up the hot water on his bath—telling him the cute little fun fact that a frog will leap out of a pot of boiling water but will blithely let you boil him alive if you just heat the water incrementally—as I started slicing vegetables into the tub.

Assuming Satan doesn't have a strong grip on your child, and it only misbehaves occasionally, you are nonetheless encouraged to smack the sin out of every little pink behind in the house with a rusty iron belt buckle if you want to keep a smile on Jesus' face. No fewer than three verses in Proverbs tell us so (23:13–14; 22:15; 13:24). Not only does Biblical beating result in children that will rarely interrupt your lovely cappuccino with whining that they need to extrude a smelly poopy, but it also ensures your boys will be of the Hardy, rather than the Nancy, variety. Just make sure that you don't whip them so often that they grow to like it. Goodness me, that can cause problems of its own, as Mrs. Thomas "Tonya" Jergens sadly found out when she discovered that her son, Little Tom, had turned her sewing room into a dungeon.

amazon.com

WELCOME **BOOKS** | YOUR ACCOUNT | HELP

SEARCH | **BROWSE SUBJECTS** | **BESTSELLERS** | **NEW & FUTURE RELEASES** | **BARGAIN BOOKS** | **AWARDS** | **RARE & USED BOOKS**

SEARCH

Banned Book Block™ is active (check with your pastor about deselecting this option)

got blood of the lamb?

Nancy Boy Chrissy

THE BEDWETTING

SISSY!

Nancy-Boy Chrissy, the Bed-Wetting Sissy

—by Pastor Deacon Fred

Now Only: **$28.99**

Summary. Do you know a little someone who seems a bit effeminate? Perhaps the son of a neighbor or acquaintance gives off some ineffable vibe that he is going to grow up craving the taste of semen. What should you, as a concerned Christian, do? Well, *Nancy-Boy Chrissy, the Bed-Wetting Sissy* is just the gift that provides the tools his parents will need to heckle and taunt him back to masculinity.

This beautifully illustrated book tells the story of Christopher Pansy, a 12-year-old boy who is gayer than a tulip tree full of parrots singing Barry Manilow. The boy's foppish femininity annoys the Lord so much that He makes sure that Christopher wakes up each and every morning awash in a clammy pool of urine. Christopher is a constant humiliation to his normal, Christian parents. While other fun-loving boys in the neighborhood are riding bikes and sticking cherry bombs into the anuses of stray cats, Christopher loves to prance about, looking through his telescope, making maps of the stars and taking hot food to shut-ins. His parents try to humiliate him with derisive rhymed chants (CD included), snakes, spankings and the hot side of a Sears iron, but nothing seems to work. Finally, some of the neighborhood's real boys corner Christopher after school behind the gymnasium. They strip the little sissy of all his girlishly clean clothes, righteously tell him that Jesus hates fats and fems ("Know ye not that the unrighteous shall not inherit the kingdom of God? Be not deceived: neither fornicators, nor idolaters, nor adulterers, nor EFFEMINATE, nor abusers of themselves with mankind" 1 Corinthians 6:9), then they sodomize him and throw stones at him until he dies. After this exciting chapter, the Lord Jesus blesses Christopher's parents with a real boy, Rodney, who is a red-blooded sports enthusiast, becoming a Division AAA All-Star in wrestling, captain of his high school's cheerleading squad and costume designer for his high school's production of *Hello, Dolly!*

From the book:

He can't go to camp
He can't have sleepovers
'Cause he gets too excited
And wets all the covers

He sleeps on plastic—
Wears diapers to gym
'Cause he pees on himself
And can't hide his SIN!

Reader Review: *Mrs. Susan Smith, South Carolina* ★★★★★
Sharper than a serpent's tooth is the idea to get rid of an ungrateful child. And when it comes to putting rebellious children to death, the Holy Book hollers, "You go, girl!" It doesn't tell you where to go, but a lake can be mighty handy! I've found that rebellion in children can show itself in many surprising ways. Like when you are fixing to go see that new Mel Gibson movie with your yummy new boyfriend, but can't afford a dang babysitter. You ask yourself, "If he can get away from his wife, why the heck can't I get away from these durn rug rats?" Interfering with your ability to hook-up is just one way that children can be rebellious. They

can also be super-rebellious when you get back to your apartment after spending a several days with the hot-to-death guy who helps the butcher at Publix. All that "where you been, Mommy?" and "we're hungry, Mommy!" rebellion is about as much as any mother should be expected to put up! So I know how Christopher's parents must have felt—big time! After all secular methods fail, his parents finally realized, as so many parents do, that the only *real* cure comes from the Word of God (the Holy Bible) and death puts a welcome end to little Christopher's selfishly ruining his parents' lives with his dang peeing. So whether you get rid of rebellious children *for* liquid or *in* liquid, it's all good!

Reader Review: Mrs. Patsy Ramsey, formerly of Boulder, Colorado ★★★★★
As the mother of a bed wetter, well, FORMER bed wetter, I really enjoyed reading a book that finally saw this annoying problem from the poor parents' side! Folks just don't realize how having a bed wetter in the house can drive you plumb crazy. You wind up doing literally ANYTHING to stop them from messing up your beautiful 100 percent 300-count Italian cotton sheets. Even when you wash the beddings separately, you are still haunted by the idea of particles of bright yellow urine floating around in your washer and spinning, spinning, spinning in your dryer—contaminating all the lovely things you own. There is nothing like being at a party and getting a compliment on a just-washed "He Has Risen!" holiday sweater and wanting to scream at the person: "You probably wouldn't be saying that if you knew it was COVERED in my daughter's piss!"

Pastor Sneezed During an Exorcism Earlier This Week and Sent 14,000 Wild Demons into Occupants of a Passing School Bus

Church members are assured that all children are safe, and the bus has been sprayed with the urine of the saved to remove demons.

Why Can't Halloween Be Both Frightening AND Religious?

Halloween Tips for Holyweeners!

1. Wait for unsaved children to come to your door, then hurl a bucketful of warm lamb's blood (goat or dog blood can be substituted later in the night if you run out) all over their hair and faces. Shout: "*I plead the power of the Blood of the Perfect Lamb over you! Take that, FOUL DEMON!*"

2. Dress up as the freshly resurrected Christ. To make your costume as realistic as possible: (a) use your mother's sewing needles to poke holes in your hands and stomach; (b) wear bluish makeup to look like someone who has been dead and lying around in a cave for a couple of days; and (c) stuff five pounds of week-old hamburger meat in your pockets to smell like rotting flesh. Sneak up behind people, grab them, turn them around, look them in the eyes and scream, "*Why have you forsaken me?*" And then slap them very hard across the face with a palmful of rancid hamburger meat. It will usually scare the living Hell out of little children, and they are sure to remember their first experience with Jesus for the rest of their pathetic lives.

3. Offer to exchange your giant, heavy treat bag with the small bag of an unsaved child—when he gets home, *surprise!* BIBLES!

4. Paint your face black, dress up in a flashy suit and wander around a predominantly colored neighborhood—talking Ebonics into a cell phone about how the Lord Jesus saved you—in a voice loud enough to wake the sleeping winos! This doesn't have to be just for Halloween. You can try this anytime. When they ask what you are talking about, simply reply, "Yo, yo, yo wazzup? I be off da chain for Jesus! I be pimpin' for da playa JC on the fly with mad props."

Once Again, Landover Baptist Leads the Nation in Hell House Innovation By Using Real Corpses This Year

Spooky Holy Ghost Halloween Costumes Are All the Rage at Landover Christian Mall

5. Perform Bible skits at your home. Vincent Price may have thought he was scary, but nothing touches the Lord when it comes to the gruesome and macabre! With baby dolls and ketchup, use your front lawn to stage a realistic reenactment of when the Lord got jealous of Samarians worshipping a rival god and ordered that their children be hacked to pieces and their pregnant women experience the Lord's abortion-by-sword calling card (Hosea 13:16).

6. When trick-or-treaters come to your door, tell them you are no different than the Lord Jesus when it comes to playing host to sinners. Then, take them into your basement (where the heater is set as hot as it will go) and give them a taste of torture.

7. Place a burning cross in your front yard, dress your kids up as ghosts, form a circle around the cross and sing hymns all night.

8. Leave a neat pile of clothing from one complete outfit (don't forget socks and used undies!) for each member of your Christian family on your front lawn. The sight of these righteously sloughed garments will naturally cause visitors to assume that you have all been Raptured away to Heaven, causing them to run screaming from your property with the abject desperation that comes with the knowledge that they have all been left behind to be mauled by the bloody iniquities that await all sinners not teleported to Glory by Jesus.

What Would Scooby-Doo?

From Bambi's aroused cartoon anus to the Little Mermaid's courtesan's décolletage, Landover Baptist youth directors have spent millions of dollars uncovering unholy messages sneakily hidden inside thousands of supposedly innocent secular cartoons. When we began smashing televisions and shooting out the lenses of movie projectors 30 years ago, licentious come-hither stares by little cartoon harlots like Snow White, a sleazy gang-banger with a fetish for men short enough to stick their noses in her business, were created with a grease pencil by filthy old men drooling over a drafting table at Disney. With the advent of computers, thousands of little Oriental anime vaginas can now be created in the time it used to take a panting pedophile at Hanna Barbera to hide one throbbing clitoris in Wilma Flintstone's clothesline.

Nothing, however, prepared us for what we found in the bestiality-friendly series *Scooby-Doo!* It goes without saying that most True Christians™ are already familiar with unattributed rumors and reliable hearsay that the term "scooby-doo" was adopted by Harley Davidson enthusiasts like Jay Leno and Tom Cruise in the late 1970s. "Scooby-doo" is Hell's Angels slang for a "fecal roll." LADIES, PLEASE MOVE ON TO THE NEXT PARAGRAPH NOW! "Scooby" is biker slang made from contracting "scat" and "doobie." It means "a filthy, frolicsome roll about while baked out of your gourd on marijuana." And in case there is any question about what it is they are rolling around in, the "doo" should tip you off—human excrement! A "fecal roll"

Drunken Mexican Spots Virgin Mother in Bowel Movement

After haphazardly relieving himself of Tuesday night's Chalupa Surprise dinner, José Hernández was shocked when he found the Mother of Jesus staring up at him from the linoleum floor of the apartment he shares with 17 friends. Four hours later, after he had transported his stool to a local Catholic church, thousands of Mary-worshippers lined up to get as close as they could stomach to the Virgin Mother. Later that week, it was found that the display violated several sanitation ordinances, thereby allowing the Godly members of Landover Baptist church to act on the Lord's behalf. Health inspectors issued 14 citations against the Roman Church. In addition to Jesus' mother, they carted away a partially decomposed shrunken saint's head and a small glass vial marked "Seed of Jesus."

Mystery Over Millions Missing from Church Account Is Solved!

It has been announced that, after a four-month investigation, Pastor has conclusively determined that Satan was the culprit.

(or "scooby-doo") occurs when a motorcycle gang of filthy, burly, hairy Hell's Angels or other unsightly pagans meet up in a public park, take off all their leather clothes, lay out a large plastic mat with poop all over it, and roll around in it until they have orgasms or are busted by the police, who undoubtedly mistake them for garden-variety homosexuals.

One doesn't have to look too far to see why the motorcycling community was so quick in adopting *Scooby-Doo*. The cartoon is chock-full of decadence. There is Shaggy, a skinny junkie who is always sleepy, hungry and paranoid. If you look closely enough and pray to Jesus, you can actually see the needle marks on his arms. At times during the filming of the cartoon, Shaggy would be so cracked-out, he would even think his own dog was talking to him. The creators were so brazen, they didn't even bother to disguise the fact that Velma is a gruff little bull dyke who represents the radical feminist movement. As

Manslaughter or Miscarriage?
God and the Fourth District Court Have Decided

Mezzanine-level ticket holder Mrs. Jack "Marcie" Davies, was convicted of third-degree murder in connection with the death of her four-day-old zygote last Tuesday. The jury returned a unanimous verdict after it learned that Mrs. Davies, despite being in the family way, continued to attend "step aerobics" classes at the Freehold YWCA. During a "reverse donkey kick" on the bench, Mrs. Davies slipped and carelessly landed on her belly. She then made her way to the restroom and her four-day-old son the jury named Jeremiah made his way into the Freehold sewer system. The jury sentenced Mrs. Davies to 20 years in a maximum security prison cell with hard labor. Pastor expressed the church's universal support for the verdict by stating: "Look, regardless of what she did to this precious, precocious bundle of joy called Jeremiah, Marcie deserved every day of prison time she got. As someone who has watched those so-called 'ladies' at the YWCA on many an afternoon from the safety of the parking lot, I am here to tell you that that those licentious gals hopping up on those plastic steps during one of those aerobics classes are indistinguishable to the disgusted Lord from one of them harlots wrapping her lusty legs around a metal pole at several seedy establishments on Bourbon Street. Particularly the ones closest to Canal Street."

such, she is, of course, an ugly-looking woman with unflattering glasses who is always reading books favored by the intellectual elite and is often bossing the stronger gender around. One never sees her little cartoon armpits, but it is safe to assume that they are shockingly hirsute.

In the character of Fred, we are subjected to a cartoon depiction of the typical wealthy homosexual male who hangs out with blond heterosexual men who do enough mind-numbing drugs to make them susceptible to buggery. His choice in fey clothing, not usually seen outside of John Travolta's cabin crew, is enough to raise the cautious eyebrows of any concerned Christian parent. Further evidence of his depravity exists in his telltale lack of interest in the character of Daphne, a female prostitute who never has anything significant to offer the group other than a harlot's smile and unclothed cartoon legs, coyly akimbo, which Landover Baptist Youth Pastor Richard N. Moff reports, "cause noticeable arousal in young boys even before they reach puberty."

The characters of *Scooby-Doo* travel in a van (an enclosed vehicle suggesting deviant activity occurring within) that may as well have an "If the van is rockin', don't come a'knockin'" sign on the back. They use this roving pothouse/bordello to go from town to town looking for ghosts that aren't holy and bloodthirsty Wiccans, and to consult with pagans who are familiar with spirits and, no doubt, the local jails. In other words, the entire show is a siren call to innocent young children to turn their hearts over to Satan and their more naughty places over to the carnal delight of itinerant strangers.

Christian parents are hereby on notice: If you allow your children to watch this secular, hedonistic propaganda, don't be surprised if you walk down to your rumpus room one morning to find them rolling about in your sculptured shag carpeting covered in their own filth!

WELCOME TO HELL HOUSE

Hell House Map Key

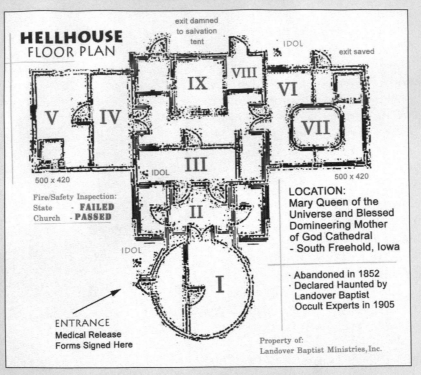

HELLHOUSE FLOOR PLAN

exit damned to salvation tent

IDOL

exit saved

IX   VIII

VI

V   IV

VII

III

IDOL

500 x 420

Fire/Safety Inspection:
State - **FAILED**
Church - **PASSED**

II

IDOL

I

500 x 420

LOCATION:
Mary Queen of the Universe and Blessed Domineering Mother of God Cathedral - South Freehold, Iowa

· Abandoned in 1852
· Declared Haunted by Landover Baptist Occult Experts in 1905

ENTRANCE
Medical Release Forms Signed Here

Property of:
Landover Baptist Ministries, Inc.

Instructions:

Stay with your group at all times. Form a single-file line when moving from room to room and cover your shoes with the plastic booties available at the gift shop if you are concerned about what blood and human excrement may do to fine leather. The gruesome tableaux of carnage will not begin until your entire party is inside a room and the iron doors are bolted and locked behind you. Horseplay or unsavory language will not be tolerated. If you thumb your nose at any of these rules, you will be yanked by the collar from your group and dragged to the Salvation tent by burly guards dressed as Catholic nuns. Landover Baptist will not be responsible for what might happen to you once you are there.

I. **The Abortion Room.** After signing your medical release form, you will enter the liberal world of 24/7, nonstop abortions-on-demand. A Jewish doctor reaches into an unsaved harlot's naughty regions and pulls out an adorable nine-week-old fetus wearing a cute velvet Little Fauntleroy outfit. With a ghastly scream, the doctor removes his bejeweled yarmulke to reveal sharp red horns. Delighted, the illegal alien mother begins screaming, "*Mate mi bebé! Mate mi bebé!*" The doctor smiles and wildly swings the umbilical cord like a sloppy lariat, splattering the spectators with a mucouslike liquid, as the centrifugal force finally sends the screaming baby over the audience where it splats against the brick wall behind them. Blood will then fall from the ceiling and cover the entire crowd as they are hurried out of the room.

II. **The Democrat Room.** Here you will experience more vile horrors of life under the extreme liberal agenda. A Hillary Clinton impersonator snatches your Chinese assault rifles out of your warm, live hands! Your children are taught that homosexuals are over 60 percent human! You pay taxes while shiftless, good-for-nothing minorities gorge on fried chicken and watch *Oprah* all day on high-definition TVs while you work! Onsite Republican voter registration is required to leave the room (minimum registration: two states).

III. **The Drunkard's Hell.** A horrific journey into the trail of full airbags and empty booze bottles left by alcoholics woozily weaving their way along America's roads. A father who had a beer an hour before driving realizes he has just killed his family. Cradling his dying child with one hand, he uses his free hand to riddle his writhing, drunk body with bullets until, finally, he lurches toward the onlookers, causing a spray of warm, liquor-laced blood to splatter the unsaved crowd. Suddenly, seeing a bottle of Jack Daniels under a smoldering car tire, he flings his screaming daughter back into the burning car so he may gulp one last drink of booze before dying.

IV. **The Teen Suicide Autopsy Room.** The doctor asks, "How can this happen?" The mother sobs, "He ignored Jesus' words!" Suddenly, we see little Tommy holding a gun to his shaggy-haired temple as the rapper M&M wails profanely in the background. Jesus appears and blithely observes, "I bet you don't have the nerve to do it, my child." In blasphemous disregard for the holy prophesy, the gun goes off. Using one of the corpses left by the tornado that ripped through Adair County last month, the Christian doctor pulls a heart out of a body and puts it into a jar of formaldehyde labeled: "Heart without a trace of respect for the Word of our Lord."

V. **Marijuana Room.** A preteen drug usage scene where everyone will be surprised who is really in control! The Devil smokes marijuana with an eleven-year-old girl, dressed with a gardenia in her hair to look like Billie Holiday. The once-innocent child instantly becomes "stoned" and screams for the Devil to impregnate her with his magnificent red rod. Given the power of a gorilla by her powerful narcotic, the little harlot tries to overpower the Prince of Darkness and rape him. Fortunately for the audience, before she can tear off Satan's britches, she becomes violently ill and dies of the all too familiar "pot overdose"—just like her idols Janis Joplin and Jimi Hendrix did before her.

VI. **The Prancing Tongued Beast.** This room shows what happens to children (and adults) who are allowed to watch television without a pastor's supervision. Children are huddled around a TV, watching a scene from a popular secular movie. A demonic homosexual monster called Jar Jar Binks appears on the screen and the kids begin to chant, "We love Jar Jar! We love Jar Jar!" Suddenly, Jar Jar appears from behind the TV and begins bumping and grinding to Michael Jackson's P. Y. T. Once Jar Jar has stripped down to his pasties and g-string, he begins slithering his enormous tongue up the shorts of the young boys. The boys squeal in wanton delight until one of them runs off with Jar Jar to get married in a state that voted for John Kerry and Al Gore.

VII. **The Lake of Fire-Dunking Booth.** Sinners from the St. Francis House Homeless Shelter dressed as Pope Benedict XVI, a Methodist, a Mormom, and a Jehovah's Witness taunt the crowd with blasphemous, evil teachings. These shameless heretics sit on a two-by-four plank over forty-eight hibachis filld with burning brimstone and charcoal briquettes to evoke the fires of Hell. The audence is given three minutes per ticket to pelt the hell-bound sinners with KJV Bibles. (Parents are asked to remind their children that while they may delight in seeing the dislodged hobos run "hot-footed" off the burning barbecue grills, there will be no escape for anyone who drops into the real Hell.)

VIII. **Meeting Jesus.** As you enter, the Lord Jesus is seen in all His holy munificence, smiling serenely, in a non-judgmental way, from the White Throne of Judgment. Once the room is filled and the doors slam shut behind the visitors, however, Jesus' face turns into a ferocious scowl as He bellows: "So, you think you have just seen the Hell that awaits you? Don't make Me laugh in your simpering faces! Landover Baptist gave you the chance to be saved and you never took it. You never even picked up one of these preprinted tithing envelopes conveniently located by each exit!" With palpable contempt, Jesus then flings the envelopes into the audience, making sure that they are evenly distributed throughout the crowd, roaring, "Get thee hence, you worthless, penny-pinching unsaved trash!" That will be your signal to pick up an envelope and move to the next room.

IX. **The Final Solution.** Now that the visitors have met the loving Lord Jesus, they will be given one last chance to accept Him as their Personal Savior before being allowed to leave Hell House. In this room they see Bill Clinton rape a live chicken. The chicken is then beheaded, plucked and cooked in tepid broth. The unrepentant souls are then given the choice of eating the demon-infested chicken or going to Hell. (Don't worry, mothers: your children will only *think* they are eating the recently sodomized chicken!) Anyone who refuses to eat the chicken as contrition for their wretchedness and accept Jesus moves to Room 10. This room is the reason for the medical waiver forms that an individual must sign before entering Hell House. Unrepentant souls are beaten and whipped until they call out the name of Christ in voluntarylike love. Come early for preferred seating on the other side of the two-way mirror to witness this miracle of faith. It is an unforgettable twenty minutes. For some, a truly unforgettable night.

MEDICAL RELEASE FORMS MUST BE SIGNED BY A PARENT, PASTOR OR LEGAL GUARDIAN ANGEL BEFORE ENTRY.

Unsaved Trash of the Month Profile: Unmasking Wiccans Without the Inconvenience or Mess of Drowning

"The Wicca Witch of the West"

Churchgoers and local Baptist police officers are now required to undergo extensive training to spot, disable and tag the latest breed of menacing unsaved trash roaming America. They call themselves Wiccans, but are more accurately described, as the True Christian™ Founding Fathers of America labeled them: *witches.* As you will recall, one of these vile, spell-casting miscreants interrupted services last weekend. In an act that can only be described as *pure evil,* a rabid, young pale-faced Wiccan girl, most likely sporting a pierced labia, burst into the 11:00 A.M. Sunday morning service and, with the force of Satan's malice, flung the bloody carcass of a headless black cat across 297 pews. Pastor Deacon Fred ducked just in time as the abomination splashed into the baptismal pool, spattering chunks of kitty flesh and water over the white robes of the choir. Scores of gunshots immediately rang out from the main floor and balconies, as congregants showed their annoyance at the intruder's rude interruption of services. But when the smoke cleared and the screams subsided, the girl had disappeared, apparently callously stepping over the bodies of the poor visitors in the Standing Room section, whom she'd caused to be wounded.

> **Pastor Orders Landover Baptist's "Declaration of Intent to Discriminate" Be Posted in the Amethyst Prayer Room, Listing Over 1,350 Different Types of People We Reserve the Legal Right to Hate Through Christ**

If you observe anyone that fits *any* of the descriptions below, anywhere on church property or in town shopping, Taser them into a catatonic state and call your pastor IMMEDIATELY!

- **Overweight**—Unlike most Christians, who are overweight simply because the Lord has blessed them with so much food, Wiccans are overweight because of gastric bloating. This is why it is very dangerous to light a match near them.

- **Piercings**—Christ had His palms, feet and side pierced on the cross. In a show of blasphemous one-upmanship, Wiccans are wont to pierce almost everything else, including genitals. If you happen to peek over to the next urinal and see a yellowish stream spraying out in three directions (to mock the Trinity), chances are you are watching a witch pee.

- **Dark Clothing**—Wiccans usually wear black. This is not because they are aping New York homosexuals, but because they are extremely sloppy eaters and couldn't get away with slurping a freshly slaughtered sacrifice in white seersucker.

- **Bad Personal Hygiene**—It is a well-known fact that Wiccans only bathe one body part each full moon. As such, they have a ripe, yeasty odor they try too hard to hide with perfumes bought on subway trains, like patchouli or wolfsbane, and light incense bought in adult bookstores, so that their apartments smell like Calcutta brothels.

- **Casting Votes for a Democrat**—If a Wiccan is sober enough to find a polling place, it will cast a vote for a Democrat. In fact, the word "democrat" is rooted in the word "demon." Fortunately, with the advent of electronic touch-screen voting, the counting of a Wiccan's vote is now a thing of the past.

- **Attending Renaissance Festivals**—Wiccans like to purchase knives and swords for ritual killings from master Wicca carnyfolk who will pitch their tents at any festival with a porta-potty. These festivals also allow Wiccans to comfortably blend into crowds of overweight people wearing black leotards and beards.

WEDNESDAY'S SERMON: "If you use faith wisely, not only can you move a mountain, you'll find it's actually an enormous pile of cash!"

Effeminate Man Asked to Leave 11:00 A.M. Service

Mormons Edge Out Moonies, Supply-Side Economics and Tom Cruise to be Named "America's Most Amusingly Far-Fetched Belief System"

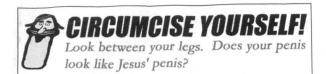

CIRCUMCISE YOURSELF!
Look between your legs. Does your penis look like Jesus' penis?

DO-IT-YOURSELF CIRCUMCISION!

FOUR EASY STEPS!   TRY AT HOME!

1. Lay your penis on a flat surface (over the sink is recommended).

2. Using a kitchen knife with a dull blade, begin pressing down on the bothersome pink ring near the uncircumcised tip of your penis.

3. Move the knife back and forth, applying liberal amounts of Crisco oil in the process. Stop when it cuts all the way through, or you hear a "popping" sound.

4. Immediately apply paper towels saturated with Crisco oil to the sacred wound. Wait seven days before returning to church.

WARNING! BEFORE YOU BEGIN:

FOR TRUE CHRISTIAN MEN - If your penis looks like "Figure A," do NOT attempt to perform this procedure! Get your penis into the "Figure B" position before you begin with step 1.

Figure A.

Figure B.

Take Your Faith into Your Own Hands:
Circumcise Yourself

Remember: When trying to be Christ-like, you should overlook no detail. Look between your legs. Does your penis look like Jesus' penis, only smaller?

Find out if you are circumcised:

By using a small mirror (use a full-length mirror if you are colored), you can verify that your personal member is a replica of the very penis Jesus took to Heaven with Him.

For this procedure you will need: A kitchen knife, a can of Crisco, a roll of paper towels, and a penis.

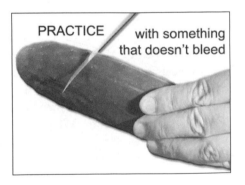

PRACTICE with something that doesn't bleed

Book Burning:
A True Christian™ Tradition

s every True Christian™ knows, everyone needs to read only one book in his life: the Bible. All the rest (except *Salvation for Dummies*) are at best useless and very likely dangerous. If you ever find yourself being grateful for the eradication of seditious works by pagan nincompoops like Socrates, Plato and Aristotle, you have a Christian to thank! The burning of books is as much a True Christian™ tradition as renouncing the stupid doctrines of all other Christians. Indeed, the Holy Bible teaches us that burning someone's books is a great way spread God's word.

> Many of them also which used curious arts brought their books together and burned them before all men and they counted the price of them and found it fifty thousand pieces of silver. So mightily grew the word of God and prevailed (Acts 19:19–20).

During Pentecost, in the early days of Christianity, new believers in Christ discovered that the Holy Spirit had lit little bonfires over their heads. This provided a convenient place to burn the supposedly sacred writings of faiths competing for the same demographic as our new faith. This joyous fad caught on quickly—even amongst believers without handy little pilot lights hovering over their heads.

Book burning reached its glorious heyday in Florence, Italy, with the advent of the first Catholic to act like a Southern Baptist, Girolamo Savonarola, during the always-hard-to-top "Bonfire of the Vanities." Sadly, it has been all downhill from there. Under the spell of Christianity's greatest enemy (the Enlightenment), people began the dangerous trend of reading and writing even more books than they burned. Then came the horrible day when children weren't even allowed to read the Bible nonstop in school. They were, however, allowed to read the smutty works of that miniskirt- and pantyhose-wearing William Shakespeare, and the unintelligible drunken ramblings of Muriel Hemingway.

"As an unwavering Republican, I have, quite naturally, burned more books than I have read."

Fire Marshall Will Conduct Safety Seminar for Christian Children:

"Don't play with matches— unless you are standing next to a big pile of books!"

Creation Scientists Prove That the Choice to Become a Homosexual Is Most Often Made Between the Hours of 10:00 P.M. and Midnight

After far too much reading for anyone's good, American Christians recently cottoned on to the ingenious concept of combining two historical eras to create a new, even better one: this century's "Renaissance of the Dark Ages." Once again, reading (especially about evolution) is frowned upon and book bannings (which are nothing more than environmentally friendly book burnings) are all the rage. Secular humanists and Atheists have been sent into a tailspin trying to make pious book burners look bad.

The real truth is, burning a book is one of the most loving things Christians can do for a person they really care about who is found flipping through a questionable novel at the grocery store checkout counter. Landover Baptist Church is proud to sponsor America's Largest Book Burning on Satan's Birthday, October 31. Each year the event is held, the number of attendees and books burned grows like a grin on the good Lord's face when He smells the sweet smoke from our book pyres pouring into Heaven, as secular ideas are turned to soot. This year we expect over 152,000 citizens of Jesusland to show up to burn over 3.4 million books! As usual, the event will start with Pastor Deacon Fred's ceremonial lighting of a first edition copy of *Valley of the Dolls*. Next, children from Landover Baptist's pre-K program will light the Koran kindling around the base of the bonfire.

As the fire rages, Deacon Fred will read his ceremonial speech, explaining the excitement behind metaphorically showing that non-Christian thinkers are blowing smoke. "The Truly Saved all across America are calling upon the name of Jesus this Halloween to decrease the number of Harry Potter books currently circulating in America by at least 70 percent. We're giving True Christian™ schoolchildren the Biblical authority to remove these evil books from their school libraries, bookstores, homes, grocery stores and anywhere they find them. All they need to say is, Give me that book! *Jesus needs it for burning!* Friends, let's help this great country return to its True Christian™, nonreading roots. Won't you please join God's people across America as they turn the heat up for Jesus by setting up a Holy Ghost book fire at your local church this Halloween? In His name, Amen."

Mind-Altering Red Bull Energy Drink Turns Senior High Bible Study into Godless Sex Orgy

Over the last year, several isolated sexual incidents involving the popular liquid methamphetamine drink Red Bull were reported to church security. The lewd nature of each case led Pastor to request that Landover Baptist's esteemed Creation Science Laboratory open up a privately funded investigation.

The lab conducted a month-long study in which no fewer than 2,000 cases of Red Bull were consumed by Landover Baptist Church deacons. These deacons served as volunteer test cases, and several of them are now hospitalized after having rubbed all of the skin off of the heads of their penises in vigorous and repeated behavior connected with the experiment. Creation Scientist Dr. Jonathan Edwards believes their condition resulted from intensive tests where each deacon was stripped of his clothes and placed in isolation for 72 hours with 200 cans of Red Bull, a plastic Ziploc bag full of Ecstasy tablets and a wide assortment of adult magazines recently confiscated from pastors returning from missionary pilgrimages in Thailand. "We were scrupulously trying to re-create the sex-crazed, raver environment of the typical person who gulps down can after can of this potent, mind-altering beverage," said Dr. Edwards.

"We knew kids were getting high off this legal crack in a can," said Dr. Edwards. "We also knew that since the product was released, the rate of teenage pregnancies has skyrocketed. And many pediatricians have reported seeing seriously calloused penises—a sign that some local men were masturbating at dangerously high speeds. The drug community calls it *speed jacking*," said Dr. Edwards. "The tests we performed just confirmed our assumptions that this so-called 'energy drink' is nothing more than liquid sin in a tin. They can't call it crank, because that is illegal, so they slyly call it Red Bull, and no one thinks anything of it."

When the Board of Deacons, through hidden cameras, discovered unreported incidents of young people in the Senior High Youth Group accidentally getting sexed up off Red Bull, the board concluded further investigation was warranted. "They chug down a few cans so they

Holy Ghost Back to Haunting the Old Williams' Mansion

can stay up and memorize Scripture verses at Bible Study, only to find that they have been taken over by the Devil in that tin can, and their Bible Study turns into a godless sex orgy!" reported Dr. Edwards. "They get so cranked up on the methamphetamine in this Devil's brew that they start to shake all over—including in their moist little teenage groin areas. And you know what happens when young folks' sinful parts start to tingle and shake—it's like popping open a hot can of just-shook Pepsi!"

Dr. Edwards revealed a startling discovery made after a few drops of Red Bull were placed under a Bible Scope in the Creation Science Lab. "You may think that this drink just tastes like harmless suntan lotion, but this so-called 'energy drink' is carbonated bull urine, with pineapple flavoring and enough crystal meth to get a whole housing project full of Negroes flapping their feet as fast as hummingbird wings, tap-dancing up and down the streets until dawn," he reported.

Local Restaurants Respond to Landover's Showing of *The Passion of the Christ*

After Landover Baptist Church began weekly mandatory matinees for Mel Gibson's *The Passion of the Christ,* local restaurateurs throughout Freehold are noticing that there is one thing their saved patrons now crave more than anything: *blood.* "None of them Baptists orders their steaks well done no more," remarked Trixie Turnstyle, waitress at the Fatted Calf Steak House. "In fact, most folks ask us not to bother cooking at all, so that all the blood from their

prime rib can pool on the plate and be slurped up in an ecstatic frenzy while the rest of the table screams Jesus' name." Many restaurants are being asked to leave the skin on meats so that the diner can flail and lacerate the hide for 90 minutes with their pocketknives.

There is so much blood being splattered around the Leviticus Outlet Mall Sizzler these days, the restaurant went through 137 lobster bibs yesterday without serving a single lobster. "We have really made a killing since we changed the name of the drink from Bloody Mary to Bloody Jesus!" squealed corpulent Dave Dial, bartender at the local Thank Our Lord and Savior It's Friday. "We now serve it with a nine-inch nail instead of a stick of celery. And we offer two kinds: Type O (well brand) and Type A (premium). While we're still lucky to get a tip other than a Bible tract from those folks, it is fun to watch them reach for their wallets after forgetting they covered their palms with V8 juice."

LANDOVER BAPTIST CHURCH

"A Rising Tithe Lifts All Yachts"

Traditional Thanksgiving Festivities Ruined by Real Injuns

Local Holiday Alert

SERMON BY PASTOR DEACON FRED

Every year, local savages insist on playing a role in Landover Baptist Church's authentic retelling of the Thanksgiving miracle. They stay boozed up all year, worshipping stuff everyone can plainly see, like the sky, instead of the invisible guy who lives in it. And then they show up one morning in November, expecting all of us proper folks to roll out *the red carpet*, as if we call it that because of them! Well, I'm putting those inebriated opportunists on notice: We Christians have learned a lot since our forefathers in angry prudery, the Pilgrims, got to America. For one thing, there is no way in tarnation we would set up shop in a Blue State known for Kennedys and marrying off nancy-boys. For another, we are a bit more selective about whom we sup with nowadays. And we're not about to issue invitations to unsaved savages who will tear our scalps off just so the Ben Afflecks of their tribe can walk around wearing hair the Lord gave to us—even if we do get their recipe for corn casserole as a thank-you! To protect our turkeys from theft and our womenfolk from licentious pleasure, dogs specially trained to sniff out feathers—and gin made from ingredients found at any drugstore—have been stationed throughout the church perimeter.

Let it be known that we hold no unusual hatred toward these Injun folks. Indeed, we don't hate them more than we hate anyone—and even less than we hate a whole mess of other folks. It is their sin that we hate: homemade booze breath, unprescribed drug use by someone who isn't a radio personality, foul or indecipherable language, calling each other by names best left to household pets, loitering, impudence, gambling, wild and noisy horseplay, lewd attire, downright audacity, misuse of leather goods and long hair on men who don't kill themselves for our sins. Landover Baptist Church will not taint our respectable Christian image by fellowshipping with Injuns (2

This Week's Sermon:

"Ask an Injun: 'How Many Casino Chips Is Your Salvation Worth?' You Will Be Pleasantly Surprised with His Answer!"
—Pastor Deacon Fred

How, buddy! You're going straight to Hell!

Corinthians 6:14) and we stand by Jesus' policy to avoid all social intermingling with those with reputations for evil, whether they be harlots, Midianites, rappers, Egyptian pharaohs, Democrats or Injuns (1 Thessalonians 5:22).

Before any of you start feeling sorry for these miserable, uninvited creatures, understand that we're not dealing with casino-owning Injuns who have the decency to cut their hair, wipe their red bottoms, don a collared shirt and tie, attend church on Sunday mornings and send a check to a Republican lobbyist! No, these local savages not only still worship false gods and have hair longer than Crystal Gayle, but not one of the useless pelt-wearing boozehounds owns even a basement roulette wheel, much less fronts a Harrah's for the enormous Caucasian gambling industry. So it is really hard to justify going to all the time and expense of bringing them to Jesus when they can't tithe one Indian nickel when they get there!

Girl Blames Pregnancy on Horny Spirit

An unwed Baptist teenager who found herself in the family way told her parents last week that she had never known a boy sexually. Instead, she blamed the pregnancy on an encounter with an invisible ghost who complimented her on being so surprisingly free of sin. She was immediately slapped senseless by her annoyed parents and sent to Pastor, who threw her out of the church. "The whole idea of a spirit flattering a young girl in hopes of diddling her lady parts is such a preposterous, lewd proposition," said Pastor Deacon Fred. "Frankly, I don't know where this little scallywag got the idea for such an outrageous, bald-faced lie."

Porn-Again Christians Bring the Gospel to X-Rated DVDs

"To the weak became I as weak, that I might gain the weak: I am made all things to all men, that I might by all means save some." —*1 Corinthians 9:19*

"To the viewer of pornography became I as a producer of pornography, that I might win those viewers to Christ." —*Rev. Douglas A. Crowther, Founder: Porn-Again Productions*

Landover Baptist's wholly owned, Bible-based company, Porn-Again Productions, is making sure that Christ's message reaches even people formerly believed to be wholly lost to Satan by less tenacious Christian ministries. Porn-Again Productions began marketing slick, sexually explicit adult entertainment two years ago— *with a big difference.* In each film, whether the star is being gang-banged in a sling by godless, hairy, uncircumcised Muslims, or simply getting popped in the eye with a money-shot from a *Watchtower*-spanking Jehovah's Witness at her doorstep, she always takes whatever happens to be in her mouth out long enough to talk about the Good News that Jesus died on the cross for the masturbating viewers' sins.

Whether based on the Old Testament (*The Garden of Eating*), the New Testament (*The Sermon on the Mounting*) or contemporary Christian fiction (*LEFT in my BEHIND*), each feature has all of its dialogue lifted directly from the pages of the Bible. In fact, the Almighty received a surprise Best Screenplay Lucite dildo trophy at last year's Adult Video Awards for the prurient things He wrote for the DVD release *Bathshe-male and David.* "Some folks think that using the Lord's Word would make our movies more chaste than your run-of-the-mill gonzo porn flick,"

Bible Quiz

Are there times when prostitution is perfectly acceptable?

A. Yes. When the money raised by a whore is used to support needy Christians (but *not* her TV ministry).

B. No. The Bible never refers to "acceptable" prostitution, as the Bible was written before Donald Trump was old enough to marry.

C. Yes. If a hooker is providing pro boner "services" to a widower out of the goodness of her heart of gold.

D. None of the above.

Answer: A. "And it shall come to pass after the end of seventy years, that the Lord will visit Tyre, and she shall turn to her hire, and shall commit fornication with all the kingdoms of the world upon the face of the earth. And her merchandise and her hire shall be holiness to the Lord: it shall not be treasured nor laid up; for her merchandise shall be for them that dwell before the Lord, to eat sufficiently, and for durable clothing" (Isaiah 23:17–18).

Guest Speakers: Phyllis Schlafly and Lynne Cheney. Topic:

"Not Letting the Horror of Waking Up to Find That Your Child Has Decided to Be a Damned Homosexual Tempt You into Rethinking Your Position on Partial-Birth Abortions"

said Rev. (and stunt dick) Douglas Crowther, "but, man, you only hear crap like that from folks who haven't really read their Bibles cover to cover!"

Indeed, Porn-Again Productions just finished a film called *The Passion of the Cum-Guzzling Slut* based on the exploits of Oholibah in Ezekiel. ("For she doted upon their paramours, whose flesh is as the flesh of asses, and whose issue is like the issue of horses" Ezekiel 23:20). "Tell me that wasn't difficult to cast and still be true to God's Word," said director Rev. Billy Armstrong. "I mean, the Lord can sure write some hot trash, but He doesn't think about the fact that we can't just make these people out of dirt or ribs like He can. We've got to go out in alleyways and Catholic girls schools to find these freaks!"

"Yes, our films are full of hot, nasty action," says Rev. Crowther. "But also, with Spirit-filled proselytizing. Each film is sort of like a Chick Bible tract—only with real chicks. While a guy is boning the babe, she gets to read Matthew to him. We work in both Luke and Matthew in the double penetration shots—they make everyone feel good 'cause we're saving twice the souls, you know. In fact, Porn-Again is reaching thousands of lost guys every week. You see, they start the downloading addicted to porno, but by the end, many wipe themselves off and find that they are addicted to Jesus! Praise!"

Christian film critic Michael Medved has praised Porn-Again for both its style and message. "Anyone who has been to a Charismatic church and seen hideously overweight people writhing on the floor, moaning and screaming 'Oh, God! Oh, Jesus! Take me! God, I'm coming now!,'" says Mr. Medved, "will enjoy seeing the same scene—only, this time, with people who don't make you lose your lunch. After all, the line between sexual and spiritual ecstasy has always been a bit blurred. Indeed, I think Porn-Again's all-girl video based on Bernini's *Ecstasy of St. Theresa* was riveting and brought clever new meaning to the phrase 'the staff of life.' And it certainly adds to the dramatic tension of each scene in *The Res-Erection!* when the Christian lady won't let any man climax until he accepts Jesus as his personal Lord and Savior. If the Almighty had thought of such incentives, there would be a lot more people in Heaven right now, my friend."

Godly Tips on How to Beat the Stuffing Out of Your Christian Child

"The blueness of a wound cleanseth away evil: so do stripes the inward parts of the belly." —*(Proverbs 20:30)*

From the Freehold Chapter of Concerned Busybodies for America

1. Be sure you leave marks. A Christian parent must understand that children will never learn a lesson unless they are beaten on their naked bottoms until the imprint of the rugged cross is plainly visible on both cheeks (Proverbs 23:13–14). A youngster who can sit comfortably after a Godly beating will think he has outsmarted you and tend to repeat the misdeed, while feeling a license to move on to more hard-core sins like blasphemy, watching the Discovery Channel and rape. If a child is able to sit down within three days of punishment without ointment or a bag of frozen vegetables, you may as well resign yourself to having created an unsaveable hellion.

Selfless Missionary Called to Ski

God has called Rev. Horace Walt to move to Beaver Creek, Colorado, and "ski for Jesus." Walt (already an avid skier) will combine his love of skiing and knowledge of Jesus in ministering to people in exclusive resorts throughout the western United States. His tax-deductible home base will be a $3.5 million chalet in Beaver Creek, right off the main trail.

2. Use a heavy object. A ruler is too light whereas a beltbuckle may cause bleeding (and intrusive inquiries from nosy liberal schoolteachers if you are careless enough to allow your child to attend a public school). We suggest a heavy King James 1611 authentic cowhide leather-bound Bible rimmed in upholstery tacks.

3. Find a comfortable place to sit so you may lure a wicked child to punishment. Act as if there is nothing amiss. We suggest that you smile or wink at your child. If it is your daughter, say, *"Come on over here and sit on daddy's lap, sweetheart. I want to talk to my little angel for a minute."* If it is your son, we suggest you say, *"Hey there, sonny, how's Dad's little quarterback? Come on over here and sit on my lap for a minute. Jesus has something He wants me to give you."*

4. As soon as you have the child on your lap, clench his hands like you've just caught a rabbit. Immediately flip the child over so that his stomach is across your knees. If the child struggles, give him a good whack across the back of his head and tell him to freeze in the name of God in Heaven. Whisper into his ear, *"You're going to get a whole lot worse from Jesus when you are in Hell, you rebellious, hateful little sissy!"*

5. Stifle the brat. At this point, the child may be acting like a little demon and screaming. Be prepared for such wicked outbursts. Have an athletic sock in your back pocket and, if need be, stuff it all the way into your child's ornery mouth until the stripes at the top of the socks touch his lips. Don't worry: If the child is smart enough to remember to breathe through his nose, he won't suffocate.

6. Pull down the child's pants and underwear to reveal the pink little heinie. Make sure both cheeks are fully exposed, as parental punishment must be balanced to be fair.

7. Ready your Bible and lift it high above your head with one hand. Keep the child secure with your free hand. Clench the back of your child's neck like a Pentecostal grabbing an angry rattler. If the child struggles, we suggest you raise your voice and say something like, *"Jesus is fixing to give you something to squirm over, you little devil!"*

8. Smack the child across the bottom with the Bible as you speak out the imp's horrible misdeed. Each word would be one healthy whack across its naked hindquarters. For example: *"YOU [WHACK!] DIDN'T [WHACK!] EAT [WHACK] YOUR [WHACK] BRUSSELS [WHACK] SPROUTS [WHACK!] YOU [WHACK!] LITTLE [WHACK!] DEMON! [WACK!],"* finishing off with lighter "cool-down" whacks: *did [whack!] "you?" [whack!]"*

9. Rebuke the child in the sweet name of Jesus, toss it aside like a used Kleenex and let it roll to the floor to contemplate its sinful nature.

10. Mentally terrorize the child. After about an hour, when the child has calmed down, have him sit on your lap again and read him some Scripture verses about Hell. We recommend Matthew 13:41–42 from the same Bible you used to beat him with. Let the child know that the punishment he received today is nothing compared to the eternal loving, sadistic tortures of Hell where Jesus burns and cooks all the bad little boys and girls who don't do what their daddy tells them to do.

Landover Garden Club disbands, declaring, "With the Rapture almost certain to happen this year, it is not only a waste of money to plant trees and perennials, it is a very dangerous rebuke to the promise of a returning Lord."

Bible Quiz

Which of the following may lead to you and all your descendants being cursed?

A. Stripping off all your clothes and lying around naked, for others to see your possibly aroused willywhacker.

B. Getting so drunk you pass out naked, allowing your whole village to see you and have the opportunity to take turns dipping your hand in hot water to see if you pee on yourself.

C. Accidentally seeing someone who has drunkenly passed out without a stitch of clothing and letting others know of this shameless debauchery.

D. A and B only.

Answer: C. "And Noah . . . planted a vineyard: and he drank of the wine, and was drunken; and he was uncovered within his tent. And Ham, the father of Canaan, saw the nakedness of his father, and told his two brethren without. . . . And Noah awoke from his wine, and knew what his younger son had done unto him, and he said, Cursed be Canaan; a servant of servants shall he be unto his brethren" (Genesis 9:20–25).

Vegans: Modern-Day Witches!

SERMON BY BROTHER HARRY HARDWICK

Friends, as the End Times approach, Satan has sent a new kind of witch to act as a siren, drawing weak-minded liberals to the horrors of Hell. The front porch cauldrons these witches maintain contain parsley and brussels sprouts rather than insects and rodent tongues, but don't let that fool you. Whether eye of newt or minestrone is the specialty of the house, when cult fare doesn't include the blood of the Lamb, there is something wickedly anti-Christian going on! And whether someone tells you she is a "vegan" or levels with you and tells you the truth—that she is a follower of Satan—don't wait until she

slips on a pointy black hat to realize you are in the presence of a vegetable-chomping witch.

One needn't look any further than Christ's words to see that so-called "vegans" are nothing more than sorcerers and troublemakers, mocking God while trying to turn His Son's lavishly catered Last Supper into something that can be whipped up in one cast iron pot. They know very well that God loves meat and has ordered humans to eat as much of it as we can. So these fiendish vegan witches spout off anti-Christian slogans like "Meat is murder" and insist their members abstain from consuming anything that comes from an animal. Hogwash! Jesus warned us about these diabolical cretins:

> Now the Spirit speaketh expressly, that in the latter times some shall depart from the faith, giving heed to seducing spirits, and doctrines of devils; Speaking lies in hypocrisy; having their conscience seared with a hot iron; Forbidding to marry, and *commanding to abstain from meats, which God hath created to be received with thanksgiving of them which believe and know the truth* (1 Timothy 4:1–2).

The Bible makes clear that God created animals for one purpose only—to wind up on our plates, backs and trophy room walls. Like the universe's first waiter, God told us: "Every moving thing that liveth shall be meat for you" (Genesis 9:3). Every moving thing—not just the ugly ones, not just the dumb ones, like chickens and fish. *Every living thing.* According to God, even the cutest animal in the world is nothing more than muscles to be stuffed into sausage casings!

When the Apostle Peter woke up hungry, what did God give him to eat? Not a cut-rate reception's platter of carrot sticks, lettuce leaves and orange slices. He gave him every type of four-footed beast on the Earth and every fowl of the air, telling him, "Rise, Peter, kill, and eat" (Acts 10:9–13). Verily, it is no wonder that He is known as the Host of Hosts! When Cain and Abel

Unsaved Witness Claims Dead Mormon Missionaries Found on Farmer Rawlings's Front Porch Were Last Seen Alive Just About to Knock on His Door

offered gifts to the Lord, Abel gave the Lord the fat he cut off the hides of his flock whereas Cain gave the Lord fruit and crudités. The Lord loved Abel's offering of something that would stick to His holy ribs and despised Cain's laughable attempt at catering. Cain became jealous and murdered the brother with the superior gift-giving eye (Genesis 4:3–8). This was the first human murder committed by these vegans (a/k/a witches/Wiccans). But, rest assured, it won't be the last.

DESIGNS ON INTELLIGENCE FUN FACT:

The amount of hogwash and gibberish they'll listen to before saying: "Wait a minute, that's the stupidest thing I've ever heard!"

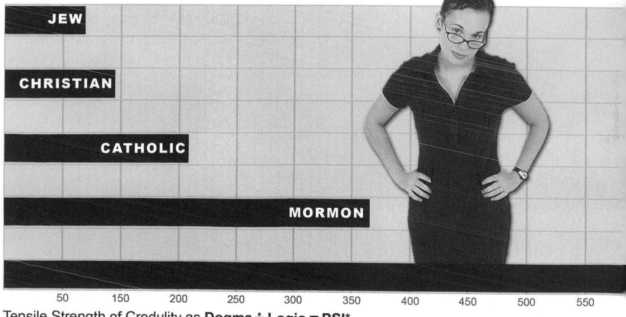

| JEW | CHRISTIAN | CATHOLIC | MORMON |

50   150   200   250   300   350   400   450   500   550

Tensile Strength of Credulity as **Dogma ÷ Logic = PSI***
*Proven Scriptural Inconsistencies

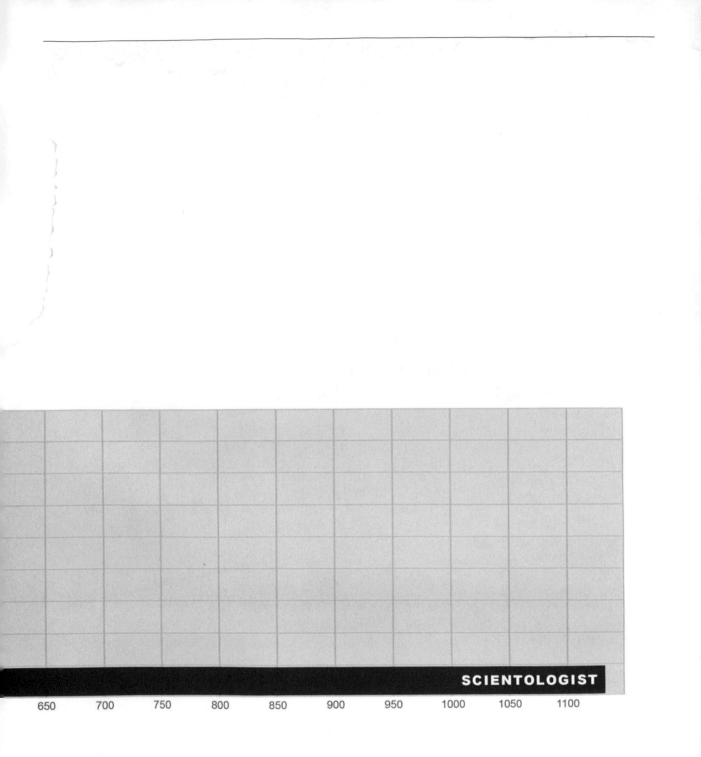

SCIENTOLOGIST

650   700   750   800   850   900   950   1000   1050   1100

Christmastime: When Santa Turns Every Macy's into Neverland Ranch

Friends, the word "Santa" is more than just an anagram for "Satan." That pompous, overweight lech you see slumped on his red throne in every mall that litters this once Godly country *is* Satan, himself! Only, instead of being surrounded by naked red demons and burning brimstone, he is surrounded by creepy little elves in tight green leotards and Styrofoam candy canes. Why, did you know that "Santa Clause" is Olde English for "Satan's Claws"? Yes indeed! Every year, greedy department stores in the Beast Master's thrall celebrate our Savior's birth by calling forth thousands of foul-smelling winos from under America's crack whores and underpasses. These filthy homeless hobos lay on their urine-stained cardboard beds 11 months out of the year, hiccupping store-brand Listerine and dreaming of Christmas, when they can drunkenly traipse into the warmth of American department stores and have innocent little Christian children squirm on their vermin-infested laps. Unwary parents happily snap scores of digital photos while these obese drunks luridly slur the hopeful inquiry: "Tell me, have you been *bad?*" Satan's disappointment with a negative response usually fuels a lewd suggestion, whispered with fetid booze-breath into the child's ear through crusty, nicotine-stained lips. These sex-starved predators "ho ho ho" simply to kill time, waiting until inattentive parents carelessly turn their attention to admire a five-foot gingerbread house. This is an opening for a fat red demon with a white beard to indulge in a furtive, lingering grope before his scantily clad little helpers hurriedly move the cherubic victim along to make way for the next victim waiting in line.

There is hope, though, for True Christians™ to stop Satan from co-opting the holiest of days.

This Week's Sermon:

"Hell: Mostly Chinese and Injun"
—*Pastor Deacon Fred*

Last Week's Favorite Hymn:

"Return O Lord
—And Step on It!"

JESUS IS THE REASON FOR THE SEASON!

And He's also the reason you are going straight to HELL!

Parental Pointers for Outsmarting Santa/Satan:

Tip one: Let your children know that every time they ask Santa for something, they are literally praying to Lucifer himself. Don't let the Devil slip down your chimney, into your True Christian™ living room, folks! Know that every Barbie and assault rifle from Santa is coming SOD (Soul on Delivery) from Satan. When Lucifer tempts your children with things like an Xbox or eternal youth, teach them to bellow: *"We are on to you, Mr. Satan! And we unmask thee, Thou Greatest Deceivereth! We spew Godly globs of sacred spit upon thee—and behold them sizzling on thy dumbstruck face! Get thee hence from Baby Jesus' birthday party! Shoo, demon!"*

Tip two: Next time your family sees some propped-up, gin-soaked vagrant in a mall wearing a red suit with white furry cuffs, set a good example for folks less fervent in their faith. Witness to the other deluded people waiting in line by saying something to get their children's attention. Try, for example, "Santa does not exist! He is a lie your unsaved parents told you because they don't love Jesus." NOTE: Now is a good time to point at Santa, raise your Bible into the air and hurl it straight at the demon's head! If you accidentally wing the child in his lap, don't fret. An unconscious child can more easily be pried from the Devil's clutches than one corrupted with promises of toys and candy.

Tip three: Incite chaos at the foot of Santa's altar by shouting, "I'm coming for you, Satan!" Knock him off his throne, hold your Bible high above your head, and point down at Santa, yelling: "This man is Satan's surrogate! He will ravage your nubile little bodies with his filthy, fumbling fingers, sully your soul with suggestions of debauchery and eventually drag your palpitating carcasses down to the fires of Hell!" At this point, you will have gotten the attention of even casual shoppers. Use this as an opportunity to hand out Gospel tracts telling them they are going to Hell, too. Remember: It is only through setting good examples such as these that we can put the *Christ* back in Christmas.

Pastor Startles Local Den Mother After Telling Her Cub Scout Troop: "I Walk Around with Confidence Because I Have Jesus, Not Because I Have the Most Enormous Penis You Are Likely to Ever Lay Eyes On!"

Rectums: The Resort of Choice for Well-Traveled Demons

Folks, you know what is the most reliable sign that Satan has entered your Christian home? No, it isn't hoofprints in your deep-pile carpeting. You see, Satan's little calling card is the smell of sulfur! God tells us in Revelation, chapter 14, that He is going to torment people with fire and brimstone. Friends, do you know what brimstone is? It's sulfur, that's what it is. It's in the center of the Earth in Hell, where Satan and his army of little red demons with pointy tails reside! God, choke me if I'm wrong, but I tell you—when you smell sulfur, you know gosh darn well that

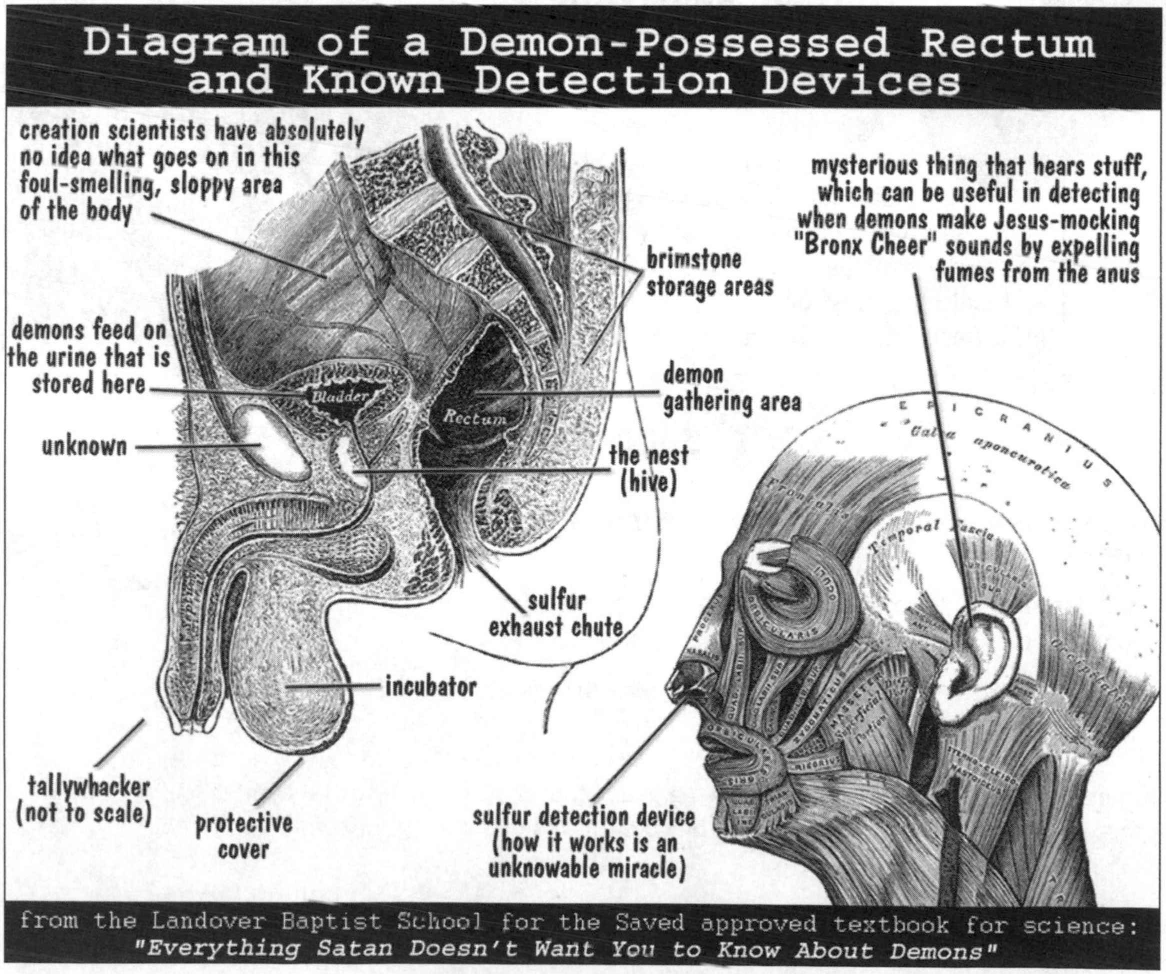

Diagram of a Demon-Possessed Rectum and Known Detection Devices

creation scientists have absolutely no idea what goes on in this foul-smelling, sloppy area of the body

mysterious thing that hears stuff, which can be useful in detecting when demons make Jesus-mocking "Bronx Cheer" sounds by expelling fumes from the anus

brimstone storage areas

demons feed on the urine that is stored here

demon gathering area

unknown

the nest (hive)

sulfur exhaust chute

incubator

tallywhacker (not to scale)

protective cover

sulfur detection device (how it works is an unknowable miracle)

Bladder

Rectum

from the Landover Baptist School for the Saved approved textbook for science: *"Everything Satan Doesn't Want You to Know About Demons"*

Landover Post Office Shut Down!

A crafty demon slipped out of an unsealed envelope from Tehran and afflicted Mrs. Alice Greenville, who was operating the Zip Code sorter, with sores that mimic secular exposure to mustard gas. Out of concern for the postal employees still alive, no mail will be sorted or delivered until further notice unless the envelope is clearly marked "TITHES."

old rascal Lucifer has been running around, making mischief where you live.

Brothers and Sisters, have you ever sat yourself down on the toilet to do nature's necessity and been overwhelmed by the smell of rotten eggs? Sometimes, it's so cotton-pickin' bad you almost wheel around and throw up all over your dirty business that's floating in the bowl. Well, it is the smell of Hell's sulfur that makes you feel so sick. And that is a clear sign that demons are living in your rear end. So, when you smell those ungodly fumes, you need to get yourself down to a Bible-believing church, pronto, and get yourself a Jesus enema, right quick!

MEMBER SPOTLIGHT

Name: Mrs. Helen Floribunda
Age: None of your beeswax
Favorite Things: George W. Bush, Jesus' love, posting on Free Republic that if I was only 65 years younger I would personally strangle every single liberal in America and just tell Jesus they died of shame, and firing off a fresh round while waiting on a pie crust.

Bible Quiz

What spoken word or words can earn you a one-way ticket to Satan's molten torture chamber?

A. None. Our faith is not one of hexes and incantations, so God would never condemn someone merely for uttering a special word.

B. Saying, "Satan is a bit misunderstood. There are things about the bloke I rather like."

C. Calling someone a fool.

D. Erroneously accusing someone of following gods other than the one with a capital "G," resulting in that person being savagely executed by bored townsfolk looking for something to do.

Answer: C. "But I say unto you, That whosoever shall be angry with his brother without a cause shall be in danger of the judgment: and whosoever shall say to his brother, Raca, shall be in danger of the council: but whosoever shall say, Thou fool, shall be in danger of hell fire" (Matthew 5:22).

KEWL KIDZ 4 CHRIST

As Filthy Sinners, Do Children Deserve Anything for Christmas This Year?

Sunday School Essay Contest!

In their effort to remind all Landover children that they are worthless, wretchedly sinful beings worthy of death and lucky to have survived this long based solely on the fickle Grace of God, all Sunday school teachers announced a contest in their classes to see which students have made the most concerted effort to follow the Lord's Word this year. The object: To find the few children who are justified in even asking for Christmas presents, much less expecting any. Students were instructed to identify at least one New Testament verse they had made a conscious effort to follow and to explain in a brief essay how they had acted as Jesus commands.

The following excerpts are from the winning essays:

1st Place: Elizabeth Helmsley, 13 (Voted "Most Coveted Christian Girl," Landover Baptist Academy for the Saved)

"I am very selective in whom I allow to be my friends. I socialize only with saved Christians (and only a few of them), and don't even speak in the hallways to any Muslims or Jews (2 John 1:10; 1 Corinthians 10:20; Romans 16:17–18). I wouldn't even have a snack, much less dinner, with the family of any Catholic girl (1 Corinthians 5:11–13)."

2nd Place: Gloria Swenson, 8 (Undergoing radical chemotherapy for non-demon-related blood cancer at Landover Baptist Hospital for the Saved)

"Whenever I attend church, pray or go out in public, I always keep my head covered at all times, like all females are supposed to do (1 Corinthians 11:5–6)."

3rd Place: Peter Hardwick, 10 (Heaviest boy, Landover Baptist School for the Saved Children)

"Like the Apostles, and as Jesus instructed, I eat lots and lots of red meat. I haven't found an animal yet I didn't consider a great meal (1 Timothy 4:1–3; Acts 10:9–13). I stay away from

City Council Bans December Holidays That Don't Involve Being Born in a Barn

Tonight's Sermon:

"2,000 Years Ago in Bethlehem, Walking Around with No Place to Sleep Made You Selfless and Humble. Today in Freehold, It Just Makes You a Nuisance and Arrested."

athletics, constantly praying instead, because I know Jesus sees little benefit to physical activity (1 Timothy 4:8)."

4th Place: Jo Cooper, 16 (Member of the ladies' golf, tennis and basketball teams, Landover Baptist Academy for the Saved)

"Unlike less-Godly girls, I don't wear fancy dresses or skirts to school. I wear simple, modest apparel, combing my hair straight and never wearing some fancy hairdo. I don't wear jewelry or any other costly things (1 Timothy 2:9)."

5th Place: George Lott, 12 (Held back in fourth grade three times, Landover Baptist School for Saved Children)

"I study the Bible rather than those secular subjects they teach at school, completely ignoring science class (1 Timothy 6:20; 2 Corinthians 10:5). I know better than to study anything other than God's Word."

6th Place: Theresa Bombay, 17 (Niece of Supreme Court Justice John Roberts, Landover Baptist Academy for the Saved)

"Early in the year, I volunteered to work at the downtown homeless shelter, serving food to those without work. When I realized that God did not want the unemployed to eat (2 Thessalonians 3:10), I quit my job and now spend my weekends protesting at the local Planned Parenthood center, screaming at the patients how they're nothing more than murderers."

"Get Your Feet Hot For Jesus" Testimony Contest Results in Angry Kicking

One mother was hospitalized after a scuffle following last Sunday's "Get Your Feet Hot for Jesus" altar call. As has become tradition, over 20 preselected youngsters spontaneously rushed to the front of the church at the end of Sunday's 8 o'clock service to provide oral evidence that they love Jesus more than their friends. Tiffany Holmes, 13, was awarded $1,500 for giving the "Most Original Testimony," and Luke Wade, 11, was given a whack on the backside for giving the "Most Derivative Testimony." Immediately after the prizes were given, Luke became overcome with demons and started bellowing in an un-Christian manner. Enraged by her child's loss, Mrs. Wade flew across the aisle and began kickboxing Mrs. Holmes until Mrs. Holmes shook loose from her walker and rolled under her pew. Mrs. Wade claimed that Tiffany had stolen all the most sensational parts of Luke's harrowing testimony. Mrs. Holmes was listed in satisfactory condition at Landover Baptist Hospital for the Saved.

7th Place: Mary Maladen, 13 (Former Debate Champion, Landover Baptist Academy for the Saved)

"I used to like to talk a lot, so it's been really difficult, but I now make certain never to open my mouth in church (1 Corinthians 14:34–35). Even in Sunday school, I let the boys answer all the questions. When my math teacher asked me to tutor some of the football players who were having trouble in our class, I declined, telling him that, as a girl, I should never try to teach. Instead, I should keep my mouth shut and just have babies (1 Timothy 2:11-15).
I probably shouldn't have said that last part in front of all the football players."

Pastor Shoots Family Dog Under Christmas Tree for Chewing off Baby Jesus' Head

The Shepherd's Purse

Public Disclosure of God's Weekly Financial Portfolio

This information is provided solely to members of Landover Baptist Church pursuant to clause 8(D)(iii) of the Landover Baptist UCC Secured Tithing Contract. All adjustments made through the Direct-Withdrawal Tithing ® program and EZ Slide Tithe™ credit card offering plates are noted.

Associate Pastor Who Asks for Cost of Living Increase at Monthly Budget Meeting Is Accidentally Shot in Leg

Heartfelt prayers go out to Brother Shenanigan who is recovering at Landover Baptist Hospital for the Saved.

Pre-Audit Attendance for Last Week	Prior Projections	Discrepancy Adjustment
Sunday School Attendance 151,219	151,319*	18 families fined $250 each for sick/truant children
Sunday 8:00 A.M. Services 83,846*	83,847*	Mrs. Esther Rutledge, 82, died on Saturday when she swung off her porch swing into a blackberry bush 20 feet away. Burial pending investigation of her reported sherry breath.
Sunday 11:00 A.M. Services 165,172 (1,781 praise-filled Christians attended and tithed in a persistent vegetative state)	162,666*	Overflow due to allowing unsaved to stand in the back for $50 as a revenue-generating test.
Sunday 1:30 P.M. Services	2,302* Invitation Only	$25,000/plate nonpolitical, humanitarian dinner with President George W. Bush and the Godly people with the power to cut checks for faith-based initiatives.
Sunday 6:30 P.M. Service 74,477*	74,477*	Perfect attendance
Sunday Pay-Per-View 2,327,945*	1,950,000	Thank you Heather Hardwick for appearing on the Crouches' show and joining Jan on a bridge near Irving, California, to throw effigies of Hillary Clinton stuffed with ripe tomatoes into passing freeway traffic and push for subscriptions from folks fed up with crazy liberals.
Wednesday Night Service 99,733	99,736*	3 families claiming "car trouble" have been fined $150.

Pre-Audit Attendance for Last Week	Prior Projections	Discrepancy Adjustment
Wednesday Pay-Per-View 1,245,329	1,821,535*	We are praying over these numbers and expect a retraction from the folks at Nielsen.
New Satellite Members 121,007	95,666*	Those unsaved telemarketers may be going to Hell, but they'll know how to sell a sin to Satan when they get there! Glory!
New Prison Members	15,500	Before folks get all alarmed, this is just an "accounting entry" done for tax purposes only.
Recorded Witnessing for Christ by the Congregation	Audited Numbers	Comments
Doorstep Visits	2	
Christian Mall Center	8,074,228*	
Prison Visits	1	Mrs. Rutledge, who is now dead, visited her unsaved criminal son, who with the Grace of God will join her shortly.
Visits to the Poor	1,238	The Ladies of Landover visited all the residents of Canaan Condominiums to discuss "Glorifying the Lord Through Window Treatments that Are Actually Attractive."
Deacon Visitation	24-hour closed-circuit "sin monitoring"	$120,450 in fines. We all know who you are. For those in doubt, names can be downloaded from the church Web site for a nominal fee.

Tithe/Donation Records	Tithing Contract Quotas	Adjustments Made by Direct-Withdrawal Tithing ® Plan
Platinum Level Tithes	SEALED	NOT EVEN GOD KNOWS
Gold Level Tithes	NOT YOUR BUSINESS!	CONFIDENTIAL
Silver Level Tithes	PASTOR ONLY	NAT. SECURITY
Bronze Level Tithes	TOP SECRET	SEALED
Tin Level Tithes	CLASSIFIED	4 GOD'S EYES
Landover Country Club Dues	(+)$4,060,120*	
Forfeited Membership Application Fees	(+)$2,010,900*	
Bottomless White House Grant for Unaudited Faith-Based Initiatives	(+)$200,925,000**	
Unaborted Baby Sales to Sterile Couples	(+)$1,120,000*	
Payment from Joel Olsteen to Settle the "Have a Ministry All About Cash" Intellectual Property Theft Lawsuit	(+)$3,120,000*	
Catholic Cathedral Razing Initiative	(+)$430,000*	
Rentals of Baptist Beards to Local Homos	(+)$627,344*	
Change That Shook Out During "Shake Some Jesus Into the Homeless" Drive	(+)$000,017.39*	
QVC sales of "Miracle 8-Ball Prayer Answerer"	(+)$2,401,230*	
Pastor's Expense Report	$17 Million***	

*   Figures based on a good faith guesstimate by Pastor.
**   Amount Pastor was called upon by God to write on the stack of blank Treasury checks.
***   Rounded down to closest publishable figure. An even closer amount is available to members in Platinum Circle with full voting rights and tight lips.

THE GOOD NEWS

New Jewish Outreach Program Will Promote Greater Understanding Between Baptists and Those Who Killed Our Savior

Out of loyalty to Jesus, Landover Baptist has snubbed the folks responsible for killing Him for as long as any of us can remember. Nevertheless, we have allowed wandering bands of Christ-killers to practice their Savior-free rituals in Freehold's gaudy 1,000-square-foot synagogue in peace, seldom interrupting their pagan rituals for either rebuke or reproach. Jewish folks love to celebrate holiday after holiday as an excuse to rub our noses in the fact that they reject Jesus' love, avoid work and wear ridiculous hats to cover their bald spots. "Every time I telephone my accountant, it seems he's out of the office for some new Messiah-renunciation celebration," noted Brother Harry Hardwick. "It's either 'Yom' this or 'Rosha' that. I no longer even ask because just hearing him pronounce the names is like listening to a cheetah cough up a fur ball."

Landover's complacency is ending, thanks to the caring Ladies of Landover who have established a new outreach program to foster better understanding between Baptists and those who killed Christ called Hebrews Are The Enemy. Mrs. Harry "Heather" Hardwick, Etiquette Chairlady for HATE, thinks that Baptist ladies too often overlook important opportunities to bring Jewesses to Christ. "Consider, for example, being in a Christ-killer's home," reminds Mrs. Hardwick. "When the hostess asks if I would like coffee, I politely reply, 'Honey, unlike you, I don't need to fill my empty life with a cheap caffeine buzz. You see, when you have the Holy Spirit running through your veins, you don't need artificial highs. I think I'll just get high on the blood of the Lamb and skip the coffee, dear.'"

This Weekend's Unsaved Speaker

Rabbi Dickmann talks about the advantage of being neither Christian nor Hindu: "I can judge until the cows come home. And then eat one of them."

"The Lord's Pre-Rapture To-Do List"

Looking at all the liberal, unsaved folks running around America, isn't it time Jesus just went ahead and flushed the commode?

Sister Inez, co-chair of HATE, offered another tip to home-makers looking to bring people who routinely spit in Jesus' face to Christ's mercy. "Those of you who have time, drive by the Saint Beth Something-or-other Jewish Preschool on Ames Highway and pick up a needy child after school lets out," offered Sister Inez. "If you get there after 2:45, the pickings are slim, but by then the kiddies are starting to worry if their mommy is going to show up at all, so you'll go through a whole lot less candy to get them into your car. Once you get them to your Christian home, they will first need to be forced to apologize for their ancestors' murder of our Lord and then made to accept Christ as their Personal Savior, whether they like it or not. If they ask for their mothers, remind them that their new Savior never had a lot of time for his Jewish mother. Gals, sometimes we are called upon to destroy a Jew family in order to save it."

At a recent press conference to announce the ambitious launch of HATE, Mrs. Betty Bowers, America's Best Christian, faced a barrage of questions about the new church program from angry secular reporters working for Jewish media conglomerates. One reporter noted that the Catholic Church created an international incident in the nineteenth century when Pope Pius IX kidnapped a Jewish child and made the boy live with him in the Vatican. The always poised Mrs. Bowers responded: "The fact that a Catholic pope and Michael Jackson share hobbies is hardly shocking, dear. Besides, we're not taking children; we're giving salvation! Hardly something to be sneezed at. What we are doing is completely different from what that Pope Pius did. I mean, kidnapping so that a Jew can become a *Catholic*? Goodness me, talk about going from the frying pan into the Hellfire!"

What to Say When Confronted by Someone Rude Enough to Wish You a "Happy Holiday."

"Pardon me, but who the H-E-double-L do you think you are muttering your saccharine, inclusive good wishes to me, an Evangelical Christian? If you can't have the *decency* to specifically acknowledge my personal brand of faith, you can kindly shut your evolution-espousing penis hangar you call a mouth!"

As Tax Year Draws to a Close, Frantic Church Members Donate Used Batteries and Coffee Filters to Needy Families

The last month of the year is always a busy time at Landover Baptist. The arrival of December not only signifies that there are only 24 frantic shopping days until Baby Jesus' birthday, it, more importantly, also means there are only 31 more days to find tax deductions. As all saved people know, the Lord God wants the Godly to give their money to His church and not send it to Washington, D.C., where it would be used to pay for minority abortions and gay marriages. So it behooves all Landoverians to get themselves unsaved accountants who can teach them how to squirrel away as much of their assets from Uncle Sam as possible, because if the government is going to keep God's Word out of public schools, it is only fair that we keep God's money out of government. And everyone wins when he turns over household junk to the poor. Not only does the donation provide an excellent way to spruce up a cluttered basement or garage, it provides valuable credits with both the IRS and God—without the donor suffering the inconvenience of any actual sacrifice!

As Mrs. Betty Bowers, president of Christians Having A Righteously Itemized Tax Year, noted, "CHARITY recommends not giving cash to the needy, as it will not bring them closer to God. After all, the Lord doesn't own a liquor store. Jesus told us 'the poor will always be with you' and we should never do anything that would risk making Him out to be a liar. But things you were going to throw out anyway make lovely gifts to people who are so thrilled to finally have a toaster that the fact that it no longer works is merely a faint footnote to their elation. Besides, it's one thing for a Jewish carpenter to tell you to give away your possessions, but when a Jewish accountant tells you to do it, you had better hop to it, sister!"

By donating old household refuse to the less-blessed, Landover Baptist Church members have saved over $2.7 million

Tax-Saving Tips for Residents of Jesusland

Attend this weekend's financial seminar and learn how to turn your one-car garage into a for-profit tax-deductible two-seater sanctuary. Next week: "Do I Count the Trinity as One or Three Dependents?"

Freehold's 750,000-square-foot Museum of Roman Catholic Idols has run out of display space and is hoping to move to a larger facility next year.

annually in charitable tax write-offs. Continuing the tradition for this tax year, the Ladies of Landover will hostess the 28th Annual Household Junk Round up on December 31. There will be no limit to what you can place curbside this year. Since the secular fascists at the Environmental Protection Agency have made it harder and harder for decent common folks to dispose of things like lead paint, asbestos and other so-called "toxic waste," poor people's homes provide the ideal place for such items.

Ladies of Landover Co-Chairwoman Mrs. Helen Floribunda noted, "It would be a waste to throw away all that old paint that's been sitting in your basement for the last 15 years. If I were a person God wanted to live in the streets, I might be sad to come home from my nonjob each night to a dirty old refrigerator box. But maybe not if it sported a fresh coat of paint with a snappy Williamsburg trim! Besides, Pentecostal and Church of God trash can use the empty cans as flower vases, mixing bowls or even sturdy purses. They all come crosstown to go through our garbage anyway. This way, we hire someone to bring it to them (which is another tax write-off), thereby saving them the trip of having to travel to our communities to pick through our trash on Jesus' birthday. Mind you, these folks that God ordained to live in the gutters don't even utter so much as a simple 'thank you, lady, there was a tasty piece of meat you left on that chicken wing I just found in your garbage can.' But Lord knows, I don't do it for the thanks. Jesus and H&R Block were right: blessings eventually come to those who help those in need."

"Kwanzaa": Ghetto Slang for "Let's Go Kill Us Some Crackas!"

Always vigilant about finding things to protest in God's name, the Ladies of Landover (after getting permission from their husbands) disguised themselves as Negresses earlier this week to attend a local Kwanzaa party. The Ladies had been tipped off to the all-night party during a routine session of listening to surreptitiously recorded tapes of their domestics' telephone conversations. At first, the Ladies had no idea what the word "Kwanzaa" meant. "It's hard enough to understand what those people are saying at the best of times," lamented Mrs. Harry "Heather" Hardwick, "but when they start making up words, you just might as well just give up." After listening to the tape five times, Mrs. Venetia Johnson, the county's only known liberal, was called in to decipher. She informed the Ladies of Landover that Kwanzaa is actually a black alternative to the celebration of Jesus' birth. "Something to compete with Baby Jesus?" asked Mrs. Billy Ray Simpkins. "Well, if that don't smack of Satan, I don't know what does!"

The Ladies decided to attend the Kwanzaa party in disguise to find out if this non-Caucasian holiday is of God or the Devil. "Lucifer just lays in wait to prey on the immoral, the lazy and the uneducated," explained Ladies of Landover co-chairwoman, Helen Floribunda. "So, when we realized it was a Negro-type event, we knew Satan had hit on a trifecta of trouble! We wanted to find out if those people were desecrating the Baby Jesus' birth. It also provided a wonderful opportunity to see if we could locate sterling flatware that was missing from our homes."

The Ladies reported that, after an interminable prelude over an inartfully catered buffet ("There were all the parts to make a whole pig on that table!" lamented Sister Inez), the entire party moved into the living room/crack den to witness a ritual killing of a stolen child dressed up as the Baby Jesus. "I was petrified," Mrs. Hardwick remembered. "In the limousine on the way over, we had speculated that sacrifices would probably somehow be a part of Kwanzaa. But, naturally, we just assumed that a small pet or a chicken would be involved. Not a human! As an African witch doctor with a tall felt hat appeared out of the shadows and took out a metallic weapon, Inez fainted onto their velvet cheetah-print sofa. That, along with our fear that one of us might soon conjugate a verb correctly, was our cue to run for our lives!"

In a police report filed pursuant to Mrs. Hardwick's 911 call, the colored hostess not only admitted what was afoot, she also revealed more Negro code words associated with the savage ritual (such as the Swahili words "bris" and "mohel"): "What were those crazy old white women doing at our bris anyway? For real, they had coal dust all over their cracker faces, screamed before the mohel got anywhere near little Jamie, and then ran out of the house, shrieking like crack heads without leaving one single gift! I tell you, white folks! Girl, they are as crazy as junkyard pit bulls with a dog bowl full of liquor." Church officials await law enforcement's translation of the hostess' Ebonics message before taking further action.

This Sunday's Sermon:

"Jesus Told You to Love Your Neighbor. Fortunately, He Never Said Anything About Liking Him."

Last Week's Most Successful Prayer

"Are you there, God? It's me, Nathanial Devonshire III, Esq., calling from my vacation home in the Hamptons, and I need another financial blessing wired to my account ASAP."

The Old Rugged Crossword Puzzle

CLUES:

ACROSS

2. Democrats' dream Ex 3:4
4. Not hard to beat Ex 21:20–21
8. Celestial square Rv 7:1
9. Woman's best skill 1 Tm 2:12
10. Dorothy should have given Oz a ____ Lv 20:27
13. Jesus called "The Prince of ____" Mt 9:34
14. Displeasing to God 1 Thes 2:14–15
17. Homosexual after-play Lv 20:13
18. Burning a mother Ge 38:24
19. God's posse Gn 18:1–4
20. Strong as God Nm 23:22
22. Penis tastes sweet as a/an____ Sa 2:3
23. God's partner in games Jb 2:3–6
25. Has melodic flatulence Is 16:11
26. From sea to shining sea Gn 1:7
28. Spoken with forked tongue Gn 3:1
31. From God's mouth Ps 18:8
32. David's bottom 2 Sm 1:26
34. God's plan for children
35. Birthday Methuselah missed Gn 5:27
37. Aaron's loud attire Ex 28:34–35
39. Dirty bird Dt 14:11–18
40. Make God drunken with anger Nm 11:1
41. God's calling card Ex 9:14
42. Gnashing in the furnace Mt 13:42

44. Make fermented poison Du 32:33
46. Prophetess spawn Is 8:3
48. Rocky refreshment Ex 17:6
49. Unused before Glory Rv 14:1–4
50. Doubtful Jn 2:29
55. Job's natty clothing Jb 7:5
56. Eli's cumming here 1 Sm 2:22
58. Must be given God in whole
61. Young fruits Lv 19:23
63. To sleep, perchance to sin Dt 23:10
64. Sun's equal Isa 30:26
65. Ruth's pimp Ru 3:3–4
67. Laura Bush forbidden to ____ 1 Tm 2:12
68. God suffers from 2 Chr 16:9
69. Cain's wife Gn 4:7
70. Rabbit food Lv 11:6
72. Wiser than Christ 1 Kas 3:12
74. Up against a wall 1 Kas 14:10
77. Both God and Jesus approved of
79. A Godly trim Is 7:20
81. Jerusalem's most popular trade
82. Never enough for Mary
83. God's nonkilling vocation Ex 4:2–9
84. God's gift to Saul 1 Sm 18:10
85. God's big creation Gn 6:4

DOWN

1. Written, then forbidden Ti 3:9
2. David's servant's miniskirts revealed 1 Chr 19:4
3. God's dog food 1 Kas 29:19
4. Jacob's bedmates Gn 29:21–30
5. Haven't you had enough, Lord? Jas 9:13
6. Swear on a stack of them Gn 24:2
7. Bible's most poorly catered events Jn 2:1
11. Floats in water 2 Kas 6:5–7
12. Peeping Ezekiel's prize Ez 1:27
15. A bane to God
16. Led Eve to be cursed and Jesus to curse Mt 21:19
21. King of kings Ez 26:7
24. Missing at church Dt 23:1
27. Not as hot in the sack as Jonathan 2 Sm 1:26
29. Where you are probably going
30. Happy parents' children's heads Pss 137:9
33. God's favorite magic act Neh 7:65
36. Gift to rapists Gn 19:8
38. Sinful splatter Gn 38:8–10
39. Betwixt and between my ____ Sa 1:13
41. Most bossy Apostle

42. Friends' feast Jer 19:7–9
43. Have unsightly foreskins Dt 10:16
45. Cover to cover Lv 18:6–19
47. Jesus was a stickler for clean ones
51. Punishment by Absalon 1 Sm 16:22
52. Biblical porn star Ez 23:20
53. Demon hotels Mk 5:12–13
54. Mecca for harlots
57. God always RSVPs "no" to a ____ Lv 11:9–12
59. Remarriage Lk 16:18
60. Chided for following Jesus' diet
61. A wise priest on stairs has Ex 20:26
62. From sneeze to shining ___ sea Ex 15:8
66. Nine scores Gn 35:28
71. Stubborn raconteur Nm 22:28–30
72. The result of Biblical sex
73. God told Isaiah to become one Is 20:2–5
75. Pimped Abraham's ho Gn 12:15
76. God loves to finish a frock with this Du 22:12
77. Unnecessary illumination Ge 1:14–19
78. Raining cats and ____ Ex 8
80. Dutiful doo-doo Ex 29:14

NOTE FROM THE PASTOR: *If you are so bereft of the Holy Spirit's inspiration that you can't solve a simple biblical crossword puzzle without looking up the answers, you are clearly too wicked for Hell itself. Get thee hence, you damned cheater!*